Culinary Prescriptions

From Textbook to Cookbook

Culinary Prescriptions
From Textbook to Cookbook

Published by UAMS College of Nursing
4301 West Markham #529
Little Rock, Arkansas 72205
501-686-5374
www.nursing.uams.edu

Cover Artist: Keith Runkle

This cookbook is a collection of favorite recipes, which are not necessarily original recipes.

Library of Congress Control Number:
        2007903235

ISBN: 978-0-9792786-0-0

Edited, Designed, and Manufactured by
Favorite Recipes® Press
an imprint of

FRP.

P.O. Box 305142
Nashville, Tennessee 37230
800-358-0560

Art Director: Steve Newman
Production Designer: Travis Rader

Printed in China
First Printing: 2008   5,000 copies

UAMS employees, patients, and friends are all proud supporters of the mission of teaching, healing, searching, and serving. To learn more about UAMS, the educational programs, hospital, clinical services, or opportunities for philanthropy, visit www.uams.edu. Proceeds from the sale of Culinary Prescriptions will benefit the UAMS capital campaign.

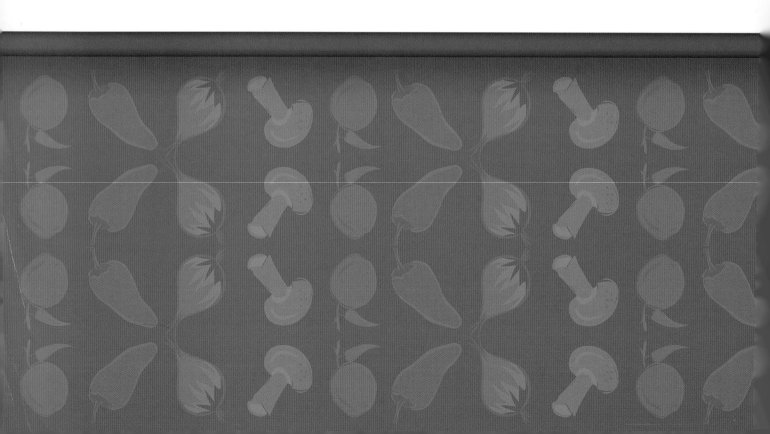

Culinary Prescriptions

University of Arkansas for Medical Sciences

From Textbook to Cookbook

Benefits of Good Nutrition

from the American Cancer Society

Good nutrition is especially important for people with cancer because the illness itself, as well as its treatments, can affect your appetite. Cancer and cancer treatments also can alter your body's ability to tolerate certain foods and to use **nutrients.**

The nutrient needs of people with cancer vary from person to person. Your doctor, nurses, and dietitian can help you identify your nutrition goals and plan ways to help you meet them. Eating well while having cancer treatment can help you to:

* feel better
* keep up your strength and energy
* keep up your weight and your body's store of nutrients
* tolerate treatment-related side effects
* decrease your risk of infection
* heal and recover quickly

Eating well means eating a variety of foods that provide the nutrients you need to maintain your health while fighting cancer. These nutrients include **protein, carbohydrates, fat, water, vitamins,** and **minerals.**

Nutrients

Protein: Protein is needed for growth, to repair body tissue, and to maintain a healthy immune system. Without enough protein, the body takes longer to recover from illness and has lower resistance to infection. People with cancer often need more protein than usual. Following surgery, chemotherapy, or radiation therapy, additional protein is usually needed to heal tissues and to help prevent infection. Good sources of protein include lean meat, fish, poultry, dairy products, nuts, dried beans, peas and lentils, and soy foods.

Fats: Fats play an important role in nutrition. Fats and oils provide a concentrated source of energy for the body. They are used to store energy, insulate body tissues, and transport fat-soluble vitamins through the blood. They also play an important role in food preparation by enhancing food flavor, making baked products tender, and conducting heat during cooking. You may have heard that some fats are better for you than others. When considering the effects of fats on your heart and cholesterol, choose the unsaturated fats.

Types of fats include:

* **Monounsaturated fats** are found mainly in vegetable oils such as canola, olive, and peanut oils. They are liquid at room temperature.
* **Polyunsaturated fats** are found mainly in vegetable oils such as safflower, sunflower, corn, flaxseed, and canola oils. Polyunsaturated fats are also the main fats found in seafood. They are liquid or soft at room temperature. Specific polyunsaturated fatty acids, such as linoleic acid and alpha-linolenic acid, are called essential fatty acids. They are necessary for cell structure and making hormones. Essential fatty acids must be obtained from foods we choose.
* **Saturated fats** (or saturated fatty acids) are found chiefly in animal sources such as meat and poultry, whole or reduced-fat milk, and butter. Some vegetable oils like coconut, palm kernel oil, and palm oil are saturated. Saturated fats are usually solid at room temperature.
* **Trans fatty acids** are formed when vegetable oils are processed into margarine or shortening. Sources of trans fats in the diet include snack foods and baked goods made from "partially hydrogenated vegetable oil" or "vegetable shortening." Trans fats also occur naturally in some animal products such as dairy products.

Carbohydrates: Carbohydrates provide the body with the fuel it needs for physical activity and for proper organ function. There are also good and bad sources of carbohydrates. The best source of carbohydrates—fruits, vegetables, and whole grains—deliver essential vitamins and minerals, fiber, and **phytonutrients** to the body's cells. Other sources of carbohydrates include bread, potatoes, spaghetti, pasta, cereals, dried beans, corn, peas, beans, and many others. Sweets as a source of carbohydrates provide very few nutrients.

Water: Water and fluids are vital to our health. All body cells need water to function. If you do not take in enough fluids or if you are vomiting or have diarrhea, you may become dehydrated. In general, a person should drink about eight glasses of water or clear liquid each day to be sure that all the body cells get the fluid they need.

Vitamins and minerals: Vitamins and minerals are needed for proper growth and development. In addition, they allow the body to use the energy (**calories**) supplied in foods. A person who eats a balanced diet with enough calories and protein usually gets plenty of vitamins and minerals. However, eating a balanced diet can be challenging when you are receiving cancer treatment and have treatment side effects that persist for long periods of time. When that is the case, your doctor or dietitian may suggest a daily multivitamin and mineral supplement. If you are thinking of taking a vitamin or supplement, be sure to discuss this with your doctor first. During treatment, it may be best to choose one with no more than the Daily Value (DV) for all nutrients and one without iron, unless your doctor thinks that you need iron. Again, discuss this with your doctor first.

Antioxidants: Antioxidants are substances that protect the body's cells from damage caused by free radicals (by-products of the body's normal processes). Examples of antioxidants include vitamin C, vitamin E, vitamin A (beta carotene), and selenium. If you want to take in more antioxidants, health experts recommend eating a variety of fruits and vegetables, which are good sources of antioxidants. Taking large doses of antioxidant supplements is usually not recommended while having chemotherapy and radiation therapy. Talk with your doctor to determine the best time to take antioxidant supplements.

Herbs: Herbs have been used to treat disease for hundreds of years. Today, herbs are found in a variety of products such as pills, liquid extracts, teas, and ointments.

While many of these products are harmless and safe to use, others can cause severe and harmful side effects and interfere with proven cancer therapies, including chemotherapy, radiation therapy, and recovery from surgery. If you are interested in using products containing herbs, talk about it with your doctor or nurse first.

Safety considerations: Many people believe that if a pill or supplement is found on store shelves, then it is safe and effective. At this time, there are no regulations controlling the safety, content, and quality or dose recommendations for these products. The U.S. Food and Drug Administration (FDA) does not require manufacturers of these products to print possible side effects on their labels. The FDA cannot pull a dietary supplement or herbal product from the market unless it can prove that the product is unsafe.

Tell your health care team about any herbal products and supplements you are using or are thinking about using. Bring the bottle(s) of the supplement to your doctor for approval of the dose and to ensure that the ingredients do not interfere with your health or cancer treatments. Some other safety tips:

* Ask your doctor or nurses for reliable information on dietary supplements.
* Check the product labels for both the quantity and concentration of active ingredients contained in each product.
* Stop taking the product immediately and call your doctor if you experience side effects such as wheezing, itching, numbness, or tingling in your limbs.

Some people with cancer take large amounts of vitamins, minerals, and other dietary supplements in an effort to enhance their immune systems or even destroy cancer cells. Some of these substances can be harmful. In fact, large doses of some vitamins and minerals can reduce the effectiveness of chemotherapy and radiation therapy.

Revised: 05/25/2006-American Cancer Society

Contents

Introduction

I learned to cook at my mother's side. I have many fond memories of learning how to measure flour, sugar, and other dry ingredients, and how to crack an egg and separate the white from the yolk. All these things I taught my own daughter, and so goes the rites of passage. The other thing that got passed down in my family was great cookbooks. I have fond memories of getting my grandmother's favorite cookbooks when she passed away. I did not want anything else, just the cookbooks. These special books were all made by her ladies aide groups or a social group, and they each had handwritten notes that my grandmother had carefully written so that I would not make the same mistakes or so I could add that extra something that made this recipe hers.

The UAMS family has done the same thing with this cookbook, *Culinary Prescriptions: From Textbook to Cookbook*, making it very special, going through each recipe with a keen eye, and making sure that each recipe would be extra special for our own UAMS family. So enjoy this extra special book; get out your favorite pen, make notes, and scribble in extras. You are creating a treasure for the ones you love and who love to cook.

Mary Twedt
Honorary Editor, UAMS Employee, Culinary Enthusiast
Host of *Arkansas Cooks*, aired on NPR affiliate KUAR

Rx

special chefs

The University of Arkansas for Medical Sciences

The University of Arkansas for Medical Sciences (UAMS) is part of the University of Arkansas System. Currently, UAMS has about 2,435 students in six academic units: the Colleges of Medicine, Pharmacy, Nursing, Health Related Professions, and Public Health, and the Graduate School. UAMS also has about 715 resident physicians completing their training at UAMS or at one of the seven Area Health Education Centers around the state.

UAMS is one of the largest public employers in the state with almost 9,000 employees, including nearly 1,000 physicians who provide medical care to patients at UAMS and its affiliates, Arkansas Children's Hospital (ACH) and the Central Arkansas Veterans Healthcare System (CAVHS).

UAMS combines the patient care resources of a state-of-the art hospital and outpatient center with the Arkansas Cancer Research Center, Harvey and Bernice Jones Eye Institute, Donald W. Reynolds Institute on Aging, Myeloma Institute for Research and Therapy, and Jackson T. Stephens Spine & Neurosciences Institute.

The outreach efforts of UAMS include seven Area Health Education Centers (AHECs) in Fayetteville, Pine Bluff, El Dorado, Texarkana, Fort Smith, Jonesboro, and Helena; networks of senior health centers and centers for young children with special health care needs; and interactive video education and medical consultation services to community hospitals around the state.

UAMS is the state's largest basic and applied research institution, with more than $107 million in annual research funding, grants and contracts, and internationally renowned programs in multiple myeloma, aging, cancer and other areas.

UAMS and its affiliates, ACH and the CAVHS, have a total economic impact in Arkansas of about $5 billion per year. UAMS receives approximately 11 percent of its funding from the state. Its operation is funded by payments for clinical services (64 percent), grants and contracts (18 percent), philanthropy and other (5 percent), and tuition and fees (2 percent).

UAMS employees, patients, and friends are all proud supporters of the missions of teaching, healing, searching, and serving. The UAMS Community strives to provide excellence in all aspects of daily work and its endeavors toward goals for the future. To learn more about UAMS, the educational programs, hospital, clinical services, or opportunities for philanthropy, see the Web site at www.uams.edu.

UAMS

**UNIVERSITY OF ARKANSAS
FOR MEDICAL SCIENCES**

Peanut-Butter Vegetable Soup

8	cups canned chicken broth
2	cups chopped cooked chicken
1	cup chopped peeled or unpeeled potato
1	cup chopped carrots
1/2	cup chopped onion
2	garlic cloves, minced
1	cup chopped zucchini
1	cup broccoli or cauliflower florets
1	cup chopped fresh or canned tomatoes
1/2	cup chopped celery
1/2	cup chopped green bell pepper
1	cup creamy natural peanut butter
1	tablespoon minced parsley
1/2	to 1 teaspoon pepper, or to taste
~	Salt to taste

Yield: 8 servings

Nutrients per serving
Calories 307
Protein 19 g
Carbo 17 g
Total Fat 19 g
Saturated Fat 4 g
Cholesterol 31 mg
Fiber 4 g
Sodium 1180 mg

11

Combine the broth, chicken, potato, carrots, onion and garlic in a stockpot and bring to a boil over high heat. Reduce the heat to medium and cook for about 10 minutes or until the vegetables are tender-crisp; do not overcook. Stir in the zucchini, broccoli, tomatoes, celery and bell pepper and simmer for 8 minutes or until the vegetables are tender but firm; do not overcook.

Add the peanut butter, parsley, pepper and salt to the soup and stir until the peanut butter is combined. Simmer for 3 minutes longer, stirring frequently; do not overcook. Ladle into soup bowls. Substitute a mixture of 4 cups canned chicken broth and 4 cups water for 8 cups canned chicken broth if too salty.

Dr. and Mrs. I Dodd Wilson—*Chancellor*

The Chancellor's Cabinet is composed of senior administrators at UAMS—Vice Chancellors, deans, and directors of various departments, institutes, or centers. Listed on the following pages are recipes from the members of the Chancellor's Cabinet in alphabetical order after the Chancellor. Where two names are listed, the spouse submitted a recipe on behalf of the cabinet member.

Gazpacho

Yield: 3 servings

Nutrients per serving
Calories 149
Protein 3 g
Carbo 16 g
Total Fat 9 g
Saturated Fat 1 g
Cholesterol 0 mg
Fiber 3 g
Sodium 1354 mg

2	to 2¹/₂ cups vegetable juice cocktail
1	cup finely chopped peeled tomatoes
¹/₂	cup finely chopped celery
¹/₂	cup finely chopped cucumber
¹/₂	cup finely chopped green bell pepper
¹/₃	cup snipped parsley
2	to 3 tablespoons wine vinegar
2	tablespoons olive oil
1	small garlic clove, minced
1	teaspoon salt
¹/₂	teaspoon Worcestershire sauce
¹/₄	teaspoon freshly ground pepper
~	Chopped avocado for garnish
~	Croutons for garnish

Combine the vegetable juice cocktail, tomatoes, celery, cucumber, bell pepper and parsley in a nonreactive bowl or glass pitcher and mix well. Stir in the vinegar, olive oil, garlic, salt, Worcestershire sauce and pepper. Chill, covered, for 4 to 10 hours. Ladle into chilled soup bowls and garnish with chopped avocado and croutons. Double the recipe and store, covered, in the refrigerator for several days.

Dr. and Mrs. Bart Barlogie—*Director, Myeloma Institute*

12

The Myeloma Institute for Research and Therapy is committed to accelerating curative therapies for multiple myeloma and related diseases. With a team of leading scientists and clinicians, the Myeloma Institute translates advances in the laboratory to breakthrough clinical treatments.

Founded in 1989 by Dr. Bart Barlogie, the myeloma program at the University of Arkansas for Medical Sciences is one of the largest in the world. Over 6,000 patients from every state in the United States and more than forty foreign countries have come to the Myeloma Institute to receive the latest and most promising treatments. More than 6,500 peripheral blood stem cell transplants have been performed.

"Firsts" at the Myeloma Institute include:

* Using tandem bone marrow/peripheral blood stem cell transplants
* Performing transplants on an outpatient basis
* Safely transplanting patients age seventy and above
* Transplanting patients with renal disease
* Introducing thalidomide as anti-angiogenesis therapy

The Institute reached a milestone in June 2004, when the Institute performed its 5,000th stem cell transplant. That same year, more than 630 patients received stem-cell transplants, more than any other facility in the nation and a record for the institution. Since the first stem cell transplant to treat myeloma was performed at UAMS in 1989, the Institute has extended the median survival rate of its patients by five years; total remission rates for patients have been increased by 45 percent.

1879

The first school facility was purchased for $5,000—the Sperindio Restaurant and Hotel at 113 West Second Street in Little Rock.

Chili

1 1/2 pounds ground round
1 tablespoon dried onion
1 garlic clove, minced
1 (29-ounce) can tomato sauce
1 (14-ounce) can tomato sauce
2 (14-ounce) cans petite
  diced tomatoes
3 to 9 ounces tomato paste
1 (16-ounce) can whole kernel
  corn, drained and rinsed
1 (16-ounce) can dark red kidney
  beans, drained and rinsed

1 (15-ounce) can black beans,
  drained and rinsed
1 (15-ounce) can Great Northern
  beans, drained and rinsed
1 tablespoon chili powder
~ Salt and pepper to taste
~ Rice, pasta, or corn chips
~ Shredded sharp Cheddar
  cheese for garnish
~ Sour cream for garnish

Yield: 8 servings

Nutrients per serving
Calories 410
Protein 30 g
Carbo 55 g
Total Fat 10 g
Saturated Fat 3 g
Cholesterol 53 mg
Fiber 14 g
Sodium 1733 mg

Brown the ground round with the dried onion and garlic in a Dutch oven, stirring until the ground round is crumbly; drain. Stir in the tomato sauce, tomatoes and 3 ounces of the tomato paste. Add the corn, beans, chili powder, salt and pepper and mix well. Stir in the remaining 3 to 6 ounces of tomato paste if a thicker consistency is desired. Chill, covered, for 8 to 10 hours. Spoon the chili mixture into a slow cooker and cook on Low for 10 to 12 hours. Serve over hot cooked rice or pasta or corn chips in soup bowls, if desired. Garnish with shredded sharp Cheddar cheese and/or sour cream.

Nutritional profile does not include rice, pasta or corn chips.

Drs. Claudia and Gary Barone—*Dean, College of Nursing and*
Division Chief, Transplant Surgery

13

Established in March 1953, the College of Nursing is committed to scholarly excellence in
1) undergraduate, master's, and doctoral nursing education programs, 2) research, and
3) service to the university, profession, and society. The College

* in 1997 became the first institution of higher education in the state to deliver courses to
distant sites through the Internet, and in 1999 began offering the entire BSN Completion
Program and BSN/MNSc Program online to RNs throughout the State.
* prepares nurses for advanced nursing practice in one of eight nursing specialties and also provides a foundation
for doctoral studies through its Master's of Nursing Science program. At least 90 percent of graduating nurse
practitioner students pass the certification examination within one year of graduation.
* has forty-seven named scholarships, two chairs, and two endowed professorships.
* is one of the few schools of nursing in the country to have funding from the National institutes of Health for a pilot
research center.
* moved from thirty-seventh to twenty-sixth place in National Institutes of Health (NIH) grant funding out of
102 nursing schools receiving NIH awards in 2005.
* In the past decade, faculty have been highly successful in gaining federal funding for their research and
currently have $9,161,042 in extramural funding.

The medical school opened Oct. 7, 1879, with 22 students.

1879

Strawberry Cake

Yield: 12 servings

Nutrients per serving
Calories 472
Protein 5 g
Carbo 69 g
Total Fat 21 g
Saturated Fat 5 g
Cholesterol 84 mg
Fiber 1 g
Sodium 379 mg

Cake
1   (2-layer) package white cake mix
1   (3-ounce) package strawberry gelatin
2   tablespoons all-purpose flour
1/2   cup vegetable oil
1/2   cup plus 3 tablespoons water
4   eggs
1   (10-ounce) package frozen strawberries

Confectioners' Sugar Icing
1/3   cup butter
2/3   (1-pound) package confectioners' sugar

To prepare the cake, mix the cake mix, gelatin and flour in a mixing bowl. Add the oil and water and beat until blended. Add the eggs one at a time, mixing well after each addition. Stir in 8 ounces of the strawberries, reserving the remaining 2 ounces strawberries for the icing. Spoon the batter into three greased and floured cake pans. Bake in a preheated 350-degree oven for 30 minutes or until the layers test done. Cool in the pans for 10 minutes and remove to a wire rack to cool completely.

To prepare the icing, bring the butter and reserved strawberries to a boil in a saucepan. Remove from the heat and mix in the confectioners' sugar, adding more or less depending on the desired consistency. Drizzle the icing between the layers and over the top of the cake, allowing the icing to flow down the side. The icing is thin, but is beautiful when it puddles around the bottom of the cake.

Mr. and Mrs. Bob Bishop—*Vice Chancellor for Compliance*

The mission of the UAMS Office of Research Compliance (ORC) is to review and report on compliance in the conduct of human subject research overseen by the UAMS Institutional Review Board. The UAMS ORC reviews studies and associated documentation for compliance to appropriate federal and state regulations, institutional policies and procedures, and accepted human subject research practices. ORC provides compliance consultations for the entire research community. ORC also may review the activities of research oversight boards such as the UAMS Institutional Review Board (IRB) and the Office of Research Support and Regulatory Affairs. Auditors provide feedback to investigators, study staff, oversight staff/groups, and the Vice Chancellors for Academic Affairs/Research Administration and Institutional Compliance concerning compliance, study conduct, and suggestions for remediation. Auditing also allows ORC staff to identify areas where additional educational programs would benefit the research community.

1880   *Dr. Tom Pinson became the first graduate of the medical school.*

Spicy New Year's Pasta

2 tablespoons olive oil
6 slices bacon, minced
2 teaspoons minced garlic
1 (35-ounce) can Italian plum tomatoes
1/2 to 1 1/2 teaspoons dried red pepper flakes, or to taste
~ Salt to taste

16 ounces penne
2 tablespoons butter, melted
3/4 cup (3 ounces) grated Romano cheese
1/2 cup (2 ounces) grated Parmesan cheese
~ Black pepper to taste

Yield: 8 servings

Nutrients per serving
Calories 440
Protein 16 g
Carbo 47 g
Total Fat 20 g
Saturated Fat 9 g
Cholesterol 34 mg
Fiber 3 g
Sodium 528 mg

Heat the olive oil in a large skillet over medium-low heat and add the bacon and garlic. Cook until the bacon is rendered or turns clear, stirring frequently. Stir in the undrained tomatoes, red pepper flakes and salt. Bring to a boil and cook for about 30 minutes or until the sauce thickens, breaking up the tomatoes with a wooden spoon during the cooking process.

Prepare the pasta using package directions and drain. Toss the pasta with the sauce in a large pasta bowl. Add the butter, Romano cheese and Parmesan cheese and mix well. Season with salt and black pepper and serve immediately.

Mr. and Mrs. John Blohm—*Vice Chancellor for Development and Alumni Affairs*

15

Since UAMS receives approximately 11 percent of its funding from the state of Arkansas, the primary mission of Development and Alumni Affairs is to secure gifts and grants that support the mission of UAMS—*To Teach, To Search, To Serve, To Heal*. This is accomplished through a comprehensive program working with individuals, foundations, corporations, and alumni. Development and Alumni Affairs supports the fundraising efforts of all colleges, centers of excellence, and departments of UAMS. To further assist in this endeavor, UAMS recently established an online giving program at www.uams.edu/giving.

The development programs of UAMS engage and involve our donors and friends in a meaningful relationship with UAMS through various special recognition events and projects throughout the year. The Development and Alumni Affairs office is also responsible for record keeping and financial management. Approximately 18,000 transactions are processed through some 1,300 foundation accounts. Thirty-four staff with fifteen development officers serve all units of the campus. During the fiscal year of 2006, payments and pledges to UAMS totaled nearly $34.7 million from 10,709 individuals, corporations, foundations, and organizations.

Enrollment increased to 80 new medical students a year. A three-story building with a lecture room and classrooms was built on Sherman Street at East Second Street.

1890

Vietnam Salad

Yield: 6 servings

Nutrients per serving
Calories 303
Protein 21 g
Carbo 9 g
Total Fat 21 g
Saturated Fat 3 g
Cholesterol 52 mg
Fiber 2 g
Sodium 876 mg

Asian Dressing
1/4 cup vegetable oil
3 tablespoons rice vinegar
2 tablespoons sugar
1 tablespoon sesame oil
1 1/2 teaspoons dry mustard
1 teaspoon salt

Salad
1 tablespoon soy sauce
1/2 teaspoon salt
1/2 teaspoon sugar
1/4 teaspoon five-spice powder
4 (5-ounce) boneless skinless chicken breasts, cut into bite-size pieces
2 to 3 tablespoons vegetable oil
1 small head iceberg lettuce, trimmed and shredded
4 ribs celery, sliced
6 to 8 green onions, sliced
1/4 cup toasted almonds for garnish
2 tablespoons sesame seeds, toasted if desired, for garnish
~ Won ton wrappers, cut into strips and fried for garnish

To prepare the dressing, combine the vegetable oil, vinegar, sugar, sesame oil, dry mustard and salt in a jar with a tight-fitting lid and seal tightly. Shake to mix. Store in the refrigerator until needed.

To prepare the salad, mix the soy sauce, salt, sugar and five-spice powder in a bowl. Add the chicken and stir until coated. Marinate at room temperature for 10 minutes.

Heat the oil in a skillet. Fry the chicken in the hot oil for several minutes or until cooked through but still juicy and tender; drain. Cool the chicken slightly and tear or cut into slivers or shred. Toss the chicken, lettuce, celery, green onions, almonds, sesame seeds and won ton strips in a salad bowl. Add the dressing and mix until coated. Serve immediately.

Mr. and Mrs. Tom Butler—*Vice-Chancellor for Administration and Governmental Affairs*

The medical school's name changed to the University of Arkansas Medical Department.

Artichoke Squares

2	(6-ounce) jars marinated artichoke hearts
1	onion, chopped
4	garlic cloves, pressed
4	eggs, lightly beaten
8	ounces sharp Cheddar cheese, shredded
1/4	cup Italian-seasoned bread crumbs
2	teaspoons minced parsley

Yield: 24 squares

Nutrients per square
Calories 71
Protein 4 g
Carbo 3 g
Total Fat 5 g
Saturated Fat 2 g
Cholesterol 45 mg
Fiber 1 g
Sodium 176 mg

Drain the marinade from the artichokes into a large saucepan. Slice the artichokes. Add the onion and garlic to the marinade and sauté until the onion is tender. Stir in the artichokes and cook for 5 minutes, stirring occasionally.

Combine the eggs, cheese, bread crumbs and parsley in a bowl and mix well. Stir in the artichoke mixture. Spoon into an 8×12-inch baking dish sprayed with nonstick cooking spray. Bake in a preheated 350-degree oven for 30 minutes. Cut into squares and serve warm.

Ms. Kari Cassel—*Chief Information Officer, Information Technology*

17

Information Technology (IT) creates and maintains the essential electronic fabric of the network and systems that facilitate UAMS communication. IT's mission is to employ information technology that extends human knowledge and facilitates discovery in support of the UAMS mission—*To Teach, To Heal, To Search, To Serve*. IT's vision is to be a continual catalyst for productivity improvement and innovation that enables and empowers UAMS in realizing its potential.

IT is a customer service organization whose ultimate goal is to get involved with, understand, and deliver service to customers. Every day creative, talented people in IT answer questions, assist UAMS faculty, staff, and students with their use of computers, fix computers, printers, and software programs, find and create solutions that improve efficiency through reports that save hours of manual effort, automate processes, and provide safety improvements.

Dr. Anna A. Shoppach became the first female graduate of U.A. Medical Department.

1901

Country Corn Bread

Yield: 8 servings

Nutrients per serving
Calories 245
Protein 5 g
Carbo 36 g
Total Fat 9 g
Saturated Fat 1 g
Cholesterol 28 mg
Fiber 3 g
Sodium 505 mg

1 tablespoon vegetable oil	1 teaspoon baking soda
2 cups stone-ground cornmeal	3 tablespoons vegetable oil
3 tablespoons all-purpose flour	1 egg, lightly beaten
1 teaspoon salt	1 1/2 cups Bulgarian buttermilk

Heat 1 tablespoon oil in a 9- or 10-inch cured cast-iron skillet in a preheated 450-degree oven until very hot. Combine the cornmeal, flour, salt and baking soda in a bowl and mix well. Stir in 3 tablespoons oil and the egg. Blend in the buttermilk just before pouring the batter into the hot skillet.

Remove the skillet from the oven and rotate the skillet to ensure the bottom of the skillet is evenly coated. Maintain the oven temperature. Pour the excess oil into the batter and mix well. Pour the batter into the hot skillet and bake for 20 minutes.

Dr. Charles Cranford—*Director, Area Health Education Centers*
Vice Chancellor for Regional Programs

18

The UAMS Regional Program is composed of the Area Health Education Centers (AHEC) Program and the Rural Hospital Program. Centers are located in El Dorado, Fayetteville/Springdale, Fort Smith, Helena, Jonesboro, Pine Bluff, and Texarkana.

The AHEC mission is to improve the supply and distribution of health care professionals in Arkansas, with an emphasis on primary care through community/academic educational partnerships, as well as increase quality health care for all Arkansans. The program sponsors six fully accredited, three-year family medicine residency programs which help improve health care services throughout the state. AHEC-trained family physicians practice in sixty-eight of the state's seventy-five counties.

The Rural Hospital Program is dedicated to serving rural hospitals throughout the state of Arkansas and surrounding areas. Through the interactive television system, residents, practitioners, students, and community members across the state can access information and programming from the state's leading health experts in their own community hospitals and clinics.

The Rural Hospital Program provides rural hospitals with resources from the University of Arkansas for Medical Sciences as well as University Hospital. The program allows UAMS to achieve its goal to establish distance learning and telemedicine within, or within thirty miles of, every hospital in Arkansas.

In addition, the Rural Hospital program offers two other programs. Consumer health education programs on wellness and health promotion subjects are offered to people from all walks of life. Med Job Arkansas is a free service to Rural Hospital Program affiliates designed to benefit rural hospitals in Arkansas by advertising employment opportunities at their facilities on the Rural Hospital Program Web site.

1909   *The U.A. Medical Department football team, the Medics, won a state championship.*

Marinated Shrimp with Oranges

3	pounds large shrimp, cooked, peeled and deveined	2	tablespoons drained capers	
~	Sections of 4 oranges	2	tablespoons minced parsley	
3	white onions, sliced	2	teaspoons garlic powder	
1 1/2	cups cider vinegar	2	teaspoons salt	
1	cup vegetable oil	2	teaspoons mustard seeds	
2/3	cup fresh lemon juice	1	teaspoon celery seeds	
1/2	cup ketchup	1/4	teaspoon pepper	
1/4	cup sugar	~	Lettuce leaves for garnish	

Yield: 12 servings

Nutrients per serving
Calories 316
Protein 19 g
Carbo 16 g
Total Fat 20 g
Saturated Fat 2 g
Cholesterol 168 mg
Fiber 2 g
Sodium 738 mg

Toss the shrimp, oranges and onions in a large bowl. Mix the vinegar, oil, lemon juice, ketchup, sugar, capers, parsley, garlic powder, salt, mustard seeds, celery seeds and pepper in a bowl. Pour over the shrimp mixture and stir gently until coated.

Marinate, covered, in the refrigerator for 8 to 10 hours, stirring occasionally; drain. Spoon the shrimp mixture onto a lettuce-lined serving platter.

Nutritional profile includes all of the marinade ingredients.

Dr. Debra Fiser—*Dean, College of Medicine, Vice Chancellor*

In 1879, eight Arkansas physicians had the foresight to establish a desperately needed medical school in Little Rock. They started with a mere twenty-two students and few resources. In 2006, enrollment approached 600 and will continue to rise to meet the growing need for more physicians in Arkansas. The UAMS College of Medicine (COM) can look back on more than 125 years of phenomenal growth and achievement in teaching, clinical care, research, and service. Excellence is a constant goal and, increasingly, a defining characteristic.

The COM is Arkansas' sole medical school, training the vast majority of the state's doctors and producing world-class physicians as well as researchers who serve on the forefront of medical breakthroughs. The students' outstanding performance on national exams in recent years is a reflection of the faculty's commitment to education, even though other important responsibilities such as clinical care and research also draw on their time. The faculty and academic leaders are truly extraordinary. The COM strives to help tomorrow's physicians acquire not only the ultimate in medical skills, but also professional and ethical standards that will aid them in their careers and ensure the very best care for patients.

The COM is one of six academic units of UAMS. Faculty are on staff at UAMS Medical Center, Arkansas Children's Hospital, the Central Arkansas Veterans Administration Hospital, the Central Arkansas Radiation Therapy Institute, and Area Health Education Centers throughout the state.

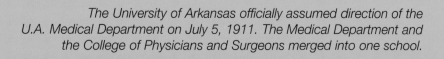

The University of Arkansas officially assumed direction of the U.A. Medical Department on July 5, 1911. The Medical Department and the College of Physicians and Surgeons merged into one school.

1911

Rum Cake

Yield: 16 servings

Nutrients per serving
Calories 338
Protein 3 g
Carbo 42 g
Total Fat 17 g
Saturated Fat 5 g
Cholesterol 64 mg
Fiber <1 g
Sodium 339 mg

20

Cake

1/3 cup chopped pecans
1 (2-layer) package butter recipe cake mix
1 (4-ounce) package vanilla instant pudding mix
1/2 cup light rum
1/2 cup water
1/2 cup vegetable oil
4 eggs

Rum Glaze

3/4 cup sugar
6 tablespoons butter
1/4 cup rum
1/4 cup water

To prepare the cake, crumble the pecans over the bottom of a greased and floured bundt pan. Mix the cake mix and pudding mix in a mixing bowl. Add the rum, water, oil and eggs and beat for 2 minutes. Spoon the batter into the prepared pan and bake in a preheated 325-degree oven for 50 minutes. Cool in the pan for 10 minutes and invert onto a cake plate.

To prepare the glaze, bring the sugar, butter, rum and water to a boil in a saucepan. Boil for 2 to 3 minutes or until the sugar dissolves, stirring frequently. Pour the glaze over the warm cake. Let stand until set.

Dr. Stephanie Gardner—*Dean, College of Pharmacy*

In 1946, a Pharmacy Department was founded at the College of the Ozarks through the collaboration of the Arkansas Pharmacists Association, the College of the Ozarks' President Wiley Lynn Hurie, and the Arkansas General Assembly. In 1951, the program was transferred to the University of Arkansas Medical Center through the collaboration of Governor Sid McMath, President Lewis Webster Jones, and the Arkansas Pharmacists Association. Milestones in the College's history include:

* 1951 Dr. Stanley G. Mittelstaedt's appointment as founding dean
* 1955 Drs. Mark Jordin's and William Heller's appointments to the Pharmacy School faculty, establishing the basis for modern clinical programs
* 1991 creation of the Nontraditional Doctor of Pharmacy Pathway, opening the PharmD degree to practicing pharmacists from the previous baccalaureate curriculum
* 1993 the inaugural graduating Doctor of Pharmacy class, establishing the PharmD as the sole professional degree program
* 1995 establishment of the Pharmacy Clinical Encounters Program, becoming the first American Pharmacy College to adopt the Standardized Patient (OSCE) method
* 2000 establishment of the Arkansas Poison Control Center as independent service and the establishment of the Arkansas Drug Information Center
* 2004 establishment of an Evidence-Based Prescribing System (EBRx) to advise Medicaid Formulary
* 2006 the Student Chapter of ASP/APhA chosen National Chapter of the Year by the American Pharmacists Association

1912

The Old State Capitol building on Markham and Center streets assigned to medical school by the state legislature.

Mississippi Mud Cake

Cake

2 1/2 cups sugar
1 cup (2 sticks) margarine or butter
3 tablespoons baking cocoa
4 eggs
1 tablespoon vanilla extract
1 1/2 cups shredded coconut
1 1/2 cups pecans, coarsely chopped
1 1/2 cups self-rising flour
1/2 teaspoon salt
1 (10-ounce) package miniature marshmallows

Chocolate Icing and Assembly

1/2 cup (1 stick) margarine or butter
1 (1-pound) package confectioners' sugar
1/2 cup evaporated milk
1/3 cup baking cocoa
1 tablespoon vanilla extract
1 1/2 cups chopped pecans

Yield: 15 servings

Nutrients per serving
Calories 741
Protein 7 g
Carbo 95 g
Total Fat 40 g
Saturated Fat 8 g
Cholesterol 59 mg
Fiber 4 g
Sodium 493 mg

To prepare the cake, beat the sugar, margarine and baking cocoa in a mixing bowl until creamy, scraping the bowl occasionally. Add the eggs and vanilla and mix until blended. Add the coconut, pecans, self-rising flour and salt and beat for 2 minutes. Spoon the batter into a greased 9×13-inch cake pan and bake in a preheated 350-degree oven for 40 minutes. Spread the marshmallows over the hot cake and bake just until the marshmallows melt; watch carefully.

To prepare the icing, melt the margarine in a microwave-safe bowl. Add the confectioners' sugar, evaporated milk, baking cocoa and vanilla and mix until blended; the icing will be very thin. Pour the icing over the hot cake and sprinkle with the pecans. Let stand until set.

Mr. and Mrs. Leo Gehring—*Vice Chancellor, Campus Operations*

The original campus of 26.1 acres was deeded to the Board of Trustees in January of 1950. Over the years an additional 60.473 acres have been acquired, and by 2006 UAMS real estate totaled 82.073 acres. As of June 2006, the original campus totaled 1,136,916 square feet (26.1 acres). Expansion numbers include:

* Elm, Pine, Cedar, and Capitol—967,357 square feet (22.207 acres includes alleys and right-of-ways, but not streets)
* Acquisition from Arkansas State Hospital—1,437,480 square feet (33 acres)
* Westmark Building land area—33,600 square feet (.771 acres)
* Ed South Building land area—38,088 square feet (.874 acres)
* Ed South vacant lots—42,000 square feet (.964 acres)
* Freeway Medical Tower—32% of the 6.082 site (1.95 acres)
* 4901 West 65th (Kennedy Head Start land)—30,800 square feet (.707 acres)

The United States entered World War I, depleting faculty numbers and drastically reducing enrollment, putting the medical school's survival at stake.

1917

Mexican-Style Creamed Corn

Yield: 4 servings

Nutrients per serving
Calories 120
Protein 4 g
Carbo 17 g
Total Fat 6 g
Saturated Fat 3 g
Cholesterol 16 mg
Fiber 2 g
Sodium 292 mg

1	(10-ounce) package frozen whole kernel corn
1/4	cup chopped green bell pepper
1/4	cup chopped red bell pepper
1/2	cup water
2	ounces cream cheese
1/4	cup minced canned green chiles
1	tablespoon skim milk
1/4	teaspoon salt
1/8	teaspoon red pepper

Mix the corn, bell peppers and water in a medium saucepan and cook for 5 minutes or until the corn is tender, stirring occasionally; drain. Add the cream cheese, green chiles, skim milk, salt and red pepper and cook until heated through, stirring frequently.

Ms. Melony Goodhand—*Vice Chancellor for Finance and Chief Financial Officer*

22

The UAMS Financial Aid office processes financial aid applications and awards funds to students in the Graduate School and in the Colleges of Pharmacy, Nursing, Health Related Professions, and Public Health. Funds are distributed through a full range of institutional, state, and federal programs.

In 2005–2006, a total of $11,818,344 was administered by the office. Of this amount, state and federal grants totaled $1,147,963; campus-based loans, $802,492; and federal loans, $9,867,889. The number of financial aid recipients totaled 1,055. As with previous years, the financial aid process mirrors the increasing enrollment and increasing number of applications, which exceeded the number of open positions for enrollment. Since the financial aid process is independent of the college's admission process, the above figures also contain data on those individuals who were not accepted but for whom aid was processed and subsequently returned.

1918 *The School's name changed to the University of Arkansas School of Medicine.*

Cuban Bread

1	envelope dry yeast	1	tablespoon sugar
2	cups lukewarm water	6	to 7 cups sifted all-purpose flour
1¼	tablespoons salt	⅓	cup cornmeal

Yield: 10 servings

Nutrients per serving
Calories 315
Protein 9 g
Carbo 66 g
Total Fat 1 g
Saturated Fat <1 g
Cholesterol 0 mg
Fiber 3 g
Sodium 875 mg

Dissolve the yeast in the water in a large bowl. Stir in the salt and sugar. Add the flour 1 cup at a time until a fairly stiff dough forms, mixing after each addition with a wooden spoon until blended. Or, beat at low speed with an electric mixer fitted with a dough hook.

Shape the dough into a ball and place in a greased bowl, turning to coat the surface. Let rise, covered with a towel, in a warm place (80 to 85 degrees) until doubled in bulk. Shape the dough on a lightly floured surface into two long French-style loaves or round Italian-style loaves.

Sprinkle a baking sheet with the cornmeal and arrange the loaves on the prepared baking sheet. Let rise for 5 minutes. Make two or three diagonal slashes in the tops of the loaves with a knife or scissors. Bake in a preheated 400-degree oven for 40 to 45 minutes or until the loaves are crusty and golden brown.

Dr. David Lipschitz—*Director, Donald W. Reynolds Institute on Aging*

23

The Donald W. Reynolds Institute on Aging and Department of Geriatrics was made possible through a $28.8 million gift from the Donald W. Reynolds Foundation. With the average American expected to live approximately eighty years and an ever-increasing number of older people in the United States living longer than ever before, they estimate that by 2020 there will be as many retired people as there are children. Arkansas already ranks fourth in the percentage of persons over the age of sixty-five. The Institute and Department of Geriatrics at UAMS has a vital mission: "to deliver quality health care to older persons, conduct research on aging and age-related diseases, provide educational programs on aging for health care professionals and the public, and to influence public policy on aging issues."

As the American population continues to live longer, the focus of health care must shift from merely keeping people alive longer to making those later years healthier and more productive. In other words, the focus is not adding years to life, but rather it's adding life to years.

The academic programs in Geriatrics continue to rank in the Top Ten in the annual *U.S. News & World Report* survey. The programs of the Reynolds Institute on Aging and Department of Geriatrics include basic and clinical research, educational programs, a primary care clinic, rehabilitation services, and administration under one roof. The facility nurtures a rich environment in which to develop a synergy between the programs.

The Senior Health Center remains one of the largest outpatient clinics on the UAMS campus. The Center also offers many valuable activities to seniors. These include the Senior Outlook Series, SeniorNet, and the UAMS Alzheimer's Seminar Series.

Courses in medical technology offered by faculty of the School of Medicine.

1921

Duck with Wild Rice

Yield: 8 servings

Nutrients per serving

Calories 529

Protein 31 g

Carbo 29 g

Total Fat 32 g

Saturated Fat 17 g

Cholesterol 153 mg

Fiber 2 g

Sodium 1073 mg

2	mallards, 4 wood or teal ducks or 3 gadwalls, dressed
1	onion, sliced
2	ribs celery, chopped
1	(6-ounce) package long grain and wild rice mix
1/2	cup (1 stick) butter
1/2	cup chopped onion
1/2	cup all-purpose flour
2	(4-ounce) cans sliced mushrooms
11/2	cups half-and-half
1	tablespoon chopped parsley
11/2	teaspoons salt
1/4	teaspoon ground pepper (Tellicherry is preferred)

Arrange the ducks in a large roasting pan and top with the sliced onion and celery. Add enough water to cover and bring to a boil. Reduce the heat to low and simmer for 2 hours or until the ducks are cooked through. Drain, reserving the stock for another use. Cool slightly and chop the ducks into bite-size pieces, discarding the skin and bones.

Prepare the rice using package directions. Melt the butter in a deep skillet or 4-quart Dutch oven and add the chopped onion. Sauté until the onion is tender and stir in the flour and undrained mushrooms. Add the rice, half-and-half, parsley, salt and pepper and mix well. Stir in the duck.

Spoon the duck mixture into a 4-quart baking dish and bake in a preheated 350-degree oven for 25 minutes. Serve with a salad and good red wine. You may prepare up to two days in advance and store, covered, in the refrigerator or freeze for future use. Extend the baking time if chilled or frozen. Quadruple the amount of pepper, if desired. Substitute with the hand- or airboat-harvested wild rice from Minnesota, if available.

Dr. Robert E. McGehee, Jr.—*Dean, Graduate School*

The Graduate School was established in 1927 with the first graduate classes at the University of Arkansas for Medical Sciences offered in 1943. The Graduate School is the home of UAMS graduate programs in neurobiology and developmental sciences, biochemistry and molecular biology, interdisciplinary biomedical sciences, interdisciplinary toxicology, microbiology and immunology, pathology, pharmacology, pharmaceutical sciences, physiology and biophysics, occupational and environmental health, nursing science, clinical nutrition, genetic counseling, and audiology and speech pathology. During the past sixty-three years, the Graduate School has awarded a total of 338 PhD degrees, 1,054 MS degrees, and 870 MNSc degrees.

1924

The City Hospital in Little Rock was dedicated, giving the U.A. School of Medicine a boost in clinical instruction for medical students.

Crab Salad

12	ounces rotini or pasta of choice	~ Old Bay seasoning to taste
16	ounces imitation crab meat, flaked and coarsely chopped	~ Dried dill weed to taste
4	ribs celery, coarsely chopped	~ Cavender's Greek seasoning to taste
1/2	cup sweet pickle relish	~ Light mayonnaise to taste
1	tablespoon dried onion	~ Light mayonnaise-type salad dressing to taste
~	Lemon juice to taste	
~	Salt and pepper to taste	

Yield: 6 servings

Nutrients per serving
Calories 311
Protein 14 g
Carbo 62 g
Total Fat 1 g
Saturated Fat <1 g
Cholesterol 15 mg
Fiber 3 g
Sodium 760 mg

Cook the pasta using package directions. Drain and rinse with cold water. Pat dry with paper towels. Combine the pasta, crab meat, celery, pickle relish, onion, lemon juice, salt, pepper, Old Bay seasoning, dill weed and Greek seasoning in a bowl and mix well. Add equal portions of light mayonnaise and mayonnaise-type salad dressing until the desired moistness and mix well. Chill, covered, for 8 to 10 hours. For variety, omit the pasta and use as a sandwich spread.

Yield: 6 servings

Dr. and Mrs. Larry Milne—*Vice-Chancellor for Academic Affairs and Research Administration*

25

The mission of the UAMS Library aligns closely with the overall mission of the University of Arkansas for Medical Sciences. As a major biomedical information source and partner in the mission of UAMS, the Library promotes the advancement of research, education, and patient care at UAMS and service to the state of Arkansas. To this end, the Library supports the creation of new knowledge, the education of health professionals, life-long learning, timely access to information, and informed health care decisions.

In 2005–2006, the Library provided online access to nearly 3,600 journals, over 3,000 books, and many reports, Web sites, and other online resources, as well as many print resources. Needed materials not owned by the Library were borrowed from other libraries and usually made available electronically within forty-eight hours. The Library implemented a new electronic document delivery service for UAMS personnel, which includes pulling and scanning older journal articles not available online and delivering them to requestors through e-mail. Other services include instruction on various information resources and topics, reference assistance and consultations, expert searching of subscription-based databases, and the Historical Research Center (HRC). The HRC contains the archives for UAMS and a collection of books, photographs, artifacts, and other materials related to the history of the health sciences in Arkansas.

The public can access valuable information through the UAMS Library. Look for information about the following special services on the UAMS Library Web site, www.library.uams.edu, or come by the Library, located in the Education II Building.

* Health Information for the Public—the best FREE health information resources on the Internet, including MedlinePlus and ARHealthLink
* Historical Research Center—books, photographs, and artifacts focusing on the history of the health sciences in Arkansas as well as UAMS
* Arkansas Public Health Virtual Library—a resource for all public health and health care professionals
* UAMS Library Catalog—listing the books and journals in the Library's Collection; open to the public

Construction began on the new six-floor medical school to accommodate 300 students.

1934

Jalapeño Corn Bread

Yield: 9 servings

Nutrients per serving
Calories 257
Protein 7 g
Carbo 22 g
Total Fat 16 g
Saturated Fat 10 g
Cholesterol 88 mg
Fiber 2 g
Sodium 376 mg

1	cup yellow cornmeal	2	eggs, beaten
1/2	teaspoon baking soda	1	cup (4 ounces) shredded sharp
2	onions, chopped		Cheddar cheese
1 1/2	cups cream-style corn	3	fresh or canned jalapeño
3/4	cup buttermilk		chiles, chopped
1/2	cup (1 stick) butter, melted		

Mix the cornmeal and baking soda in a bowl. Stir in the onions, corn, buttermilk, butter and eggs. Spread half the batter in a greased 9×9-inch baking pan. Sprinkle with 1/2 cup of the cheese, the jalapeño chiles and the remaining 1/2 cup cheese. Top with the remaining batter and bake in a preheated 350-degree oven for 1 hour. Cool in the pan for 15 minutes and cut into 9 squares.

Dr. and Mrs. T. Glenn Pait—*Director, Jackson T. Stephens Spine Institute*

Dedicated in April 2003, the Jackson T. Stephens Spine & Neurosciences Institute was made possible by a $48 million gift from the late Jackson T. Stephens, a Little Rock businessman and philanthropist. The vision that became the Spine Institute arose from a long-term relationship between Stephens and Dr. T. Glenn Pait, the Institute's director and co-author with Stephens of a book on golf and the spine. Stephens recognized the need for a facility dedicated to treating all aspects of spine-related problems and worked with Pait to make his dream become a reality.

The Institute houses some of UAMS' most visible departments, including the Center for the Athletic and Aging Spine, University Rehabilitation, the Departments of Neurosurgery, Neurology, and Otolaryngology/Head and Neck Surgery of the UAMS College of Medicine, as well as related neurosciences programs. It is also home to the Myeloma Institute for Research and Therapy.

The Center for the Athletic and Aging Spine in the Stephens Institute has an expansive physical therapy room with special equipment that measures minute improvements to accurately document patients' progress. The Center also has an 80,000-gallon therapy pool that is wheelchair accessible and designed for water therapy. Since walking in waist-deep water is a common resistance therapy designed to improve mobility and strength, the pool has a unique walking path with a handrail that extends all the way around its perimeter.

The Institute's twelfth floor contains the Fred W. Smith Conference Center, which includes the 335-seat Fred W. Smith Auditorium and James H. Hamlen II Boardroom. The conference center, the result of a generous gift from the Donald W. Reynolds Foundation given in honor of its chairman, gives UAMS the capability of hosting national seminars, conferences, and educational symposiums. The center's state-of-the-art audiovisual equipment allows UAMS to offer teleconferencing on a large-scale basis. The boardroom is named for the late James Hamlen, a Little Rock businessman who was a generous supporter of UAMS.

1935

The new medical school, facing McAlmont Street, was completed and linked with City Hospital.

Blueberry Walnut Bread

1 3/4 cups all-purpose flour
2/3 cup sugar
1 1/2 teaspoons baking powder
1/2 teaspoon salt
~ Juice of 1 orange
2 tablespoons margarine, melted
2 teaspoons grated orange zest
1 egg, beaten
1 cup fresh blueberries
1 cup chopped walnuts
1/4 cup all-purpose flour

Yield: 12 slices

Nutrients per slice
Calories 216
Protein 4 g
Carbo 31 g
Total Fat 9 g
Saturated Fat 1 g
Cholesterol 18 mg
Fiber 2 g
Sodium 187 mg

Mix 1 3/4 cups flour, the sugar, baking powder and salt in a bowl. Combine the orange juice and margarine with enough boiling water in a heatproof measuring cup to measure 3/4 cup. Stir the orange juice mixture into the dry ingredients. Add the orange zest and egg and mix just until moistened.

Toss the blueberries, walnuts and 1/4 cup flour in a bowl. Fold the blueberry mixture into the batter. Spoon the batter into a greased 5×9-inch loaf pan and bake in a preheated 350-degree oven for 55 to 60 minutes or until the loaf tests done. Cool in the pan for 10 minutes and remove to a wire rack to cool completely.

Mr. Dick Pierson—*Vice-Chancellor for Clinical Programs*

27

As Arkansas' only true teaching resource, UAMS Medical Center remains on the forefront of new medical procedures and technologies. We believe we provide better patient care because we have a coordinated and integrated system that includes clinical care, medical research, and education. Because we are a teaching medical center and all our physicians are on staff, the knowledge and experience of many different specialties can quickly be applied to the patient's problem. In addition, our research and educational programs inspire new knowledge and methods that help improve patient care and are a unique and valuable part of the way UAMS Medical Center doctors practice medicine.

Our quality care has not gone unnoticed either. Nationwide authorities frequently rate many of our physicians among the best in the nation and state. And, every year since 1996, *U.S. News & World Report* has listed our hospital as "One of America's Best." No other hospital in Arkansas has ever been named to this prestigious list.

The Arkansas legislature assessed a new tax on beer and liquor to fund appropriations for the School of Medicine.

1939

White Chicken Enchiladas

Yield: 12 enchiladas

Nutrients per enchilada

Calories 206

Protein 20 g

Carbo 18 g

Total Fat 5 g

Saturated Fat 2 g

Cholesterol 50 mg

Fiber <1 g

Sodium 174 mg

12 (6-inch) white or yellow corn tortillas

4 ounces reduced-fat cream cheese, softened

1 tablespoon skim milk

1 teaspoon ground cumin

4 cups chopped cooked chicken breast

1/2 cup chopped green onions

1/2 cup chopped red bell pepper

1 (10-ounce) can reduced-fat reduced-sodium cream of chicken soup

1 cup skim milk

1 cup fat-free sour cream

2 jalapeño chiles, seeded and chopped

1/4 teaspoon cayenne pepper

1/2 cup (2 ounces) shredded reduced-fat Cheddar cheese

Wrap the tortillas in foil and heat in a preheated 350-degree oven for 3 to 4 minutes or until softened. Maintain the oven temperature. Combine the cream cheese, 1 tablespoon skim milk and the cumin in a bowl and mix until blended. Stir in the chicken. Sauté the green onions and bell pepper in a skillet coated with nonstick cooking spray until tender. Stir the green onion mixture into the chicken mixture.

Combine the soup, 1 cup skim milk, the sour cream, jalapeño chiles and cayenne pepper in a bowl and mix well. Stir 2 tablespoons of the soup mixture into the chicken mixture. Spoon 1/3 cup of the chicken mixture down the center of each tortilla and roll tightly to enclose the filling. Arrange seam side down in a 9×13-inch baking dish sprayed with nonstick cooking spray. Top with the remaining soup mixture and bake, covered with foil, for 30 minutes or until heated through. Remove the foil and sprinkle with the Cheddar cheese. Bake for 5 minutes longer or until the cheese melts.

Dr. James Raczynski—*Dean, College of Public Health*

The UAMS Fay W. Boozman College of Public Health (COPH) was established as the sixth and newest academic unit at UAMS in July, 2001. The development of the College was made possible by Initiated Act 1 of 2000, the Tobacco Settlement Proceeds Act, with over 64 percent voting in favor during the November 2000 election. The COPH is the only school of public health in the country to be established with tobacco settlement funds. The Mission of the COPH is focused on improving the health and promoting the well-being of individuals, families, and communities in Arkansas through education, research, and service.

The COPH brings a different perspective to the Medical Center's traditional health care services, which have historically focused primarily on the treatment of individual patients. In contrast, public health focuses on 1) an emphasis on improving the quality of life for the entire community in what is known as a population or community-wide perspective; 2) a heavy emphasis on health promotion and disease prevention as a cost-effective way to maintain the health and well-being for all Arkansans; and 3) a fundamental commitment to the policy development and information-gathering that is necessary to develop sound policy and environmental changes to promote health and well-being.

1940

A two-story connection was established between the medical school facility and City Hospital. It included a waiting room, two emergency rooms and a clinical laboratory.

Blackberry Cake

Cake

1	(2-layer) package yellow cake mix
1	(3-ounce) package raspberry gelatin
1	(16-ounce) package frozen blackberries, thawed
1/3	cup sugar
4	eggs

Cream Cheese Frosting

1	(1-pound) package confectioners' sugar
8	ounces cream cheese, softened
1	teaspoon vanilla extract

Yield: 12 servings

Nutrients per serving
Calories 497
Protein 7 g
Carbo 90 g
Total Fat 14 g
Saturated Fat 5 g
Cholesterol 92 mg
Fiber 2 g
Sodium 393 mg

To prepare the cake, combine the cake mix, gelatin, blackberries, sugar and eggs in a mixing bowl. Beat at medium speed for 2 minutes, scraping the bowl occasionally. Spoon the batter evenly into three 8-inch cake pans or a 9×13-inch cake pan sprayed with nonstick cooking spray. Bake at 350 degrees for 35 minutes. Cool in the pans for 10 minutes and remove to a wire rack to cool completely.

To prepare the frosting, combine the confectioners' sugar, cream cheese and vanilla in a mixing bowl and beat until of a spreading consistency. Spread the frosting between the layers and over the top and side of the cake.

Dr. and Mrs. John Shock—*Executive Vice-Chancellor and Director, Jones Eye Institute*

29

The Harvey and Bernice Jones Eye Institute, a 100,000-square-foot, free-standing Center of Excellence on the UAMS campus was founded in 1994. The Institute is dedicated to the study and treatment of the eye. It provides patient care in every ophthalmic specialty while serving as the principle training site for medical students and ophthalmology resident physicians. Annual patient visits to the Institute's Eye Clinic now exceeds 22,000—a significant increase from 6,900 patient visits in 1980. Patients come to the Jones Eye Institute from every county in our state and even from surrounding states and other countries. Patients can enjoy a multitude of services ranging from our unique optical shop to our LASIK surgery programs.

The modern facility serves as home for the Pat and Willard Walker Eye Research Center, established in 1987, and is considered a driving force behind the Department of Ophthalmology's overall growth. A broad spectrum of basic science and clinical research is ongoing, with special emphasis on ocular virology and age-related macular degeneration.

The Arkansas Lions Eye Bank and Laboratory, Arkansas' only eye bank, also is located in the Jones Eye Institute. Arkansas ranks third in the nation in new cases of blindness each year. Through a nationwide network, the Eye Bank provided the gift of sight to more than 600 individuals last year.

The Department of Ophthalmic Technologies, located in the Jones Eye Institute, is one of only seven accredited programs in the United States to provide advanced ophthalmic training for students. Graduates earn a BS degree with a major in Ophthalmic Medical Technology and are eligible to undergo the national certification process to become a certified ophthalmic medical technologist (COMT). The Department of Ophthalmic Technologies is a partnership between the College of Health Related Professions and The Harvey and Bernice Jones Eye Institute that began in 2000.

Dr. W. C. Langston initiated the concept of a medical center, which began to take shape.

1940

Mandarin Salad

Yield: 6 servings

Nutrients per serving
Calories 176
Protein 3 g
Carbo 17 g
Total Fat 12 g
Saturated Fat 1 g
Cholesterol 2 mg
Fiber 2 g
Sodium 266 mg

1	(12-ounce) package romaine, torn
1	(11-ounce) can mandarin oranges, drained
1/2	cup crumbled crisp-cooked bacon
1/4	cup sliced almonds
6	green onions, thinly sliced
1/4	cup vegetable oil
2	tablespoons sugar
2	tablespoons vinegar
1/2	teaspoon salt
1/8	teaspoon hot red pepper sauce

Toss the romaine, mandarin oranges, bacon, almonds and green onions in a bowl. Whisk the oil, sugar, vinegar, salt and hot sauce in a bowl until combined. Pour over the salad and mix until coated.

For variety, increase the sugar to 1/4 cup and the vinegar to 1/4 cup and omit the hot sauce. Toss the dressing with a mixture of the romaine, 4 chopped green onions, two (11-ounce) cans mandarin oranges, 2/3 cup dried cranberries, 2/3 cup sunflower kernels and 1 pint grape tomato halves.

Nutritional profile does not include the variation.

Dr. G. Richard Smith—*Director, Psychiatric Research Institute*

The UAMS Department of Psychiatry and Behavioral Sciences is one of the largest and fastest-growing departments within the College of Medicine. The department's mission is to improve treatment for people with mental disorders and their families through professional education, research, and standard-setting clinical care. To accomplish this, the UAMS Psychiatric Research Institute (PRI) has been established as one of nine UAMS Centers of Excellence. The facility housing the PRI is scheduled to open in the spring of 2008. It is estimated that the PRI will bring approximately 60,000 visits annually, which is similar to the other institutes and centers on campus. There are only nine other such institutes in the nation of more than 125 academic health science centers such as UAMS.

In 2005, the UAMS College of Medicine ranked third in the nation in the number of medical students who chose to go into psychiatry. This is a testament to our exceptional residency training program. Our commitment to education extends to the training of medical students, fellows, interns, and students in other health profession fields. Our weekly grand rounds, other continuing medical educational opportunities, and various community outreach programs also provide outstanding opportunities for professionals and the general public to learn about cutting-edge research and innovative clinical treatments available in psychiatry.

1941   *The School of Medicine blood bank established.*

Soy Sauce Chicken

1	(2¹/₂- to 3-pound) chicken, cut up
¹/₂	cup (1 stick) butter, melted
¹/₄	cup soy sauce

Arrange the chicken in a single layer in a large baking dish. Mix the butter and soy sauce in a bowl. Brush the chicken with some of the soy sauce mixture. Bake in a preheated 350-degree oven for 1 hour, turning and basting the chicken every 15 minutes with the remaining soy sauce mixture. Serve with hot cooked rice.

Dr. and Mrs. James Suen—*Director, Arkansas Cancer Research Center*

Yield: 5 servings

Nutrients per serving
Calories 483
Protein 35 g
Carbo 1 g
Total Fat 37 g
Saturated Fat 17 g
Cholesterol 155 mg
Fiber 0 g
Sodium 1284 mg

31

Founded in 1984, the Arkansas Cancer Research Center (ACRC) is the official cancer research institution in Arkansas. The ACRC is a leader in the fight against cancer in Arkansas through research, treatment, prevention, outreach, and education while providing personalized patient care with a helpful, compassionate attitude.

The ACRC's approach to cancer management has earned UAMS a place among the "Top Fifty Cancer Treatment Centers" in the country by *U.S. News & World Report*. UAMS is the only Arkansas hospital to receive this prestigious recognition. Several programs attract patients from all over the United States and foreign countries. These programs include multiple myeloma, neurosurgery, head and neck cancer, and vascular lesions. The ACRC also has outstanding clinical programs in breast cancer, medical oncology, prostate cancer, orthopedic oncology, neuro-oncology, and gynecology oncology. About 150 UAMS faculty are ACRC members.

In fiscal year 2006, the ACRC handled a record 113,868 patient visits—more than one-third of all UAMS outpatient visits. With so many patient visits, the ACRC Volunteer Services and Auxiliary plays an important role at the Center, providing information, service, compassion, and hope to those whose lives are touched by cancer.

With World War II underway, more than one-third of the part-time faculty was on active duty with the military from 1942-1943.

1942

Jalapeño Cheese Grits

Yield: 8 servings

Nutrients per serving

Calories 344

Protein 13 g

Carbo 20 g

Total Fat 24 g

Saturated Fat 15 g

Cholesterol 118 mg

Fiber 1 g

Sodium 864 mg

3	cups water
1/2	teaspoon salt
1	cup quick-cooking grits
1/4	to 1/2 cup (1/2 to 1 stick) butter or margarine
6	ounces Velveeta cheese, sliced or shredded
1/2	cup milk
2	eggs
1/4	teaspoon pepper
1/2	cup pickled jalapeño chiles, chopped
6	ounces Monterey Jack cheese, shredded

Bring the water and salt to a boil in a saucepan over high heat and stir in the grits. Reduce the heat and cook for 3 to 4 minutes or until thickened. Add the butter and Velveeta cheese and stir until blended.

Whisk the milk, eggs and pepper in a bowl until blended and stir into the grits mixture. Mix in the jalapeño chiles. Spoon into a greased 2-quart baking dish and bake in a preheated 300-degree oven for 45 minutes or until set. Sprinkle with the Monterey Jack cheese and bake until the cheese melts.

Mrs. Pat Torvestad—*Vice-Chancellor for Communications*

The UAMS Office of Communications and Marketing is responsible for managing UAMS communications to the public and to UAMS employees and students. This includes working closely with local, state, and national media and writing and coordinating the timing of news releases and feature stories, as well as preparing and placing newspaper, radio, and television advertising. The department also produces e-mail announcements, fliers, posters, the *Update* employee newsletter, and other newsletters, Podcasts, and Webcasts and updates the UAMS Internet and the intranet to communicate internally and externally.

1943

The School of Medicine blood bank expanded to serve the entire state.

Low-Fat Chocolate Muffins

1 1/2 cups all-purpose flour
3/4 cup granulated sugar
1/4 cup baking cocoa
2 teaspoons baking powder
1 teaspoon baking soda
1/2 teaspoon salt
2/3 cup vanilla low-fat yogurt
2/3 cup skim milk
1/2 teaspoon vanilla extract
~ Confectioners' sugar (optional)

Yield: 14 muffins

Nutrients per muffin
Calories 109
Protein 3 g
Carbo 24 g
Total Fat <1 g
Saturated Fat <1 g
Cholesterol 1 mg
Fiber 1 g
Sodium 233 mg

Combine the flour, granulated sugar, baking cocoa, baking powder, baking soda and salt in a bowl and mix well. Add the yogurt, skim milk and vanilla and mix just until moistened. Fill paper-lined baking cups 2/3 full with the batter.

Bake in a preheated 400-degree oven for 15 to 20 minutes or until a wooden pick inserted in the centers of the muffins comes out clean. Cool in the pan for 2 minutes and remove to a wire rack. Sprinkle confectioners' sugar over the tops of the muffins and serve warm.

Mr. Charles White—*Assistant Vice Chancellor for Employee Relations*

33

The Office of Human Resources (OHR) has developed a new information site on the Web which employees can reference when trying to deal with work/life issues. The link on the OHR Web site is to help employees find and understand all the benefits and resources available to them from UAMS.

The information can be found at www.uams.edu/ohr and then click on work/life balance. The site has information on the following:

* campus services
* family care and education
* cultural resources
* entertainment and recreation in the area
* flexible work arrangements
* health and fitness
* life events
* transportation

The City Hospital was renamed University Hospital.

1944

Lentil Soup

Yield: 6 servings

Nutrients per serving

Calories 128

Protein 8 g

Carbo 26 g

Total Fat <1 g

Saturated Fat <1 g

Cholesterol 0 mg

Fiber 6 g

Sodium 264 mg

4	cups water	1	garlic clove, minced
1	onion, chopped	1	(6-ounce) can tomato paste
4	carrots, chopped	1/4	teaspoon ground pepper
2	ribs celery, chopped	1/16	teaspoon thyme
2/3	cup dried lentils, sorted		

Combine 4 cups water, the onion, carrots, celery, lentils and garlic in a large saucepan and bring to a boil. Reduce the heat to low and simmer, covered, for 3 hours, adding additional water or a little white wine as needed. Stir in the tomato paste, pepper and thyme and simmer just until heated through. Taste and adjust seasonings as desired and ladle into soup bowls. The flavor is enhanced if prepared one day in advance and stored, covered, in the refrigerator. Reheat just before serving.

Dr. and Mrs. Ronald Winters—*Dean, College of Health Related Professions*

34

The College of Health Related Professions (CHRP) serves the state of Arkansas as the primary arm of the University of Arkansas in offering programs that provide education, service, and research in the allied health professions.

The college was organized as a separate college within the University of Arkansas for Medical Sciences in 1971, although one of its programs (Medical Technology) began at UAMS in 1918 and another (Radiologic Imaging Sciences) in 1946. The CHRP currently offers programs at various degree and certificate levels in seventeen different professional areas, offering career preparation to suit many different interests—from laboratory work to the patient's bedside, information management to oral health care, diagnostic imaging to cancer therapy, emergency services to eye care, and genetics to nutrition.

Educational programs range from academic requirements of one semester to programs that require four or more years. Academic awards include the certificate and the associate's, bachelor's, master's, and doctoral degrees. Nearly all the programs stipulate prerequisites for admission that must be completed at another general undergraduate institution. Some programs are offered only in Little Rock, but since 1989, many have become available in whole or in part at other locations around Arkansas—such as at UAMS' Area Health Education Centers (AHEC) or online via the Internet to students in Arkansas and other states. All programs in the college require clinical rotations, which may occur in a wide variety of settings, such as hospitals, clinics, and laboratories.

Other roles of the CHRP include public and professional service and research. The college offers professional continuing education opportunities to enhance the abilities of practicing allied health professionals, serves as a resource center for allied health planning, education, and delivery systems in Arkansas, and develops applied research programs in allied health.

1947

Although the official name became the University of Arkansas School of Medicine, the campus was referred to as the University of Arkansas Medical Center (UAMC) until 1974.

Arkansas Country Rice

1	cup chopped celery	2	(10-ounce) cans cream of
1	onion, chopped		chicken soup
1/2	cup (1 stick) butter	1	(14-ounce) can chicken broth
4	cups cooked rice	1	teaspoon liquid smoke
		~	Salt and pepper to taste

Sauté the celery and onion in the butter in a large skillet until tender. Stir in the rice, soup, broth, liquid smoke, salt and pepper. Spoon the rice mixture into a 9×13-inch baking dish and bake in a preheated 350-degree oven for 30 minutes.

U.S. Representative Marion Berry *(D–AR)*
Congressman Berry was first elected to the United States House of Representatives in 1996. He graduated from DeWitt High School in 1960 and earned a Bachelor of Science degree from the University of Arkansas College of Pharmacy in 1965.

Yield: 8 servings

Nutrients per serving
Calories 283
Protein 5 g
Carbo 30 g
Total Fat 16 g
Saturated Fat 8 g
Cholesterol 37 mg
Fiber 1 g
Sodium 839 mg

35

Poppy Seed Chicken

8	(5-ounce) chicken breasts	8	ounces club crackers or butter
~	Salt and pepper to taste		crackers, crushed
2	(10-ounce) cans cream of	1/2	cup (1 stick) butter, melted
	chicken soup	2	tablespoons poppy seeds
2	cups sour cream		

Season the chicken with salt and pepper and place in a slow cooker. Add enough water to cover and cook on Low for 6 to 8 hours or until the chicken is tender. Cool the chicken slightly and chop into bite-size pieces, discarding the skin and bones. The chicken may be cooked on the stove top, if desired. Mix the chicken, soup and sour cream in a bowl and spoon into a 9×13-inch baking dish. Toss the cracker crumbs, butter and poppy seeds in a bowl until coated and sprinkle the crumb mixture over the top of the prepared layer. Freeze, if desired, at this point or bake in a preheated 325-degree oven for 50 minutes. If frozen, thaw in the refrigerator before baking.

U.S. Representative John Boozman *(R–AR)*
Congressman Boozman, a successful businessman and life-long resident of Arkansas, is in his third term representing the Third District of Arkansas in the United States House of Representatives. After graduating from Northside High School in Fort Smith, Boozman played football at the University of Arkansas while completing his pre-optometry requirements.

Yield: 10 servings

Nutrients per serving
Calories 475
Protein 28 g
Carbo 21 g
Total Fat 31 g
Saturated Fat 15 g
Cholesterol 112 mg
Fiber <1 g
Sodium 818 mg

The First African-American student, Edith Irby, admitted to the School of Medicine and the first issue of student newspaper, The Medico, was published.

1948

Chicken à la Scampi

Yield: 5 servings

Nutrients per serving
Calories 684
Protein 47 g
Carbo 57 g
Total Fat 30 g
Saturated Fat 12 g
Cholesterol 136 mg
Fiber 4 g
Sodium 662 mg

1/4 cup (1/2 stick) butter
1/4 cup olive oil
1 bunch green onions, trimmed and chopped
1 teaspoon minced garlic
2 pounds boneless skinless chicken breasts, cut into 1/2-inch pieces
~ Juice of 1 lemon, strained
1 teaspoon salt
1/2 teaspoon ground pepper
2 large tomatoes, coarsely chopped
1/4 cup chopped fresh parsley
12 ounces fettuccini or rigatoni, cooked and drained
2 tablespoons butter, softened

Heat 1/4 cup butter and the olive oil in a skillet until the butter melts. Stir in the green onions and garlic and sauté until the green onions are tender. Stir in the chicken, lemon juice, salt and pepper.

Cook for 8 to 10 minutes or until the chicken is cooked through, stirring constantly. Add the tomatoes and parsley and cook for 5 to 6 minutes longer or until the tomatoes are heated through, stirring frequently. Toss the hot pasta with 2 tablespoons butter in a pasta bowl. Spoon the chicken mixture over the buttered pasta and serve immediately.

Don J. Bingham—*Certified Executive Chef*
As a former "Arkansas Chef of the Year," Don J. Bingham is a Certified Executive Chef with the American Culinary Federation and served as chairman of the Board for the Central Arkansas Chapter of the American Culinary Federation. Chef Bingham is also an active member of the American Academy of Chefs. Over the years, he has held various positions in the hospitality and food industry, including owning and operating the Zinzenddorf's Tea Room and Restaurant in Conway. In 1998, he became the Governor's Mansion Administrator under the Huckabee administration. In this position, he was responsible for the day-to-day operations of the mansion, in addition to serving as host and event planner. Chef Bingham has been featured on A Taste of the South, a national five-state cooking show featuring Arkansas, Alabama, Mississippi, Louisiana, and Georgia. Chef Bingham and his wife Nancy have co-authored two cookbooks. He always has eagerly shared his knowledge of the culinary arts with a variety of audiences. He has appeared on numerous TV shows, including WB-affiliate KKYK's Arkansas View; as host of the ABC's of Cooking on PBS affiliate, AETN; and on the 700 Club with special Christmas segments. He has also presented numerous seminars and demonstrations for churches, civic groups, and political functions.

1950

A forty-acre track of land on West Markham Street was deeded to the university by the State Hospital.

White Chili

1 onion, chopped
2 garlic cloves, minced, or 1/4 teaspoon garlic powder
1 tablespoon olive oil
2 (4-ounce) cans mild or medium chopped green chiles
2 1/4 tablespoons cayenne pepper
2 tablespoons ground cumin
1 1/2 teaspoons oregano
4 (15-ounce) cans Great Northern beans
6 cups chicken broth
8 (5-ounce) boneless skinless chicken breasts, cooked and chopped
3 cups (12 ounces) shredded Monterey Jack cheese
~ Sour cream for garnish
~ Salsa for garnish

Yield: 12 servings

Nutrients per serving
Calories 402
Protein 38 g
Carbo 33 g
Total Fat 13 g
Saturated Fat 6 g
Cholesterol 80 mg
Fiber 8 g
Sodium 917 mg

37

Sauté the onion and garlic in the olive oil in a stockpot until the onion is tender. Stir in the green chiles, cayenne pepper, cumin and oregano. Add the undrained beans and broth and mix well. Stir in the chicken.

Cook for 20 to 30 minutes or to the desired consistency, stirring occasionally. Add 1 cup of the cheese and cook until the cheese melts, stirring constantly. Ladle into soup bowls and serve with the remaining 2 cups cheese, sour cream and salsa for toppings.

U.S. Senator Blanche L. Lincoln *(D–AR)*
Senator Lincoln made history on November 3, 1998, when she became the youngest woman ever elected to the United States Senate. She is only the second woman to win a U.S. Senate seat representing Arkansas, following in the footsteps of Hattie Caraway.

Commencement was held in Little Rock for the first time instead of Fayetteville.

1950

Sausage Balls

Yield:
72 sausage balls

Nutrients per ball
Calories 49
Protein 2 g
Carbo 3 g
Total Fat 3 g
Saturated Fat 2 g
Cholesterol 9 mg
Fiber <1 g
Sodium 98 mg

| 1 | pound medium Cheddar cheese, shredded | 1 | pound hot bulk sausage |
| 2 | cups baking mix | | |

Combine the cheese, sausage and baking mix in a bowl and mix well; the dough will be stiff. Shape the dough into 1-inch balls and arrange in a single layer on a baking sheet. Bake in a preheated 400-degree oven for 20 minutes; drain. You may freeze the unbaked sausage balls for future use. Increase the baking time to 30 minutes.

U.S. Representative Mike Ross *(D–AR)*
Congressman Mike Ross, of Prescott, was first elected to the United States Congress in 2000 and is currently serving his fourth term. In 1990, Mike was elected, at age 29, as the youngest member of the Arkansas State Senate, where he served for ten years.

Cheese Sandwich

Yield: 1 sandwich

Nutrients per sandwich
Calories 700
Protein 22 g
Carbo 24 g
Total Fat 58 g
Saturated Fat 29 g
Cholesterol 126 mg
Fiber 4 g
Sodium 876 mg

| 4 | teaspoons mayonnaise | 1/3 | to 1/2 cup shredded medium Cheddar cheese |
| 2 | slices whole wheat bread | 2 | tablespoons butter |

Spread 1 teaspoon of the mayonnaise on each side of both slices of the bread. Place the cheese between the two slices to form a sandwich. Melt the butter in a nonstick skillet over low heat. Toast the sandwich over low to medium heat until the cheese melts and the sandwich is brown on both sides.

U.S. Representative Vic Snyder *(D–AR)*
Congressman Snyder has served in the United States House of Representatives since 1996. Following his graduation from medical school in 1979, he moved from Oregon to Little Rock to become a family practice resident at the University of Arkansas for Medical Sciences.

1951 *The state legislature appropriated $7.4 million for the university, using a newly passed two-cent cigarette tax.*

Scotch Fudge Cake

Cake

1	cup (2 sticks) margarine
1	cup water
3	tablespoons baking cocoa
2	cups all-purpose flour
2	cups sugar
1	teaspoon ground cinnamon
1	teaspoon baking soda
1/2	cup buttermilk
2	eggs, lightly beaten
1	teaspoon vanilla extract

Chocolate Icing

1/2	cup (1 stick) margarine
6	tablespoons milk
3	tablespoons baking cocoa
1	(1-pound) package confectioners' sugar
1	teaspoon vanilla extract
~	Chopped nuts (optional)

Yield: 24 servings

Nutrients per serving
Calories 291
Protein 2 g
Carbo 45 g
Total Fat 12 g
Saturated Fat 2 g
Cholesterol 18 mg
Fiber 1 g
Sodium 199 mg

39

To prepare the cake, combine the margarine, water and baking cocoa in a saucepan and cook until blended, stirring occasionally. Combine the flour, sugar, cinnamon and baking soda in a bowl and mix well. Stir the buttermilk, eggs and vanilla into the flour mixture. Add the baking cocoa mixture and mix well.

Pour the batter into a sheet cake pan and place the pan on the top oven rack. Bake in a preheated 375-degree oven for 25 minutes or until the edges pull from the sides of the pan.

To prepare the icing, bring the margarine, milk and baking cocoa to a boil in a large saucepan, stirring frequently. Remove from the heat and mix in the confectioners' sugar and vanilla. Fold in the nuts. Spread the icing over the warm cake and let stand until set.

Senator Mark Lunsford Pryor *(D–AR)*
On January 7, 2003, Mark Lunsford Pryor was sworn in as Arkansas' thirty-third senator. In 1998, he was elected Arkansas' Attorney General, making him the youngest chief law enforcement officer in the nation. The Scotch Fudge Cake was a favorite recipe of his grandmother, Susie Pryor.

Ground was broken for the new University Hospital.

1951

Arkansas Cancer Research Center Auxiliary: Cooks Tour History

In fiscal year 2006, the ACRC handled a record 113,868 patient visits—more than one third of all UAMS outpatient visits. With so many patient visits, the ACRC Volunteer Services and Auxiliary plays an important role at the Center, providing information, service, compassion, and hope to those whose lives are touched by cancer. The 2005–2006 auxiliary membership included 550 individuals, with 300 of these members working at the ACRC on a regular basis or helping with special events each year. Most visible are the patient care volunteers who serve in the public waiting areas and the volunteers who staff the gift shop. In fiscal year 2005–2006, over $165,000 was directly donated to the ACRC or the UAMS Family Home and ACRC Auxiliary Cancer Support Center with financial gifts and in-kind contributions. One project sponsored by the Auxiliary is the Miracle Star Project. During the holiday season, trees decorated with Miracle Stars are placed in the waiting rooms of the ACRC Building. Individuals may sponsor a star on a Miracle Star Tree as a special holiday greeting or to pay tribute to a special person or in their memory. In 2005, proceeds of $3,600 were given to the ACRC Patient Support fund to assist patients with taxi and bus fare, meals, and other needs that cannot be met by other means.

Perhaps the most ambitious project of the volunteers was raising more than $1 million between 1997 and 2007 for the UAMS Family Home and ACRC Auxiliary Cancer Support Center in Little Rock. The house provides shelter for patients and families who are in town for long-term cancer treatment at ACRC and for parents of newborns in UAMS Medical Center's neonatal intensive care unit.

Cooks Tour '91

The first Cooks Tour was held on Saturday, May 19, from 10 a.m. to 2 p.m., in the East Palisades Drive homes of Lisa McNeir and Frank McGehee, who baked pizza in his outdoor oven, Diane and Bill Bray, where David Cone presented an informal lecture on food and wine, and Stephanie and Jerry Atchley. Mr. Atchley gave tours of the wine cellar in his home. The original concept for this event was a tour of wonderful homes, which focused on the most important room in a house— the kitchen. Live music was presented at each site to complement the experience. Tickets were $10 and about 150 people attended. Terri Bonner was chairman. Cooks Tour I was not conceived as a fund-raising event, but rather a means of increasing awareness of ACRC within the community. Nonetheless, the tour netted over $2,500, which was used to purchase refreshments, plants, and TVs for our patient waiting areas.

Cooks Tour '93

Cooks Tour II was moved from Saturday to Sunday and from May to April. On April 4, three Edgehill homes were visited by more than 250 people in spite of rainy weather. Tickets were $12 per person, and the tour was scheduled from noon to 3:30 p.m. Betty Meyer and Kay Beavers chaired the event for the Auxiliary. The homes on the tour and chefs were: Dr. and Mrs. Henry Thomas, with Jeff Medbury of Cassinelli 1700 and Elizabeth McMullen of Catering to Your Cravings with wine tasting conducted by Melissa Kinser of the Silbernagel Company; Mr. and Mrs. Dudley Shollmier with Robin Parker; and Mr. and Mrs. Ted Skokos with Rhonda Williams from the Arkansas Cattlemen's Association. The tour netted more than $5,000, which was used to underwrite an educational breast cancer conference and to open a gift cart as a service to our patients, selling items such as turbans, for example, at no profit.

Cooks Tour '94

Cooks Tour grew this year with the addition of a cocktail buffet for our supporters. About 150 $50 tickets were sold for a dinner on Saturday, April 9, at the Vantage Point home of Sue and Bill Gaskin. A live auction of five special parties boosted the proceeds from the dinner. Betsy Blass, who had received the 1994 Outstanding Volunteer Fund-Raiser Award from the National Society of Fund-Raising Executives, was honored.

On Sunday, April 10, four houses on Sunset were open for tours from 1 to 4 p.m. Food demonstrations and a wine lecture by David Cone enhanced the tour. Those opening their homes were Marian and Frank Lyon, Stuart and Jim Cobb, Ybeltje and Jim Conner, and Margaret and Mike Kemp. Chefs were Janan Jackson of the Arkansas Egg Council, Jeff Medbury of Cassinelli 1700, and Greg Matthews of Simply the Best Catering. Tickets were $20.

Robin Dean, chairman of Cooks Tour III, reported a profit of $18,000. Proceeds helped support a national educational breast conference for physicians and begin a patient partners program for our bone marrow transplant patients.

Cooks Tour IV began with a Saturday night cocktail buffet, attended by 170 people, at the Chenal Circle home of Drs. Janet and Steve Cathey on April 29. Complete with a live auction, this $50-per-person evening preceded a Sunday afternoon tour of four Chenal Circle residences on April 30. Local chefs Jiri Bar, Woody Powell, Norman Geisselbrecht and John Smurawa provided food demonstrations and tastings in the kitchens of Scott and Dr. Melanie Davie, Mr. and Mrs. Jerry Davis, Mr. and Mrs. Mark Brockinton, and Dr. and Mrs. Harold Betton. **Around the World with Cook's Tour** drew more than 600 people (tickets were $20). Chairman Lou Ellen Treadway reported a profit of $25,000. Proceeds were set aside to purchase inventory for a gift shop to be opened in conjunction with ACRC's building expansion project.

The patrons dinner on Friday, April 19, honored ACRC Director Dr. Kent Westbrook. A sell-out crowd of 250 guests bought $60 tickets to dinner at the home of University of Arkansas President Dr. B. Alan Sugg and his wife, Jean. Co-hosts for the evening were Harry P. Ward, M.D., UAMS chancellor, and his wife Betty Jo. Pulaski Bank & Trust sponsored the dinner. The Auxiliary presented Dr. Westbrook with lifetime memberships in the ACRC Auxiliary and the Arkansas Game and Fish Commission. Skipworth, Inc., and the Auxiliary also contributed a framed portrait of Dr. Westbrook to be hung at ACRC. A lively auction of six special events raised a whopping $8,150 to conclude the evening.

The theme of Cooks Tour V, held in four houses on the banks of the Arkansas River on Sunday, April 21, was **Canal Pointe Cuisine**. Chefs were Peter Brave of Brave New Restaurant, Kent Griffiths of Zaffino's, Greg Matthews of Andre's, and Paul Novicky of Spaule. The homes on the tour were those of Carolyn and Louis Schaufele, Mary and Frank Heigel, Nancy McKenzie and Ann Blair and Bert Park. Again, Lou Ellen Treadway was chairman and tour tickets were $20. More than $32,000 was raised during Cooks Tour V, and the proceeds were committed to the gift shop project, patient headphones for the aphaeresis area, and, with the UAMS Auxiliary, a $10,100 Hema-Tek Slide Stainer and Bone Marrow Filing System for the Hematology/Bone Marrow Clinical Laboratory.

The patrons dinner for 175 guests on Friday, April 18, was hosted by John and Grace Steuri in their River Ridge home. Co-hosts for the evening were Kent and Johnnie Westbrook and I. Dodd and Ginger Wilson. Dr. James Suen was the honoree, and the Auxiliary presented him with a set of golf clubs and a portrait by Skipworth, Inc. An auction of special items concluded the evening.

Three Courses & Dessert, an educational forum, was incorporated as a new event on Saturday by Ginger Wilson, co-chair of Cooks Tour '97. Dr. Wilson welcomed a crowd of more than 100 to the Sam Walton Auditorium. Dr. Westbrook presented an overview of ACRC, followed by course sessions by Drs. Laura Hutchins, Sundar Jagannath, and Steve Harms. TCBY, forum sponsor, provided *dessert* for the participants at the conclusion of the sessions.

The Cooks Tour, **an Afternoon of Delicious Treats on River Ridge,** followed on Sunday. Approximately 500 $20 tickets were sold for the tour of homes, which were identified this year by new sandwich board signs. Again this year, five chefs volunteered to provide cooking demonstrations during the tour. They were Peter Brave of Brave New Restaurant at the home of Kay Spencer; Paul Novicky of Spaule at the home of Drs. Sally and E. F. Klein; Jeff Medbury and Andrea Cassinelli of Cassinelli 1700 at Ramona Caldwell's; and Mark Abernathy of Loca Luna at the home of Dr. and Mrs. Robert Power. Chairman Martha Markland directed a committee of nineteen auxiliary members and a team of more than eighty volunteers. More than $22,000 in proceeds will support research in the use of magnetic resonance imaging (MRI) to improve the diagnosis, treatment, and outcomes of breast cancer.

The patrons dinner on Friday, April 17, was held at he home of Gus and Ellis Walton and honored Dr. Laura Hutchins. Co-hosts for the 175 guests were Betty Jo and Dr. Harry Ward and Kathy and Dr. Bart Barlogie. The Auxiliary presented Dr. Hutchins with a painting and a Skipworth portrait following a live auction of special items.

Three Courses and Dessert, the educational component of Cooks Tour, was held on Saturday afternoon in Sam Walton Auditorium. Around sixty people were welcomed by Dr. I. Dodd Wilson. James Suen, M.D., introduced the speakers, Drs. Graham Greene, Jayesh Mehta, and Suzanne Klimberg. TCBY provided the desserts at the conclusion of the program.

The Cooks Tour on Hill Road in Historic Hillcrest followed on Sunday, April 19. Approximately 500 people purchased $20 tickets for the four-home tour and chef demonstration. ACRC Gift Shop set up a "gift shop" in the dining room of one of the homes. The homes and chefs were Evette Brady of 1620 at Dr. Denise Greenwood's; Paul Novicky of Spaule at the home of Chris and Trip Strauss (and also gift shop); Mark Abernathy of Loca Luna at Ruth Ann and Don Jack's; and Jeff Medbury of Cassinelli 1700 at the home of Dr. Frances Wilson and Dr. David Lipschitz.

Chairmen Stuart Cobb and Barbara Hoover directed a committee of twenty auxiliary members and a team of more than eighty volunteers. Over $25,000 was raised during Cooks Tour and will be used to help fund the Charles William Rasco III Endowed Symposium on Oncology.

Cooks Tour '99

Cooks Tour '99 began with the free educational forum on Thursday, April 15, in conjunction with UAMS Mini-Medical School. The session, Genes and Cancer: From the Bedside to the Bench and Back Again, was presented by John D. Shaughnessy, Jr., Ph.D, and Robert L. Saylors III, M.D., with Director of ACRC Bart Barlogie, M.D., Ph. D., presiding. Over 100 people attended the session held in Pauly Auditorium in the Education III Building.

The Patrons Dinner was held on Friday, April 16, at the home of ACRC Foundation Board President Dr. Bill Tranum and honored Dr. Bart Barlogie. Co-hosts for the 225 guests (who paid $60 per ticket) were Dr. and Mrs. Harry Ward and Dr. and Mrs. James Suen. Following the auction (which raised over $8,000) by Craig O'Neill, Dr. Barlogie was presented with a life membership to the auxiliary and a portrait to hang at ACRC.

The Cooks Tour on Beechwood Street in the Heights neighborhood drew over 600 people ($20 each) to enjoy the perfect weather and sample dishes prepared by Executive Chefs Mark Abernathy of Loca Luna, Evette Brady of 1620 Restaurant, Peter Brave of Brave New Restaurant, and Eric Isaac of Cassinelli 1700. The homeowners are Sue and Jim Gaston, Robin and Stephen Davis, Carole and Chuck Meyer, and Karen and Randy Mourot. Kay Spencer and Jane Teed chaired a committee of twenty auxiliary members and more than 150 volunteers. Over $44,000 was raised during Cooks Tour '99, which will be used to develop easy-to-read cancer education materials for the Women's Oncology Clinic at ACRC.

Cooks Tour 2000

The 2000 Cooks Tour began with the patrons cocktail buffet at the Edgehill home of Lee and Greg Hatcher, on Friday, April 28. Robin Dean welcomed the crowd of 230 people and introduced Dr. James Suen. Dr. Suen presented Dr. Richard Nicholas as the ACRC Auxiliary 2000 Distinguished Honoree. Attorney General Mark Pryor also gave personal remarks about Dr. Nicholas. Dr. Harry Ward, with Former Senator David Pryor, announced the David Pryor Chair for Orthopedics. Pat McClelland announced that the ACRC Gala performer will be Gladys Knight. Following the program, guests went to the back veranda and lawn for the live auction with auctioneer Bill Glasscock. Following the auction (which raised over $8,000), the dining room doors were opened for the buffet prepared by Rob Best of Simply the Best Catering.

The educational program consisted of free screenings of skin, thyroid, oral, and throat cancer by the Department of Otolaryngology-Head and Neck Surgery, prostate cancer screening by the Section of Genitourinary Oncology, Department of Urology, and instruction in breast self-examination by UAMS-trained Breast Teaching Professionals. Over sixty people participated in the screenings.

An Afternoon of Delicious Treats in the Heights was held in the Armistead/Edgehill neighborhood. It drew almost 500 people who enjoyed the perfect weather and sampled treats prepared by Mark Abernathy of Loca Luna at the home of Ginger Crews; Evette Brady of 1620 Restaurant at the home of Vicki and Mark Saviers; Peter Brave of Brave New Restaurant at Sandy and Gene Jones' home; and Gregory York of Cassinelli 1700 at Betsy and Dr. Mike Bauer's.

Doll Wilkins and Linda Weems chaired a committee of twenty-six auxiliary members and more than 150 volunteers. Almost $30,000 was raised during the Cooks Tour 2000 weekend and will be used to partially fund a guesthouse/cancer support center for cancer patients to be located near the ACRC/UAMS campus.

The 2001 Cooks Tour got off to a great start with a cocktail buffet at the home of Chuckie and Curt Bradbury on Edgehill Road, on Friday, April 20. Jane Teed welcomed the largest patrons dinner crowd ever and introduced Dr. Bart Barlogie and Dr. James Suen who presented Dr. Graham Greene, the 2001 recipient of the ACRC Auxiliary Distinguished Honoree. Bill Allen, a patient of Dr. Greene's, talked about his positive experience with Dr. Greene. The presentation was followed by a live auction led by Andy Pearson of KTHV Channel 11. The auction raised almost $10,000. Following the auction, the buffet prepared by Rob Best of Simply the Best Catering was served.

The Sunday afternoon tour was in four homes in the Beverly Place/Longfellow Lane neighborhood. Almost 500 people enjoyed the beautiful weather and sampled fare prepared by Executive Chefs Mark Abernathy of Loca Luna at Kathleen and Bobby Brown's; Evette Brady of 1620 Restaurant at Pat and Dr. David Wilkes'; James Hale of Acadia Restaurant at Julie and Dr. John Jones'; and Michael Selig of Vermillion Bistro at Wendy and Dr. Ted Saer's. A successful boutique with items from the ACRC Auxiliary Gift Shop was in the pool house of one of the homes.

Julie Fulgham and Beth Jackson were chairs of the committee that included twenty-five auxiliary members and 150 volunteers for the events. Over $35,000 was raised during the two events with another $15,000 donated by the Affiliated Foods Classic bringing the total to over $50,000. The proceeds of Cooks Tour 2001 will go toward a $200,000 commitment to the UAMS Guesthouse/ACRC Cancer Support Center to be located across the street from the UAMS campus.

The 2002 Cooks Tour was kicked off with the Patrons Cocktail Party on April 26 in the Pleasant Valley home of Marge and Tom Schueck. It was the largest crowd ever for the Patrons Party with over 350 in attendance. Linda Weems welcomed the crowd and introduced Dr. James Suen who presented **Dr. Suzanne Klimberg** as the recipient of the ACRC Auxiliary Distinguished Honoree. Following the presentation, a live auction was held. One of the items auctioned was commissioned art by Gay Bechtleheimer, of El Dorado, to be hung in ACRC. Proceeds from this item was used to start the Cole Bechtleheimer Endowment Fund. Cole was Gay's son and a patient at ACRC before he died of brain cancer. Following the auction, guests enjoyed the buffet dinner provided by Rob Best of Simply the Best Cantering.

Suzanne Klimberg, M.D., is currently the director of the Breast Cancer Program and a professor in Surgery and Pathology at UAMS. When she is not directing programs, performing surgery, or writing manuscripts, she is wife to Sam and mother to Sade and Spencer. Suzanne loves the time she spends with her family and large group of friends. Suzanne also loves to cook and uses this cooking time to be with her girls. About once a month, the three of them get together and bake in preparation for Sunday Tea.

The recipe is as follows for Suzanne's Almond Macaroons: Ingredients: 1 can of almond paste, 2 egg whites, 1 1/4 cups sugar. Preheat oven to 325 degrees. Using a food processor or mixer, combine almond paste and egg whites until smooth. Add sugar and blend until the paste is smooth. Place parchment paper on cookie sheet. (This will make removing cookies so much easier after cooling.) Use a teaspoon to drop dough onto parchment paper. Bake at 325 degrees for 18 minutes. Remove paper and cookies together and cool. After cooling, remove cookies gently from paper.

The Sunday tour, held in four homes in Pleasant Valley, drew almost 400 people. For the first time, houses were not near each other and attendees drove from house to house. The weather was perfect and the almost 400 people who attended enjoyed the fare prepared by Executive Chefs Mark Abernathy of Loca Luna at Kathy and Spence Churchill's; Evette Brady of 1620 Restaurant at Carolyn and Matt Harrison's; James Hale of Acadia Restaurant at the home of Rebekah and Keith Hardin; and Michael Selig of Vermillion Bistro at Julie and Bryan Watkins. A boutique with items from the ACRC Auxiliary Gift Shop was held at one of the homes.

Kelly Harbert chaired the event. The Cooks Tour committee included over twenty auxiliary members and 120 volunteers for the events. Approximately $40,000 was raised from the event and another $15,000 was donated by Affiliated Foods bringing the total over the $50,000 that was committed to the UAMS Family Home/ACRC Auxiliary Cancer Support Center which will open in the fall of 2002.

Cooks Tour 2003

The 2003 Cooks Tour got off to a good start with the Patrons Cocktail Buffet on Friday, April 25, at the Heights home of Heather and Warren Overton. Over 225 people attended the event. A silent auction was held on the Overton's veranda overlooking the Country Club of Little Rock golf course. Over $8,000 was made on the auction. Marge Schueck welcomed the guests and Dr. James Suen introduced the 2003 ACRC Auxiliary Distinguished Honoree, Dr. Ralph Sanderson, Director of Basic Research. Before and after the presentation, guests dined on wonderful treats prepared by Rob Best of Simply the Best Catering.

The Sunday tour was held in four lovely homes in the Prospect Terrace neighborhood of the Heights. The weather was picture perfect, and the crowd of over 400 was delighted with delicious treats from Executive chefs Mark Abernathy of Loca Luna and Bene Vita at Jackie and Gerald Johnson's; Peter Brave of Brave New Restaurant at Anne Hickman's; Evette Brady of 1620 Restaurant at Claudia and Hartsill Ragons's; and Michael Selig of Vermillion Bistro and Vermillion Water Grille at the home of Belinda and Bob Shults.

The event was chaired by Kelly Harbert and Ashley Carper. With a major sponsorship from Affiliated Foods, $50,000 was raised. This completed the $200,000 commitment to the UAMS Family Home/ACRC Auxiliary Cancer Support Center, which is due this year.

Cooks Tour 2004

Cooks Tour 2004 was the most successful ever. The Patrons Party on April 23, at the Edgehill home of Cindy and Chip Murphy, honored Dr. Ronda Henry-Tillman as the ACRC Auxiliary Distinguished Honoree for her work in the area of breast and colon cancer. Over 250 people attended and enjoyed the welcome by Julie Fulgham, the presentation by Dr. James Suen to Dr. Henry-Tillman as well as the dinner and band. Silent and live auctions were held and brought in over $13,000.

The Sunday tour was held in four new homes in the Sologne neighborhood of Chenal Valley. With approximately 600 in attendance, this was one of the largest crowds in the thirteen-year history of Cooks Tour. Those attending received special treats prepared by Executive Chefs Mark Abernathy of Loca Luna and Bene Vita at Cindy and Gene Osment's; Peter Brave of Brave New Restaurant at Kelly and John Hammer's; Evette Brady of 1620 Restaurant at Tina and Haitham Alley's; and Michael Selig of Vermillion Bistro and Vermillion Water Grille at the home of Debbie and John Rees.

The event was chaired by Ashley Carper and Gloria Redman. Over 130 volunteers were involved in the event. Over $60,000 was raised from Cooks Tour 2004 and will be used for patient support programs at ACRC and the UAMS Family Home and ACRC Auxiliary Cancer Support Center.

Cooks Tour 2005

Cooks Tour 2005 proved once again to be a delight for everyone who participated in the weekend festivities. It got off to a good start with the Cooks Tour Patrons Party, Friday, April 15, at the home of Drs. Janet and Steven Cathey. The evening welcomed more than 200 guests who enjoyed dinner prepared by Brian Cochrane, Executive Chef and owner of Taste of Heritage in Bryant. The crowd was welcomed by auxiliary president Beth Jackson, and Dr. James Suen introduced the ACRC Auxiliary Distinguished Honoree, Dr. Deborah Erwin, Ph.D., who has played such an important role in so many areas of cancer education and prevention. Jancey Sheets and Bob Clausen served as Emcees. The silent and live auctions (with Jack McCray of Chenal Properties) were held and brought in over $12,000.

The Sunday, April 17, tour was held in four new homes in the Germay neighborhood of Chenal with more than 600 people touring. Those supporters were treated to special samples prepared by Executive Chefs Mark Abernathy of Loca Luna and Bene Vita at Anne and John Koch's; Peter Brave of Brave New Restaurant at the home of Kristen and Dr. Randy Minton; Evette Brady of 1620 Restaurant at Jenny and Hal Purdy's; and Michael Selig of Vermillion Bistro and Vermillion Water Grille at the home of Jan and Dr. Tom Paulus.

The event was chaired by Gloria Redman and Claudia Stallings. Over 140 volunteers were involved in Cooks Tour 2005, and over $50,000 was raised from the weekend's events. Projects to be supported from this will be patient support programs at ACRC and the UAMS Family Home and ACRC Auxiliary Cancer Support Center.

Cooks Tour 2006 got off to a smashing start with the Patrons Cocktail Buffet at the home of Ann Bradley on Friday, April 21, in the Prospect Terrace neighborhood of the Heights. More than 200 people attended to have dinner catered by Taste of Heritage in Bryant and to see the presentation of the 2006 ACRC Auxiliary Distinguished Honoree to John Shaughnessy, Ph.D., who has done extensive research in the Multiple Myeloma area. He was introduced by Dr. James Suen. Christina Munoz of KATV served as emcee for the evening and introduced Claudia Stallings, who recognized the sponsors, and Brad Wooley, who conducted the live auction of four parties. The auction brought in $18,000.

The Sunday, April 23, tour was held in four homes on Chenal Circle with approximately 550 people in attendance. They sampled wonderful food prepared by Executive Chefs Mark Abernathy of Loca Luna and Bene Vita at the home of Penny and John Burkhalter; Evette Brady of 1620 Restaurant at Mary Lynn and David Pickering's; Scott McGehee of Boulevard Bread at the home of Shannon and Dr. Scott Davis; and Michael Selig of Vermillion Water Grille at the home of Robyn and Keith Richardson.

The event was chaired by Claudia Stallings with Diana Smithson. Over 160 volunteers were involved in Cooks Tour 2006, and $50,000 was raised from the weekend's events. The proceeds of Cooks Tour 2006 will be used for the first installment of a four-year, $200,000 pledge for the new digital mammogram machine in the UAMS/ACRC Breast Center.

45

Celebrity Chefs for ACRC Cooks Tour (Alphabetically)

Portabella Mushrooms on Toastette

Mushrooms: Choose firm whole portabella mushroom caps. Brush off any dirt. Sauté in unsalted butter with a dash of Worcestershire until soft, 3 to 4 minutes.

Toastettes: Cut 3/4-inch slices of french bread. Butter and top with grated fresh Parmesan cheese. Bake at 250 until crisp and brown.

Aioli: Blend 1 cup mayonnaise, 1 Tbsp. fresh basil, and 1 Tbsp. fresh parsley.

Assemble: Spread a little aioli on toastette. Top with a slice of fresh tomato. Add red pepper strips and onion slices that have been sauteed in olive oil. Add a large piece of portabella mushroom. Melt Mozzarella or Monterey Jack cheese over top. Finish with a small dollop of aioli. Salt, if desired.

1998—An Afternoon
of Delicious Treats
on Hill Road
Courtesy of
Mark Abernathy
Executive Chef,
Loca Luna

Roasted Chicken & Brie Quesadilla with Pineapple-Mango Salsa

Strips of grilled chicken
Sauted onion & red bell pepper
Chopped cilantro
Thin strips of Brie cheese
Shredded Monterey Jack cheese
On half of a flour tortilla, layer these ingredients. Fold the tortilla over (like a taco), butter one side and grill until brown; repeat on other side. Cut into wedges and top with salsa and sour cream.

To make the salsa, dice and toss together:

1/2 cup fresh pineapple	1 Tbsp. lime juice
1/2 cup fresh mango	1/4 cup red bell pepper
1/4 cup red onion	1 jalapeno, seeded
1 Tbsp. basil (cut in thin ribbons)	1/2 cup ripe tomato

1999—Delicious
Treats on
Beechwood Street
Courtesy of
Mark Abernathy
Executive Chef
and Owner,
Loca Luna and
Bene Vita Restaurants

Wild Ozark Mushroom Pasta

2000—Cooks Tour
Visits Armistead &
Edgehill Roads
Courtesy of
Mark Abernathy
Executive Chef
and Owner,
Loca Luna Restaurant

Sauté together until onions are clear:

1 Tbsp. olive oil
1 cup yellow onion, diced

1 cup red bell pepper, diced
1/2 cup carrots, shredded

Add 1 1/2 cups fresh assorted mushrooms sliced 1/2-inch thick. Sauté until soft.

Add and heat:

1/2 cup pesto

1 1/2 cups whipping cream

Directions: Stir in 1/2 cup shredded Parmesan cheese. Pour over 8 cups of cooked penne pasta. Add shredded meat from 2 grilled/baked partridge/game hens or 1 chicken. Sprinkle top with shredded Parmesan, strips of fresh basil, lightly toasted pine nuts or hazelnuts, and crumbled crisp-fried bacon. (Serves 8)

Squash Soup with Chicken and Chipotle-Lime Broth

2001—Cooks Tour
Visits Longfellow
Lane & Beverly Place

Courtesy of
Mark Abernathy
Executive Chef
and Owner,
Loca Luna Restaurant

46

Cut 1 acorn squash in half, clean cavity, brush with lightly with vegetable oil, and bake, cut side down, at 400 degrees for 15 minutes or until barely tender. Remove skin and slice into 1/4- to 1/2-inch chunks. Heat 1 Tbsp. oil in skillet and saute 1 medium onion, chopped, until soft. Add 2 cloves garlic, finely chopped, and cook on low 2 minutes. Remove 2 chipotle chiles in adobo sauce from can; rinse, seed, and cut in strips.

Bring 6 cups chicken stock to simmer in a large saucepan. Add chiles and cook 2 minutes. Add squash, onion, 1 1/2 cups fresh or frozen corn, 1 can black beans (rinsed), and 1 can pink or red beans (rinsed). Simmer 10 minutes. Stir in 2 cups of shredded roasted or grilled chicken breast. Turn off heat and let soup sit 15 minutes for flavors to meld. Season to taste with salt and pepper. To serve, add 3 Tbsp. fresh lime juice, 1/2 cup chopped cilantro, and 2 ripe avacados, thinly sliced. Serve over a bed of crisp fried corn tortilla strips.

Simple "Fresh Taste" Italian Tomato Sauce over Capellini

2002—An Afternoon
of Delicious Treats in
Pleasant Valley
Courtesy of
Mark Abernathy
Executive Chef and
Owner, Loca Luna
Restaurant

Sauté over low heat:

1/4 cup olive oil
1/2 cup chopped yellow onion

16 to 20 oz. canned "fresh cut" tomatoes
5 cloves garlic

Add and simmer 10 to 15 minutes:

1/3 cup fresh parsley, chopped
2 Tbsp. sugar
1 tsp. pepper

30 fresh basil leaves
1 tsp. salt

Serve immediately over capellini (angel hair) pasta.

Shrimp Bruschettas

2003—Treats in the
Prospect Terrace
Neighborhood of the
Heights
Courtesy of
Mark Abernathy
Executive Chef
and Owner,
Loca Luna and Bene
Vita Restaurants

Italian Herb Spread: Mix together:

1/2 cup mayonnaise
1 tablespoon basil, chopped
1 tablespoon parsley, chopped

2 teaspoons Italian dried herbs or oregano
Pinch of black pepper

Combine 1 tablespoon butter, 1 tablespoon olive oil, 2 cloves garlic (minced), 1 red bell pepper cut into thin strips, 1 yellow bell pepper cut into thin strips, and 1 red onion cut into thin strips in sauce pan. Cook over low heat 3-4 minutes until vegetables are soft. Add 1/2 lb. medium size shrimp (peeled and deveined) and cook about 3-4 minutes until shrimp are firm. Add 1 cup shredded mozzarella and stir until melted. Remove from heat.

Butter and toast 1/2 slices of bread. Spread Italian herb mix on the toast, top with shrimp mixture, cover with a slice of cheese and bake (or broil) until the cheese is melted.

Zuppa Lumbarda (Tuscan Bean Soup)

4 garlic cloves, finely chopped and sautéed in 1 tablespoon olive oil until soft

Add and lightly sauté:

2 tomatoes, chopped, or 2 cups canned chopped tomatoes

2-3 Portabella mushrooms, sliced thin

1 cup prosciutto (Italian Ham), sliced thin and chopped

Add:

4 cups veal stock (or 3 cups chicken stock and 1 cup beef stock)

2 cups canned cannellini or navy beans

1/2 cup chopped fresh basil

2 teaspoons ground black pepper

2004—Sologne neighborhood of Chenal Valley
Courtesy of
Mark Abernathy
Executive Chef and Owner, Loca Luna and Bene Vita Restaurants

Tuscan Vegetable Cheese Casserole

Sauté in 1 tablespoon olive oil until soft:

2 cups red onions, chopped into large chunks

2 large red bell peppers, sliced into rings

2 cloves garlic, minced or chopped small

Combine sautéed vegetables in large bowl with:

2 cups yellow squash, sliced into sticks

1 cup zucchini squash, sliced into sticks

1 cup portabella mushrooms, sliced thick

2 cups grape tomatoes, sliced in half

1/2 cup fresh basil, chopped

1/2 cup salted butter, melted

1 cup mozzarella cheese, shredded

1 cup sharp white Cheddar cheese, shredded

1 cup Parmesan cheese, shredded (don't use dry, canned cheese)

1 tablespoon black pepper

1 tablespoon crushed red pepper

1 tablespoon salt

Spray non-stick spray on 9×13 inch glass casserole dish. Pour all ingredients into the greased casserole dish. Bake at 350 degrees for 20 minutes. Remove from oven and cover the top with 2 cups shredded mozzarella cheese and sprinkle with shredded Parmesan cheese. Garnish with sprinkle of roasted pine nuts and finely chopped fresh parsley.

2005—Afternoon Delight in Germay Court
Courtesy of
Mark Abernathy
Executive Chef and Owner, Loca Luna and Bene Vita Restaurants

47

Penne Pasta with Grilled Salmon & Gorgonzola Alfredo Sauce

2 (8-oz.) salmon filets

1 tablespoon unsalted butter

1/2 pint heavy cream

1/4 cup crumbled Gorgonzola blue cheese (or other mild blue cheese)

1 cup frozen English peas

Salt and pepper

A block of quality Parmesan cheese

4 cups dried penne pasta

2 cloves garlic, minced fine or pressed

1/2 cup shredded Parmesan cheese (not powdered)

Pinch of nutmeg

1/2 cup pine nuts, lightly roasted

Fresh basil, cut into thin ribbons

2006—Afternoon Delight in Chenal Circle
Courtesy of
Mark Abernathy
Executive Chef and Owner, Loca Luna and Bene Vita Restaurants

Brush salmon with olive oil, sprinkle with salt and pepper and grill. It should be a little overcooked and very firm. Set aside, keep warm. In a saucepot, on low heat, melt butter and garlic and cook until garlic is opaque. Raise heat to medium, add the cream and Gorgonzola cheese. Stir until melted throughout. Add salt, pepper, and a pinch of nutmeg. Boil pasta in a large pot of salted water until al dente (cooked but firm); then drain. Toss pasta with Gorgonzola sauce. Add peas & pine nuts. Mix in large chunks of salmon. Do not overmix or the salmon will fall apart. Top with grated fresh Parmesan cheese and shredded basil.

Fresh Salmon Mousse with Dill

1998—An Afternoon of Delicious Treats on Hill Road
Courtesy of
Evette Brady
Certified Executive Chef and Owner, 1620 Restaurant

16 oz. fresh salmon, skin removed
8 oz. mayonnaise
1 large shallot, peeled
Juice of 1 fresh lemon

Salt to taste
Cayenne pepper to taste
Fresh dill

Cook salmon about 10 minutes in a medium pot of boiling salted water. Drain and place in bowl to cool. Blend salmon in food processor until smooth. Add shallot, mayonnaise, dill, lemon juice, salt, and pepper; blend until smooth. Place in a mold and chill for one hour. Serves 8 to 12 as an appetizer with toast or crackers.

Shrimp Butter Appetizer

1999—Delicious Treats on Beechwood Street
Courtesy of
Evette Brady
Certified Executive Chef and Owner, 1620 Restaurant

1 lb. shrimp, cooked, peeled and deveined
8 oz. cream cheese
Juice of 1 lemon, seeded
Salt to taste

1 small white onion, finely chopped
1/2 lb. unsalted butter
Cayenne pepper to taste

Cook shrimp in salted boiling water until pink. Drain and place in bowl to cool. Chop onion fine in food processor. Add shrimp and blend until smooth. Add cream cheese, butter, lemon, salt, and pepper to taste. Place in small mold or bowl. Serve with toast points or wafer crackers. (Makes 10 appetizer servings)

1620 Seafood Jambalaya

2001—Cooks Tour Visits Longfellow Lane & Beverly Place
Courtesy of
Evette Brady
Certified Executive Chef and Owner, 1620 Restaurant

Make a roux with 1 stick butter, 1/2 cup diced salt pork, 1 to 1 3/4 cups flour, and spices.

Season with spices and sauté:

3 cups celery, chopped
3 bunches green onions, chopped
3 cloves garlic, chopped
1 large bell pepper, chopped

1 bunch parsley, chopped fine
1 large can stewed tomatoes
1 can mild Rotel

Season with spices and sauté:

3 cups chicken, in chunks
3 cups ham, in chunks
1 lb. sweet Italian sausage, sliced

Combine these three mixtures and add: 1 qt. tomato juice, 2 cups chicken stock, 1/2 lb. medium shrimp, raw, peeled, deveined, 1/2 lb. lump crabmeat, flaked (do not drain), 4 cups cooked rice. Adjust seasonings, pour into 4 qt. pan. Bake loosely covered at 350 degrees for 45 minutes to 1 hour. Let stand 5 minutes before serving.

Salmon with Caribbean Salsa or Cucumber Dill Sour Cream Sauce

2002—
An Afternoon of Delicious Treats in Pleasant Valley
Courtesy of
Evette Brady
Certified Executive Chef and Owner, 1620 Restaurant

Caribbean Salsa: Blend ingredients and chill before serving atop grilled salmon.

1/2 cantaloupe, peeled, seeded and diced
1/2 pineapple, peeled, cored and diced
1 mango, peeled and diced
1 jalapeño chile, seeded and finely chopped
Juice of 1 lemon and 1 lime
1/4 cup raisins
3 Tbsp. brown sugar

Poached Salmon: Fill roasting pan with 2 quarts water. Add 2 Tbsp. vinegar, 1/4 tsp. olive oil, 5 to 6 sprigs fresh parsley, 1 cup carrots (cut in 1/4-inch chunks), and 1 lemon, sliced. Bring to a boil, then reduce to simmer. Poach salmon about 2-3 minutes/side. Drain on absorbent towels. Serve each portion with sauce.

Cucumber Dill Sour Cream Sauce: Blend 1 cup cucumber, peeled, seeded, and diced; 2 to 3 sprigs fresh dill, chopped; juice of 1/2 lemon; 1 cup sour cream; dash of salt. Chill before serving.

Italian and Smoked Meats

Italian and smoked meats:	Cheeses:
Italian sausages	blue cheese
Smoked salmon	Brie
Salami	Havarti
Smoked quails	Striped Jack
Ham	Provolone

Served with marinated vegetables and crudités along with assorted stuffed peppers.

Greek Salad with Meat and Cheese Trays

Italian and smoked meats:	Cheeses:
Italian sausages	Blue cheese
Stuffed leg of lamb	Brie
Pork tenderloin	Havarti
Smoked quails	Striped Jack
	Provolone

Served with marinated vegetables and crudités along with assorted stuffed peppers.

1620 Marinade for Smoked Meats

1/2 cup fresh ground coriander	2 tablespoons ground black pepper
3 cups Worcestershire Sauce	4 large minced shallots
1 cup chili powder	6 minced garlic cloves
1/4 cup salt	1 cup prepared mustard
3 cups brown sugar	

Combine all ingredients in a heavy saucepan and stir. Bring to a rolling boil for 10 minutes, remove from heat, let stand for 5 minutes, and apply to meats.

Coriander Rub for Beef Fillets

8 ounces whole coriander seed
2 tablespoons chili powder
3 tablespoons minced shallots
1/4 cup salt
1/4 cup packed dark brown sugar
2 tablespoons olive oil

Grind the coriander seeds. Combine all ingredients in a bowl and mix thoroughly.

Smoked Salmon Mousse

16 oz. smoked salmon*
1 cup heavy whipping cream
Juice of 1 lemon
2 tsp. fresh dill, chopped (1 tsp. dried)
Salt and pepper to taste

Puree salmon in food processor. Slowly add cream. Add lemon juice and dill and season to taste. Pour in pastry bag to pipe or a souffle dish. Spread on crackers or toast points. Garnish with fresh dill.

*Slice salmon very thin and soak in a brine solution made of 6 Tbsp. salt, 6 Tbsp. sugar, and 2 tsp. Worcestershire sauce, in 6 gallons of water. Remove after 10 minutes and pat dry. Place on grate and smoke according to instructions (using hickory, mesquite or apple wood— your choice) for 15 to 20 minutes.

2003—Treats in the Prospect Terrace Neighborhood of the Heights
Courtesy of
Evette Brady
Certified Executive Chef and Owner, 1620 Restaurant

2004—Sologne neighborhood of Chenal Valley
Courtesy of
Evette Brady
Certified Executive Chef and Owner, 1620 Restaurant

2005—Afternoon Delight in Germay Court
Courtesy of
Evette Brady
Certified Executive Chef and Owner, 1620 Restaurant

2006—Afternoon Delight in Chenal Circle
Courtesy of
Evette Brady
Certified Executive Chef and Owner, 1620 Restaurant

1996—Down By The Riverside
Courtesy of
Peter Brave
Owner and Executive Chef, Brave New Restaurant

Smoked Tomato Soup

1997—Afternoon of
Delicious Treats on
River Ridge
Courtesy of
Peter Brave
Owner and
Executive Chef,
Brave New Restaurant

5 lb. ripe red tomatoes, peeled, seeded, and cooked in a smoker 45 minutes
1/2 yellow onion, chopped
1 tsp. garlic
2 Tbsp. olive oil
2 qt. chicken stock
Salt, pepper, lemon juice, and Worcestershire sauce to taste

In a stockpot, sauté onion and garlic in olive oil until translucent. Add tomatoes and chicken stock. Simmer 45 minutes. Purée with an immersion blender. Season, garnish with fresh chives, and serve. (Serves 12)

Chocolate Ganache with Fresh Berries

1999—Delicious Treats
on Beechwood Street
Courtesy of *Peter Brave*
Owner and Executive Chef,
Brave New Restaurant

1 cup heavy cream
2 Tbsp. granulated sugar
2 Tbsp. unsalted butter
12 oz. semisweet chocolate, chopped

Heat cream, butter, and sugar in saucepan until almost boiling. Place chocolate in stainless steel bowl and pour heavy cream mixture over it. Cover bowl with plastic wrap. Let sit at room temperature for approximately 5 minutes until chocolate melts. Remove plastic wrap and stir with spatula until smooth. Place berries in dessert dishes and top with chocolate ganache. Garnish with mint sprigs or additional berries.

50

Roast Pork Tenderloin with Whole-Grain Mustard Sauce

2000—Cooks Tour
Visits Armistead &
Edgehill Roads
Courtesy of
Peter Brave
Owner and
Executive Chef,
Brave New Restaurant

Pork: Combine and marinate 1 (12-14 oz.) pork tenderloin for 2 to 6 hours:

1/2 cup honey	1/2 Tbsp. minced garlic
1/2 cup sesame seed oil	1/2 Tbsp. seasoned salt
1/2 cup red wine	

Roast in a 425-degree oven 20 minutes, basting 2-3 times with marinade. Let stand 5 minutes.

Sauce: Combine in saucepan:

1 cup heavy cream	1/4 tsp. minced garlic
2 Tbsp. Parmesan cheese	1/4 tsp. seasoned salt

Reduce by 2/3. Stir in 3 Tbsp. whole grain mustard. Serve slices of tenderloin and sauce over basmati rice pilaf.

Dessert Tarts Filled with Mousse and Garnished with Fresh Berries

2003—Treats in the
Prospect Terrace
Neighborhood of
the Heights
Courtesy of
Peter Brave
Owner and
Executive Chef,
Brave New Restaurant

10 oz. chocolate
12 oz. butter
5 eggs, separated
2 oz. sugar
8 oz. whipped cream

Combine chocolate and butter and heat until melted; then whip yolks and 1/2 of sugar until mixture forms ribbons. Whip whites and other 1/2 of sugar to stiff peaks. Fold whites and yolks. Fold butter and chocolate mix into egg mix. Fold in whipped cream. Spoon into tart shells and chill until serving time. Garnish with fresh berries.

Shrimp and Basil

8 oz. angel hair pasta, cooked and strained
2 tbsp. olive oil
1 lb. peeled and deveined shrimp
2 cups diced tomatoes
3 tbsp. fresh basil leaves, chopped
1 tbsp. fresh garlic, minced
1 tbsp. butter
Salt and pepper to taste

Heat oil in skillet. Sauté shrimp, tomatoes, garlic and basil until shrimp is thoroughly cooked, about 2-3 minutes. Stir in butter and serve over pasta. Yields 2 servings.

2004—Sologne
Neighborhood of
Chenal Valley
Courtesy of
Peter Brave
Owner and
Executive Chef,
Brave New Restaurant

Shrimp on a Skewer with Mango Horseradish Buerre Blanc

Marinate shrimp in olive oil with plenty of garlic and cracked black pepper; broil in oven for approximately four minutes.

Sauce

1 cup white wine
1/2 cup mango purée
1/8 cup puréed horseradish

3 shallots, finely chopped
1/2 cup white wine vinegar

In a saucepan, reduce all above ingredients by 3/4 volume. Then whisk in 1 lb. unsalted butter 2 oz. at a time until all is incorporated; add salt and pepper to taste.

2005—Afternoon
Delight in Germay Court
Courtesy of
Peter Brave
Owner and Executive
Chef,
Brave New
Restaurant

Seafood Bisque

3 cups seafood, your choice
1/2 cup chopped onion
1/2 cup chopped celery
3/4 cup chopped green pepper
1 Tbsp. minced garlic
20 leaves fresh basil, torn
2 (16 oz.) cans tomatoes, chopped

24 oz. shrimp stock
1/4 cup whipping cream
3/4 cup olive oil
1/2 cup flour
1 Tbsp. black peppercorns, crushed
1 1/2 tsp. salt
1/2 cup sugar

Sauté seafood, onion, celery, and green pepper with olive oil until onions are translucent. Add garlic and set aside. In a large sauté skillet, make a dark brown roux of olive oil and flour. Add pepper, first mixture, tomatoes and stock. Stir well. Add remaining ingredients. Simmer 10 minutes.

1996—Down By
The Riverside
Courtesy of
Kent Griffiths
Executive Chef,
Zaffino's Italian
Restaurant

Pan-seared Sea Scallops with Granny Smith Apple Horseradish Salsa and Blue Cheese Grits

Grits: Bring 5 1/3 cups water to a boil. Add 1 1/3 cups grits, salt to taste, and 1 Tbsp. garlic. Cover and simmer over low heat 5 to 7 minutes, stirring occasionally. When thickened, fold in 1/3 cup blue cheese.

Salsa: Dice 2 Granny Smith apples, 1 red bell pepper, and 1 green bell pepper. Toss with 1 Tbsp. garlic, 1/3 cup vinegar, 2 Tbsp. horseradish, and salt and pepper to taste.

Scallops: Season 16 oz. of scallops with salt and pepper. Heat 3 Tbsp. butter in skillet until just brown. Add scallops and sear on both sides until golden brown. Spoon grits into middle of plate. Surround with scallops. Garnish with salsa.

2001—Cooks Tour
Visits Longfellow
Lane & Beverly Place
Courtesy of
James Hale
Executive Chef &
Co-owner,
Acadia Restaurant

Smoked Duck Cole Slaw with Rosemary Potato Cakes

2002—An Afternoon
of Delicious Treats in
Pleasant Valley
Courtesy of
James Hale
Executive Chef &
Co-owner,
Acadia Restaurant

Slaw: Combine ingredients:

1 duck breast,
smoked and sliced thin
1 carrot, julienned
1/2 tsp. minced garlic

1/2 cup shredded cabbage
5 scallions, chopped
Salt & pepper to taste

Serve at room temperature over hot potato cakes.

Potato cakes: Combine ingredients:

1 baking potato, grated
1 Tbsp. minced garlic
1/2 cup flour
2 Tbsp. fresh rosemary

3 eggs
2 Tbsp. cooking oil
2 Tbsp. cream
Salt & pepper to taste

Pat into pancake-size portions and cook in small amount of hot oil in non-stick skillet.

Maiale in Latte (Pork in Milk)

1999—Delicious Treats
on Beechwood Street

52

Courtesy of
Eric Isaac
Executive Chef,
Cassinelli 1700

5 lb. pork loin
3 cups white wine vinegar
20 cloves garlic, peeled
5 cups milk
1 cup olive oil

Sear pork with garlic in olive oil. Add white wine vinegar and reduce by half. Add milk. Cover and bake in a 350-degree oven for 1 hour. Remove pork from pan. Blend and strain pork juices and serve with the sliced pork.

White Chocolate Raspberry Brûlée

1996—Down By
The Riverside
Courtesy of
Greg Matthews
Executive Chef,
Andre's Hillcrest

350 grams grated white chocolate
2 qts. whipping cream
1 cup brown sugar

14 egg yolks
7 oz. sugar
56 frozen raspberries

Bring whipping cream and brown sugar to a boil and turn off heat. Combine white chocolate, egg yolks, and sugar in mixing bowl. Carefully add whipping cream mixture. Stir slowly until chocolate is completely melted. Strain mixture into individual ramekins. Add 3 or 4 raspberries to each cup. Bake in water bath at 350 degrees for 1 hour. Cool completely before serving. (If brûlée is undercooked it will be runny; if overcooked, the egg yolk will scramble).

Florentine Chicken Fricassee

1997—Afternoon
of Delicious Treats
on River Ridge
Courtesy of
Jeff Medbury
Andrea Cassinelli
Cassinelli 1700

11/2 oz. dried porcini mushrooms, soaked 30 minutes, drained, and cleaned
1 chicken (about 3 lb.), cut into 8 pieces
Cheesecloth bag: 1 red onion, 1 celery rib, 10 sprigs Italian parsley, leaves only;
1 carrot, scraped; 1/2 tsp. fresh rosemary leaves
1 Tbsp. unsalted butter
2 Tbsp. olive oil
11/2 Tbsp. unbleached all-purpose flour
21/2 cups chicken or meat broth, heated
3 extra-large egg yolks, beaten

Sauté chicken in butter & oil over medium heat 10 to 12 minutes. Set aside. Add flour and cook until golden. Add 11/2 cups broth, mixing well. Return chicken pieces, add cheesecloth bag, cover and simmer 20 minutes. Remove bag and season with salt and pepper. Add mushrooms and more hot broth, if needed. Cover and simmer 10 minutes more. Remove from the heat, and quickly add the egg yolks which have been beaten, stirring continuously.

Tuscan Chicken Liver Pate

2 Tbsp. extra virgin olive oil
1/2 cup small diced shallots
8 oz. chicken liver
Salt and pepper to taste
2 Tbsp. marsala wine

2 Tbsp. vin santo
1/4 cup rinsed capers
4 sprigs fresh sage
2 anchovies
2 Tbsp. butter

Add olive oil to sauté pan and cook shallots over medium heat, stirring often, until caramelized. Add the chicken livers and sauté until just cooked through, about 2 minutes. Add marsala and vin santo (increase the amount of marsala if you don't have vin santo), and reduce by 1/2. Allow the liver and shallot mixture to cool slightly and transfer to a food processor. Add the capers, sage and anchovies. Process until slightly smooth; add butter and process until the butter is incorporated. Correct seasoning, spread on grilled crostini and enjoy!!!!

2006—Afternoon Delight in Chenal Circle
Courtesy of
Scott McGehee
Executive Chef & Owner, Boulevard Bread Company

Girello Agnello con Erbe

Coat rack of lamb with Dijon mustard and bread crumbs. Grill and serve with sauce. Sauce: Bake 6 lb. veal bones, split in 2-inch pieces, at 500 degrees for about 25 minutes until edges start to turn black. Chop and add 1 carrot, 1 onion, 4 ribs celery, and 6-8 cloves garlic. Lower oven temperature to 450 degrees and cook 5 minutes. Add 1/2 cup tomato paste; cook 5 minutes. Add 32 oz. dry red wine and cook until reduced by half. Add 1 quart water and cook 25 minutes. Stir in 1 cup flour and immediately place in large stockpot. Deglaze baking pan with 1/2 gallon water. Add this plus another 3 1/2 gallons to stockpot. Make sachetto by tying 1 1/2 Tbsp. black peppercorns, 3-inch sprig fresh rosemary, 1 Tbsp. thyme, 1 Tbsp. marjoram, 1 tsp. rubbed sage in a small cheesecloth bag; add it to the pot. Bring to a boil, then lower heat and simmer about 3 hours. Add 1 tomato, coarsely chopped, 10 springs parsley, and 1/8 cup fresh mint. Reduce stock by half. Add 2 gallons cold water and return to boil. Then simmer for 6 to 8 hours. Remove sachetto and bones; strain sauce. Chill to remove any remaining fat.

1998—An Afternoon of Delicious Treats on Hill Road
Courtesy of
Jeff Medbury
Certified Executive Chef, Cassinelli 1700

Risotto

Cook 1/2 cup chopped onions and 1 tsp. chopped garlic in 3 tsp. butter. Add 1 1/4 cups of Arborio rice. Cook until transparent. Add 1 quart chicken stock. Cook for 15 minutes, or until rice absorbs stock, stirring occasionally. Add 3 Tbsp. room temperature butter and blend. Add 1/2 cup freshly grated Parmesan cheese. Salt and pepper to taste. You can also add a variety of ingredients to this dish, such as mushrooms, artichoke hearts, sun-dried tomatoes, and fresh vegetables.

Risotto is a traditional Italian rice dish which means "little rice."

1996—Down By The Riverside
Courtesy of
Paul Novicky
Certified Executive Chef, Spaulé

Lemon Mousse Croustades with Red Currant Coulis

Cut puff pastry in 2×3-inch rectangles and bake at 400 degrees until golden brown. Let cool while preparing lemon mousse.

2 egg yolks
6 Tbsp. sugar
2 Tbsp. cornstarch

6 limes, juiced
2 lemons, juiced
2 egg whites, whipped to soft peaks

Whip yolks and sugar until frothy. Add cornstarch and juices; bring to a boil. Let cool, then fold in whites. Cut out puff pastry centers and fill with mousse.

To Make Coulis: Place 1 lb. fresh red currants (no stems), 3 Tbsp. water, and 1 cup sugar in saucepan. Simmer on low/medium heat until reduced by 1/2. Let cool and pour over mousse.

1997—Afternoon of Delicious Treats on River Ridge
Courtesy of
Paul Novicky
Certified Executive Chef, Spaulé

Dark Chocolate Bavarian Cream Napoleon

1998—An Afternoon of Delicious Treats on Hill Road
Courtesy of
Paul Novicky
Certified Executive Chef, Spaulé

Cookies: Whip 2 egg whites, 1 tsp. vanilla, and 2 oz. sugar until soft peaks form. Combine 2 oz. flour, 4 oz. sugar, and 1/2 cup heavy cream. Fold whites into mixture. Spoon 30 discs onto non-stick cookie sheet and bake at 350 degrees until golden brown. Let cool before removing from pan.

Mousse: Combine 1 cup sugar, 1 tsp. vanilla, and 1/2 cup butter in saucepan. Heat to dissolve sugar. Add 1 lb. melted bittersweet chocolate. Place mixture in mixer. Add 4 eggs slowly. Whip 1 qt. heavy cream and 3 Tbsp. sugar until stiff. Fold into chocolate mixture.

Assemble: Layer mousse and cookies, using 3 cookies per serving. Serves 10.

Shiitake & Peking Pork Crisp

2001—Cooks Tour Visits Longfellow Lane & Beverly Place
Courtesy of
Michael Selig
Executive Chef & Co-owner, Vermillion Bistro

Combine ingredients and marinate 8 oz. pork tenderloin for 30 minutes:

3 oz. hoisin
1 Tbsp. chili garlic
4 oz. soy sauce
3 Tbsp. sesame oil
2 oz. orange juice
1 1/2 Tbsp. cilantro, minced

Bake tenderloin at 350 degrees for 20 minutes. Let cool, then slice into strips.

Julienne 1 red pepper and 1 large red onion. Sauté 1/4 of each with 1 Tbsp. sesame oil and set aside. Remove stems from 10 shiitake mushrooms; steam, cool, set aside. Place 1 nori (seaweed paper) on dry surface. Shingle shiitakes on bottom third. Add strips of pork, then pepper and onion. Roll the nori in egg roll fashion. Repeat until you have 8 rolls. Coat with beaten egg, then Japanese bread crumbs. Bake or deep-fry until crispy. Serve with dipping sauces like spicy mustard, pineapple plum, or peanut.

Sea Scallops with Crab Pepper Greens

2002—An Afternoon of Delicious Treats in Pleasant Valley
Courtesy of
Michael Selig
Executive Chef & Co-owner, Vermillion Bistro

Scallops: Combine 4 basil leaves, finely minced, with blackening seasoning. Coat 6 sea scallops with mixture. Sauté in 1 tsp. butter until done.

Chipotle Aioli: Combine in food processor:

6 oz. mayonnaise
2 oz. Dijon mustard
1 oz. each roasted garlic, honey, and chipotle

Greens: Reduce together until mixture begins to stick to the bottom of the pan:

1 jar pepper vinegar sauce
1 1/2 onions, diced
1/4 lb. bacon, chopped

Add and cook until greens are done:

2 lb. collard greens (fresh or frozen)
1 ham hock

When ready to serve, fold 1 lb. lump crab into greens. Top with scallops and aioli.

Lump Crab Crusted Roasted Chipotle Shrimp

For Shrimp:

16 shrimp (16-20 peeled and deveined)

1 lb. lump crab (picked, clean)

2 tbs. mayo

1 tsp. Dijon mustard

1/2 tsp. Old Bay

1 chipotle pepper

1/2 cup orange juice

1/2 oz. minced cilantro

Combine chipotle, cilantro and orange juice. Marinate shrimp in mixture for one hour. Combine mayo, mustard, Old Bay and crab in separate bowl. Surround shrimp with crab, leaving the tail exposed. Preheat oven to 450 degrees and roast shrimp.

For Polenta:

3/4 cup polenta (quick)

3 cups chicken stock

5 oz. candied pistachios

4 oz. Brie cheese

3 oz. butter

3 oz. heavy cream

Bring chicken stock to a boil with candied pistachios and Brie. Let boil for five minutes and add polenta. Simmer for two minutes and add butter and heavy cream. Cook for two more minutes.

For Sun-Dried Cherry Butter:

4 oz. butter

2 oz. onion, roughly chopped

3 oz. sun-dried cherries (soaked)

1/2 cup white wine

2003—Treats in the Prospect Terrace Neighborhood of the Heights

Courtesy of

Michael Selig

Executive Chef & Co-owner, Vermillion Bistro

Sesame Ahi Mango Risotto Chip with Spicy Mustard

2 lb. ahi (sashimi grade)

1 lb. Arborio rice

1 fresh mango, puréed

2 ounces cilantro, chopped

2 tbsp. chili garlic

3 ounces soy sauce

1 Tbsp. sesame oil

2 oz. orange juice

2 oz. honey

8 egg roll wrappers

1 egg, beaten

Combine cilantro, soy sauce, sesame oil, orange juice and honey; mix well and set aside. Cook risotto with Arborio rice; once risotto is done, while still hot, fold in 1/2 of marinade and puréed mango. Let cool to room temperature. Slice ahi in strips and place in remaining marinade; lay out egg roll wrappers and brush with egg. Place approximately 6 tbsps. risotto on each wrapper, leaving 1/2-inch space on all sides. Place ahi strip in middle of risotto and fold vertical side into ahi; roll from one end to close. Bake at 400 degrees until golden brown or fry until golden brown and enjoy.

2004—Sologne neighborhood of Chenal Valley

Courtesy of

Michael Selig

Executive Chef & Co-owner, Vermillion Bistro and Vermillion Water Grille

Cilantro Ahi Pico Shooters with Chipotle Aioli

2005—Afternoon
Delight in Germay Court
Courtesy of **Michael
Selig** Executive Chef &
Co-owner, Vermillion
Bistro and Vermillion
Water Grille

Ahi (4 oz. diced and marinated in oriental marinade)
Oriental marinade (1 oz.) Vermillion Secrets
Pico de gallo (6 oz. purée) Vermillion Secrets
Chipotle aioli (4 oz.)
Place pico de gallo in a shot glass (1 oz.); put diced ahi on top of pico and finish with aioli.

Crab Cakes

2006—Afternoon
Delight in Chenal Circle
Courtesy of **Michael
Selig** Executive Chef &
Co-owner, Vermillion
Bistro and Vermillion
Water Grille

1lb. lump crab (steamed and picked)
3$1/2$ tablespoons mayonnaise
$1/2$ tablespoon Dijon mustard
$1/2$ teaspoon Old Bay seasoning
Combine all ingredients and form six 3-ounce crab cakes. Place in freezer for 2 minutes. Heat a non-stick skillet over medium heat. Remove crab cakes from freezer and spray with non-stick cooking spray. Place in pan and brown both sides until middle is hot. Enjoy with your favorite sauces.

Tips from the Chef: Combine mayonnaise, mustard and Old Bay seasoning, and then add crab. This helps keep the lump crab intact.

56

Canederli

2000—Cooks Tour
Visits Armistead &
Edgehill Roads
Courtesy of
Gregory York
Executive Chef,
Cassinelli 1700

Beat 4 eggs, $3/4$ cup milk, and a little salt. Cut 9 oz. stale bread into cubes and soak them in this mixture about 20 minutes.

Finely chop and sauté over medium heat for a few minutes (but do not brown):
2 oz. pancetta
2 oz. hard salami
1 medium white or yellow onion
1 sprig Italian parsley

Add to bread mixture, along with:
3 Tbsp. all-purpose flour
Salt and freshly ground black pepper to taste
Put a heaping Tbsp. of this mixture in a ladle containing a small amount of flour. Turn the mixture until you have created a round or egg-shaped dumpling. Cook a few at a time in boiling water for 4-5 minutes. Drain and toss with melted butter and Parmesan cheese OR melted butter and finely chopped fresh sage OR a rich flavorful broth.

Appetizers and Beverages

A Recipe for Safe Food

Food-borne illnesses may be prevented by the proper storage, safe handling, and appropriate preparation and cooking. From the grocery store to the table, consumers can take simple measures to protect themselves and others from bacteria that may cause illness, by washing hands and preparation surfaces frequently; avoiding cross-contamination; cooking food to proper temperatures; and storing food at proper temperatures as soon as possible.

At the Supermarket

- Minimize thawing—Choose perishables shortly before you finish shopping.

- Ensure freshness—Inspect packaging to ensure it is intact, leak free, and within expiration dates.

- Separate fruits and vegetables from meat, poultry, and fish to avoid cross-contamination.

Home Storage

- Refrigerate perishables within two hours.

- Maintain refrigerator temperature at ≤ 40 °F and freezer at 0 °F.

Cook or Freeze

- fresh poultry, fish, ground meats, and variety meats within two days

- other beef, veal, lamb, or pork, within three to five days

- Wrap/store meats and store below other foods to prevent juices from contacting other food.

Shelf Life of Canned Foods

- high-acid (tomatoes, grapefruit, and pineapple) ≈ twelve to eighteen months

- low-acid (meat, poultry, fish, most vegetables) ≈ two to five years (if the can remains in good condition and has been stored in a cool, clean, and dry place).

Preparation

- Always wash hands with warm water and soap for twenty seconds before and after handling food.

- Sanitize cutting boards and countertops with hot, soapy water before and after all food preparation.

- Sanitize preparation area and utensils, after preparing meats and before preparing foods that will be consumed without cooking.

- If possible, use one cutting board and preparation area for fresh fruits and vegetables and a different cutting board and preparation area for meat, poultry, and fish.

Meats

- Don't cross-contaminate. Keep raw meat, poultry, fish, and their juices away from other food.

- Marinate meat and poultry in a covered dish in the refrigerator.

Vegetables/Fruits

- Clean the sink with hot, soapy water or cleanser before and after washing and preparing fresh fruits and vegetables.

- Wash all fruits and vegetables under running water, just before cooking.

- When possible, scrub fruits and vegetables with a clean scrub brush or hands.

- Remove outer green leaves from items like lettuce or cauliflower before washing.

- Trim the hull or stem from items like tomatoes, strawberries, and peppers after washing with warm water.

Thawing and Cooking

- Use the refrigerator for safe slow thawing; use cold water for fast thawing.

- Cook meat and poultry immediately after thawing.

- Cook beef, veal, and lamb steaks, roasts, and chops to 145 °F.

- Cook pork, ground beef, veal, and lamb to 160 °F.

- Cook all poultry to a minimum internal temperature of 160 °F.

Serving/Re-serving

- Keep hot foods at >140 °F and cold foods at < 40 °F.

- Perishable foods should not be left at room temperature for more than two hours.

- Use cooked leftovers within four days.

Cocktail Nibbles

1 1/2 cups vegetable oil
2   envelopes ranch salad dressing mix
2   teaspoons lemon pepper seasoning
1   teaspoon dill weed
1   teaspoon garlic powder
3   (10-ounce) packages oyster crackers

Whisk the oil, dressing mix, lemon pepper seasoning, dill weed and garlic powder in a large bowl until combined. Add the crackers and mix until coated. Let stand for 1 hour before serving. Store in an airtight container.

Yield: 60 servings

Nutrients per serving
Calories 111
Protein 1 g
Carbo 11 g
Total Fat 7 g
Saturated Fat 1 g
Cholesterol 0 mg
Fiber <1 g
Sodium 242 mg

Bruschetta

1   (16-ounce) loaf crusty French bread, cut into 1/2-inch slices
1   tablespoon chopped garlic
1   tablespoon olive oil
1 1/2 pounds Roma tomatoes, seeded and chopped
1/2   cup fresh basil leaves, chopped
1   tablespoon chopped fresh oregano leaves
1   tablespoon balsamic vinegar
1   teaspoon fresh lemon juice
~   Salt and pepper to taste

Rub both sides of the bread slices with the garlic and brush with the olive oil. Grill the bread slices or toast in a preheated 400-degree oven until brown on both sides. Mix the tomatoes, basil, oregano, vinegar, lemon juice, salt and pepper in a bowl. Spoon the tomato mixture on the toasted bread slices and serve immediately. Do not prepare in advance as the bread will become soggy.

Yield: 12 servings

Nutrients per serving
Calories 146
Protein 6 g
Carbo 26 g
Total Fat 2 g
Saturated Fat <1 g
Cholesterol 0 mg
Fiber 3 g
Sodium 251 mg

To make reading recipes and keeping them clean an easier task, clip recipes to skirt holder clips and hang from kitchen cabinet knobs.

The School of Pharmacy was established. 1951

Toasted Butter Pecans

Yield: 16 servings

Nutrients per serving
Calories 222
Protein 3 g
Carbo 4 g
Total Fat 23 g
Saturated Fat 4 g
Cholesterol 8 mg
Fiber 3 g
Sodium 192 mg

1/4 cup (1/2 stick) butter, softened
1   tablespoon seasoned salt
1   pound pecan halves (about 4 cups)

Mix the butter and seasoned salt in a bowl. Arrange the pecans in a 11/2-quart microwave-safe dish. Dot the pecans with the butter mixture. Microwave on High for 5 to 6 minutes and stir to coat the pecans with the butter mixture. Remove to a platter to cool. Store in an airtight container.

Hot Artichoke and Feta Cheese Dip

Yield: 32 servings

Nutrients per serving
Calories 92
Protein 2 g
Carbo 1 g
Total Fat 8 g
Saturated Fat 2 g
Cholesterol 11 mg
Fiber 1 g
Sodium 220 mg

1   (14-ounce) jar marinated artichokes
1   cup mayonnaise
1/2 cup (2 ounces) grated Parmesan cheese
4   ounces feta cheese, crumbled
4   ounces garlic and herb feta cheese, crumbled
1   garlic clove, minced
1/2 cup (2 ounces) grated Parmesan cheese

Chop the artichokes, reserving the marinade. Combine the artichokes, reserved marinade, mayonnaise, 1/2 cup Parmesan cheese, the feta cheese, garlic and herb feta cheese and garlic in a bowl and mix well. Spoon into a baking dish and sprinkle with 1/2 cup Parmesan cheese. Bake at 350 degrees for 20 to 25 minutes or until brown and bubbly. Serve warm with assorted party crackers.

Often during pregnancy, women think eating everything in sight is OK. What is more crucial is eating healthy foods. Women should gain approximately twenty-five to thirty pounds during pregnancy. This amount of weight gain accounts not only for the weight of the baby but also the placenta and maternal blood/fluids. Usually in the first trimester of pregnancy, only ten pounds is gained. During the latter half of pregnancy, women should typically gain one pound a week. Pregnant women's diets should be filled with fresh fruits and vegetables, dairy, and protein. At times, indulgence on desserts is OK, but it should not be every day.
—Stephanie Wyatt, APN, and Paul Wendel, MD

1952   *The first School of Pharmacy students graduated.*

BLT Dip

1	pound sliced bacon	1	teaspoon Dijon mustard
1	cup sour cream or reduced-fat sour cream	2	large tomatoes, seeded and chopped
1	cup mayonnaise or reduced-fat mayonnaise	1/2	cup sliced scallions
		~	Salt and pepper to taste

Cook the bacon in a skillet until brown and crisp. Drain on paper towels and crumble. Combine the sour cream, mayonnaise and Dijon mustard in a bowl and mix well. Fold in the bacon, tomatoes and scallions. Season with salt and pepper. Serve with chips and/or assorted party crackers. You may substitute with packaged pre-cooked bacon.

Yield: 24 servings

Nutrients per serving
Calories 125
Protein 3 g
Carbo 1 g
Total Fat 12 g
Saturated Fat 3 g
Cholesterol 14 mg
Fiber <1 g
Sodium 206 mg

Hot Broccoli Dip

1   (5-ounce) roll garlic cheese
1   (10-ounce) can cream of mushroom soup
2   (10-ounce) packages frozen chopped broccoli, cooked and drained
1   onion, chopped
1   (6- to 8-ounce) can mushroom pieces, drained

Combine the cheese and soup in a saucepan and cook until the cheese melts, stirring frequently. Stir in the broccoli.

Sauté the onion with the mushrooms in a nonstick skillet until the onion is tender. Add to the broccoli mixture and mix well. Cook just until heated through. Serve hot with assorted chips.

Yield: 10 servings

Nutrients per serving
Calories 98
Protein 4 g
Carbo 8 g
Total Fat 6 g
Saturated Fat 2 g
Cholesterol 9 mg
Fiber 2 g
Sodium 402 mg

Dipping bacon in cold water before cooking will cut down on the edges curling. To separate frozen bacon, heat a spatula with hot water and the bacon will separate easily.

The School of Nursing was established. 1953

Chocolate Dip

Yield: 15 servings

Nutrients per serving
Calories 183
Protein 3 g
Carbo 32 g
Total Fat 6 g
Saturated Fat 4 g
Cholesterol 9 mg
Fiber 1 g
Sodium 46 mg

1 cup (6 ounces) chocolate chips
1 (14-ounce) can sweetened condensed milk
2 tablespoons milk or cream
1 (7-ounce) jar marshmallow creme
1 teaspoon vanilla extract

Heat the chocolate chips, condensed milk and milk in a double boiler over simmering water until blended, stirring occasionally. Stir in the marshmallow creme and vanilla. Serve warm with assorted fruit or anything edible.

Orange Pecan Dip

Yield: 8 servings

Nutrients per serving
Calories 164
Protein 3 g
Carbo 8 g
Total Fat 14 g
Saturated Fat 7 g
Cholesterol 36 mg
Fiber <1 g
Sodium 122 mg

8 ounces cream cheese, softened
1/4 cup thawed frozen orange juice concentrate
2 tablespoons whipping cream
2 tablespoons sugar
1/2 teaspoon lemon juice
1/8 teaspoon salt
1/4 cup chopped pecans

Combine the cream cheese, orange juice concentrate, whipping cream, sugar, lemon juice and salt in a bowl and mix well. Stir in the pecans.

Spoon the dip into a serving bowl. Chill, covered, until serving time. Serve with assorted fruit.

Keep sliced apples, bananas, pears, and other fruit from discoloring by tossing with orange juice or diluted lemon juice.

1954

The VA Hospital in Little Rock was included as part of the School of Medicine's clinical teaching program.

Confetti Crab Dip

16	ounces cream cheese
12	ounces crab meat, drained and flaked
1/4	cup minced green onions
3	tablespoons mayonnaise
2	tablespoons sour cream
1 1/8	teaspoons garlic powder
1/4	teaspoon salt
1/4	teaspoon dry mustard
1/8	teaspoon sweet red pepper flakes
1	(2-ounce) jar diced pimento, drained
1	tablespoon sauterne
1	tablespoon chopped fresh chives

Yield: 20 servings

Nutrients per serving
Calories 114
Protein 5 g
Carbo 1 g
Total Fat 10 g
Saturated Fat 5 g
Cholesterol 40 mg
Fiber <1 g
Sodium 163 mg

Place the cream cheese in a 1-quart microwave-safe baking dish. Microwave on High for 1 to 1 1/2 minutes or until softened; stir. Add the crab meat, green onions, mayonnaise, sour cream, garlic powder, salt, dry mustard and red pepper flakes and mix well.

Microwave, covered with heavy-duty plastic wrap, on High for 2 to 3 minutes or until heated through, stirring after 1 minute. Stir in the pimento and wine and sprinkle with the chives. Serve warm with assorted party crackers.

63

Plan on serving about eight different types of appetizers for a party with more than forty-five guests. For less than forty-five guests, serve six different appetizers; for fourteen to sixteen guests, serve four or five different appetizers; and for eight to ten guests, serve three different appetizers.

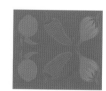

The first class of the new School of Nursing arrived—all eight of them.

1955

Lobster Dip Elegante

Yield: 12 servings

Nutrients per serving
Calories 118
Protein 4 g
Carbo 1 g
Total Fat 10 g
Saturated Fat 5 g
Cholesterol 33 mg
Fiber <1 g
Sodium 173 mg

8	ounces cream cheese
1/4	cup mayonnaise
1	garlic clove, crushed
1	teaspoon grated onion
1	teaspoon prepared mustard
1	teaspoon sugar
1/8	teaspoon seasoned salt
1	cup canned flaked lobster meat or crab meat
3	tablespoons cooking sauterne

Heat the cream cheese in a saucepan over low heat until melted, stirring constantly. Stir in the mayonnaise, garlic, onion, prepared mustard, sugar and seasoned salt. Add the lobster and wine and mix gently.

Cook over low heat until heated through, stirring occasionally. Serve warm with fresh vegetables and/or assorted party crackers.

64

Black Bean Salsa

Yield: 15 servings

Nutrients per serving
Calories 66
Protein 3 g
Carbo 17 g
Total Fat 1 g
Saturated Fat <1 g
Cholesterol 0 mg
Fiber 4 g
Sodium 460 mg

2	(15-ounce) cans black beans, drained and rinsed
1	(15-ounce) can whole kernel corn, drained
1	red bell pepper, chopped
1	bunch green onions, trimmed and sliced
1/3	cup fresh cilantro leaves
1/4	cup lime juice
1	(10-ounce) can tomatoes with green chiles, partially drained
2	teaspoons ground cumin
1/4	teaspoon garlic salt

Combine the beans, corn, bell pepper, green onions and cilantro in a bowl and mix well. Mix the lime juice, tomatoes, cumin and garlic salt in a bowl and stir into the bean mixture. Serve at room temperature or chilled with assorted chips.

1956

UAMC moved to the West Markham campus. Unfortunately, patient rooms were not air-conditioned until 1966.

Watermelon Salsa

2 cups chopped watermelon
1 onion, chopped
1/4 cup water chestnuts, chopped
1 or 2 jalapeño chiles, chopped
~ Balsamic vinegar to taste

Combine the watermelon, onion, water chestnuts, jalapeño chiles and vinegar in a bowl and mix gently. Serve with assorted chips.

Yield: 8 servings

Nutrients per serving
Calories 21
Protein <1 g
Carbo 5 g
Total Fat <1 g
Saturated Fat <1 g
Cholesterol 0 mg
Fiber 1 g
Sodium 2 mg

Salsa is traditionally a combination of chiles, tomatoes, and assorted spices. The origins can be traced back to the Aztecs, Mayans, and Incas. It was originally served to complement fish and other meats. Today, salsa has grown in popularity, use, and variations, as indicated by the version of salsa on this page.

The first nursing school class graduated. The Education I Building was completed and construction began on the new student residence building and student union.

1957

Swiss Walnut Cheese Spread

Yield: 16 servings

Nutrients per serving

Calories 153

Protein 5 g

Carbo 2 g

Total Fat 14 g

Saturated Fat 7 g

Cholesterol 28 mg

Fiber <1 g

Sodium 115 mg

8	ounces Swiss cheese, shredded
1/2	cup (1 stick) butter, softened
3	tablespoons milk
1/4	teaspoon salt
1/8	teaspoon cayenne pepper
1	cup finely chopped walnuts

Combine the cheese, butter, milk, salt and cayenne pepper in a mixing bowl and beat until creamy. Stir in the walnuts. Pack the cheese spread in a 2-cup crock or other nonreactive dish.

Chill, lightly covered, for 24 hours or for up to two weeks. Let stand at room temperature for 1 hour before serving. Serve with assorted breads and/or crackers.

Tapenade

Yield: 8 servings

Nutrients per serving

Calories 52

Protein 1 g

Carbo 6 g

Total Fat 3 g

Saturated Fat <1 g

Cholesterol 0 mg

Fiber 1 g

Sodium 286 mg

1	cup dry-pack sun-dried tomatoes
10	to 15 kalamata olives, pitted
1/4	cup olive oil
5	garlic cloves
1	tablespoon balsamic vinegar
1	tablespoon fresh thyme leaves
1	teaspoon chopped fresh rosemary
~	Salt and pepper to taste

Rehydrate the sun-dried tomatoes in boiling water in a heatproof bowl for 1 minute; strain. Combine the tomatoes, olives, olive oil, garlic, vinegar, thyme, rosemary, salt and pepper in a food processor. Process until the desired consistency.

Store, covered, in the refrigerator for up to two weeks. Serve with warm toasted bread.

1958 *The School of Nursing became the first in Arkansas to be fully accredited by National League of Nursing.*

Crab Delights

1	(6-ounce) can crab meat, drained and flaked
1	(5-ounce) jar Old English cheese spread
1/2	cup (1 stick) butter, softened
2	teaspoons mayonnaise
1 1/2	teaspoons garlic salt
6	English muffins, split

Yield: 12 servings

Nutrients per serving

Calories 181

Protein 7 g

Carbo 13 g

Total Fat 12 g

Saturated Fat 7 g

Cholesterol 39 mg

Fiber 1 g

Sodium 527 mg

Combine the crab meat, cheese spread, butter, mayonnaise and garlic salt in a bowl and mix gently until combined. Spread the crab meat mixture evenly on the cut sides of the muffins. Arrange the muffin halves cut side up on a baking sheet.

Broil on High until brown and bubbly and serve immediately. You may wrap each uncooked muffin half in plastic wrap or place in a sealable plastic freezer bag and freeze for future use. Broil frozen until brown and bubbly. Serve as an appetizer or with tomato soup.

67

You are the model for your children's eating behavior. Children model all of the behaviors they see, especially eating habits. As a parent, it is important to teach children from an early age that eating a balanced diet is both healthy and fun. It is much healthier to eat at home and not at a fast food restaurant. Remember when cooking or preparing meals, make it a learning experience for children. This will encourage children to spend time together in a family setting and provide a platform for educating children on how to eat nutritious snacks and meals.

As a guide, children ages two to six should over the course of the day consume **two servings from the milk group** (e.g. 1 cup of milk or yogurt or 2 ounces of cheese), **two servings from the meat group** (e.g. 2 to 3 ounces cooked lean meat, poultry, or fish), **three servings from the vegetable group** (e.g. 1/2 cup chopped raw or cooked vegetables or 1 cup raw leafy vegetables), **two servings from the fruit group** (e.g. 1 piece of fruit or melon wedge, 3/4 cup juice, 1/2 cup canned fruit), and **six servings from the grain group** (e.g. 1 slice bread, 1/2 cup cooked rice or pasta, 1/2 cup cooked cereal, or 1 ounce ready-to-eat cereal).

The School of Pharmacy moved to Education I Building and the inpatient unit for adult psychiatric patients opened.

1958

Peach Quesadillas

Yield: 16 servings

Nutrients per serving

Calories 73
Protein 2 g
Carbo 11 g
Total Fat 2 g
Saturated Fat 1 g
Cholesterol 5 mg
Fiber 1 g
Sodium 112 mg

2	tablespoons Arkansas honey
2	teaspoons fresh lime juice
1/2	teaspoon grated lime zest
2	large ripe Arkansas peaches, peeled and thinly sliced (about 1 cup)
1	teaspoon brown sugar
3	ounces Brie cheese, thinly sliced
4	(8-inch) flour tortillas

Whisk the honey, lime juice and lime zest in a bowl until combined. Gently toss the peaches and brown sugar in a bowl until coated. Spoon half the peaches on one of the tortillas and arrange half the cheese over the peaches. Top with another tortilla.

Heat a large nonstick skillet over medium-high heat and coat with butter-flavor nonstick cooking spray. Cook the quesadilla in the hot skillet until light brown and crisp on both sides. Repeat the process with the remaining tortillas, remaining peach mixture and remaining cheese. Cut each quesadilla into eight wedges and serve with the honey sauce.

In 1966, Louis Grace and his son, Richard, engineers with a propensity toward innovation, started a machine tool and die business in Michigan. In 1978, Richard moved the company to Russellville, Arkansas, after he and his family took a liking to the area, and the company began producing precision parts for computer peripheral markets.

The Microplane Divison of Grace Manufacturing was started in 1990 in a small corner of the Grace building after a Canadian homemaker discovered that one of their rasps (carried by her husband in his hardware store) made a perfect zester for the orange zest needed on her Armenian Orange Cake. Rasps began flying off hardware shelves when chefs and "foodies" discovered what great kitchen tools they were . . . now know as zesters. The products have been featured on *The Today Show*, multiple Food Network programs, *Martha Stewart Living*, *Oprah*, and *QVC*.

1959

The Student Union opened and was named in memory of Dr. Jeff Banks, a longtime and much-liked anatomy professor in the College of Medicine when he died in 1959.

Filipino Spring Rolls

1	pound shrimp, peeled and deveined	1	teaspoon pancake syrup	
1	pound ground chicken	1/4	teaspoon salt	
1	(8-ounce) can water chestnuts, drained and chopped	1/4	teaspoon pepper	
1	onion, finely chopped	3	drops of sesame oil	
1	small carrot, shredded	1	(50-count) package small spring roll wrappers	
1	egg	~	Vegetable oil for frying	

Combine the shrimp, ground chicken, water chestnuts, onion, carrot, egg, syrup, salt, pepper and sesame oil in a food processor and process just until blended. Prepare the wrappers using package directions.

Place 1 heaping teaspoon of the shrimp mixture at the end of each wrapper and roll to resemble a cigar, enclosing the filling. Moisten the edges of the wrappers with water to seal. Arrange the spring rolls on a baking sheet and freeze until firm. Store in a resealable plastic bag in the freezer until ready for use.

Cut each frozen spring roll into thirds and fry in hot oil in a skillet until brown on all sides; drain. Keep warm in a preheated 300-degree oven. Serve warm with sweet-and-sour sauce. Spring roll wrappers are available at Asian markets; do not use won ton wrappers.

Nutritional profile does not include the vegetable oil for frying.

Yield: 50 spring rolls

Nutrients per spring roll
Calories 51
Protein 3 g
Carbo 8 g
Total Fat 1 g
Saturated Fat <1 g
Cholesterol 21 mg
Fiber <1 g
Sodium 33 mg

69

Eggnog

8	cups (2 quarts) milk	1	cup sugar
2	cups half-and-half	2	teaspoons vanilla extract
2	(4-ounce) packages vanilla instant pudding mix		

Combine the milk, half-and-half, pudding mixes, sugar and vanilla in a mixing bowl and beat until blended. Pour into a large pitcher and chill, covered, until serving time. Stir before serving.

Yield: 20 (1/2-cup) servings

Nutrients per serving
Calories 153
Protein 4 g
Carbo 25 g
Total Fat 6 g
Saturated Fat 4 g
Cholesterol 19 mg
Fiber <1 g
Sodium 185 mg

The dormitory building opened, accommodating 315 single students and 95 married couples with mix of traditional dormitory-style rooms and efficiency apartments.

1959

Holiday Punch

Yield:
200 small cups

Nutrients per serving
Calories 62
Protein <1 g
Carbo 16 g
Total Fat <1 g
Saturated Fat <1 g
Cholesterol 0 mg
Fiber <1 g
Sodium 3 mg

8   cups (2 quarts) hot water
8   cups sugar
3   (2-liter) bottles ginger ale
2   (46-ounce) cans pineapple juice
2   (46-ounce) cans apricot nectar
4   (10-ounce) packages frozen strawberries
8   ripe bananas, mashed or puréed

Dissolve the sugar in the hot water in a large container. Combine the ginger ale, pineapple juice, apricot nectar, strawberries and bananas in a large container and mix well. Stir in the sugar mixture. Chill until serving time. Ladle into punch cups.

French Mint Tea

Yield: 16 servings

Nutrients per serving
Calories 99
Protein <1 g
Carbo 25 g
Total Fat <1 g
Saturated Fat <1 g
Cholesterol 0 mg
Fiber <1 g
Sodium 8 mg

16   cups (1 gallon) water
6   tea bags
1¼   cups sugar
1   (6-ounce) can frozen lemonade concentrate
1   (6-ounce) can frozen orange juice concentrate
~   Fresh mint leaves to taste

Bring the water to a boil in a large saucepan and add the tea bags. Steep for 20 minutes; discard the tea bags. Combine the sugar and tea in a 2-gallon container and stir until the sugar dissolves. Mix in the lemonade concentrate, orange juice concentrate and mint leaves. Chill, covered, for 24 hours. Pour over ice in glasses.

The Clinical Computer Training Center, located in the Clinical Programs Education Department, is responsible for training UAMS staff and students on computer programs used at UAMS. They provide training in basic computer skills, SAP, eChart, UAMS scheduling and registration software, Microsoft Office programs, and other hospital-specific software packages.

1961

The T.H. Barton Research Building was completed and was the first building on campus devoted solely to research.

The Toad

3/4 ounce **Absolut Mandarin vodka**
3/4 ounce **Bacardi lemon rum**
2 ounces **sweet-and-sour mix**
2 ounces **orange juice**
1/2 ounce **Midori**

Combine the vodka, rum, sweet-and-sour mix and orange juice in a shaker cup and spindle blend. Pour over ice in a hurricane glass. Top with the liqueur. Garnish with an orange/cherry flag.

Yield: 1 serving

Nutrients per serving

Calories 236
Protein 1 g
Carbo 29 g
Total Fat <1 g
Saturated Fat <1 g
Cholesterol 0 mg
Fiber <1 g
Sodium 2 mg

71

Mike's Place Restaurant is located in Conway, Arkansas, a short drive from Little Rock. It opened in the summer of 2005 and features Cajun/Louisiana-style dishes and Gulf Coast seafood. Based on the history of Conway and Toad Suck Daze, one of the restaurant's signature drinks was developed—The Toad.

How did Toad Suck Daze get its name? According to legend, long ago, steamboats were able to travel the Arkansas River when the water was at the right depth. When it wasn't, the captains and their crews tied up their boats to wait where the Toad Suck Lock and Dam now spans the river. While they waited, they refreshed themselves at the local tavern, much to the dismay of the folks living nearby who commented, "They suck on the bottle 'til they swell up like toads." Hence, the name Toad Suck. The tavern is long gone, but the legend and fun live on at the annual Toad Suck Daze Festival, which was established in 1981 in Conway, Arkansas. Today the festival is held the first weekend in May over a three-day period and includes varied festivities and a carnival atmosphere that ranges from the famous toad and 10K races to musical performances to arts and crafts displays.

UAMC acquired its first kidney dialysis machine.

1961

Cossatot

Yield: 1 serving

Nutrients per serving
Calories 222
Protein <1 g
Carbo 34 g
Total Fat 0 g
Saturated Fat 0 g
Cholesterol 0 mg
Fiber <1 g
Sodium 1 mg

1/2 ounce Absolut Citron vodka
1/2 ounce Bombay gin
1/2 ounce Bacardi "O" rum
4   ounces sweet-and-sour mix
~   Splash of soda
~   Lemon wedge for garnish

Combine the vodka, gin, rum, sweet-and-sour mix and soda in a shaker cup and spindle blend. Pour over ice in a hurricane glass and garnish with a lemon wedge.

—*Courtesy of* **Mike's Place Restaurant**

Tequila Surprise Punch

Yield: 8 servings

Nutrients per serving
Calories 189
Protein <1 g
Carbo 32 g
Total Fat <1 g
Saturated Fat 0 g
Cholesterol 0 mg
Fiber 0 g
Sodium 6 mg

1   (12-ounce) can frozen limeade concentrate
1   (12-ounce) can Sprite
1   (12-ounce) bottle beer
1/2 limeade can tequila (6 ounces)

Mix the limeade concentrate, Sprite, beer and tequila in a pitcher. Pour over ice in glasses. Add green food coloring to enhance color, if desired.

The UAMS Department of Psychiatry's Child Study Center (CSC) provides comprehensive diagnostic evaluations and treatment for children and adolescents with behavioral, emotional, learning, and adjustment difficulties. The mission is to provide quality innovative behavioral health care to those we serve in a therapeutic environment.

CSC staff includes psychiatrists, psychologists, psychological examiners, social workers, licensed professional counselors, a psychiatric nurse, educational specialists, and mental health para-professionals. The Child Study Center is also an education and training site. Because of this, the center's professional staff includes psychiatric residents and interns in psychology and social work.

1965

The Arkansas Legislature began funding "full pay" beds for University Hospital, removing hospital from "charity" classification.

Soups and salads

Entertaining Tips

Whether entertaining a large or small group in a formal or informal setting, careful planning can help keep you from becoming a frazzled host or hostess by the time of the event. Once you have determined the theme of the party (if applicable), a guest list has been developed, and invitations sent or phone calls made, it is time to begin the pre-party steps.

Menu

While a party's theme may make it easier to plan a menu, consider the following when planning any menu.

- Be sensitive to your guests' food preferences.

- Plan a menu that has a variety of tastes, textures, and colors (you don't want everything to be spicy, crunchy, or bland in color).

- If serving appetizers, be careful not to repeat the food flavors that will be served in the meal.

- This is not the time to experiment with new recipes. If you have something new you want to serve, do a test run.

- Include one menu item that has the "WOW" factor—perhaps a beautifully decorated cake or a beautiful mold—the recipe doesn't need to be complicated.

- Choose items that can be prepared ahead of time—do not prepare any more than one item that requires split-second timing immediately before serving (and if you can avoid that, do so).

- If your guests will not be seated at tables to eat, choosing foods that do not require cutting can prevent some mishaps. Serve meats that have been precut into bite-size pieces or foods that can be cut easily with a fork.

- Once the menu has been planned, write down every ingredient of every dish, check this against your food inventory, and then prepare your grocery list. Don't forget items such as extra ice and butter for the rolls.

- Never plan to do any grocery shopping the day of the event.

- Prepare do-ahead dishes at least two days before if possible.

Table Decorations

- Decorations do not have to be elaborate. If your party is not theme-centered, fresh-cut flowers in vases and lit candles from votives to tapers can always help create a wonderful atmosphere.

- Be creative. Fill a hurricane lamp or other unusual container with fresh lemons or pine cones or place individual large flower blooms in individual containers.

- Create several small decorations for the table instead of one large centerpiece.

- Remember that napkins, place mats, table runners, and tablecloths can contribute to the decorations as well, since they come in such a variety of colors, textures, and patterns.

- Consider mixing glassware and dish patterns to enhance your table decorations.

Getting Your Home Ready

- Do any necessary cleaning well ahead of time. This may include cleaning out your refrigerator so that you have ample room to store your pre-prepared items.

- Check several days in advance to be certain that you have all the necessary serving pieces, dishes, glassware, and so forth. If using table linens, make certain they look fresh and crisp.

- Set up as much as you can the day before the party.

- The day of the party, give a final check to the bathroom the guests will be using.

- Turn down the thermostat before the party. It is amazing how quickly a room can become too warm once guests have arrived.

With good pre-planning, you will be able to focus on one thing when the guests arrive—their comfort and enjoyment.

A Few Last Hints

- Do not wait more than thirty minutes for late guests to arrive before serving the meal. Offer a simple and kind apology to latecomers.

- Continue to keep tabs on the room temperature.

- If possible, have someone reliable help during the party so you can stay out of the kitchen as much as possible and enjoy yourself as well as your guests.

Chili

1	pound ground beef, chili meat or ground turkey	1	teaspoon salt	
1	tablespoon dried minced onion	1/2	teaspoon ground cumin	
1/4	teaspoon granulated garlic	1/2	teaspoon sugar	
1	(8-ounce) can tomato sauce	2	cups hot cooked rice	
1	cup water	~	Corn chips for garnish	
1	tablespoon New Mexico chili powder	~	Chopped onion for garnish	
1	tablespoon all-purpose flour	~	Shredded Cheddar cheese for garnish	

Yield: 6 servings

Nutrients per serving

Calories 215

Protein 16 g

Carbo 20 g

Total Fat 8 g

Saturated Fat 3 g

Cholesterol 47 mg

Fiber 1 g

Sodium 649 mg

Brown the ground beef with the dried minced onion and garlic in a large saucepan, stirring until the ground beef is crumbly; drain. Stir in the tomato sauce, water, chili powder, flour, salt, cumin and sugar.

Simmer, covered, for 30 minutes, stirring occasionally. Ladle over the rice in soup bowls. Garnish with corn chips, chopped onion and cheese.

Black Bean, Yellow Pepper and Cumin Chili

2	large onions, coarsely chopped	4	(15-ounce) cans diced tomatoes with roasted garlic
2	yellow bell peppers, chopped	4	cups vegetable broth or chicken broth
2	to 3 tablespoons cumin seeds	~	Salt and pepper to taste
6	tablespoons olive oil		
4	teaspoons (or less) finely minced canned chipotle chiles		
4	(15-ounce) cans black beans, drained		

Yield: 12 servings

Nutrients per serving

Calories 217

Protein 8 g

Carbo 39 g

Total Fat 8 g

Saturated Fat 1 g

Cholesterol 0 mg

Fiber 10 g

Sodium 1671 mg

Sauté the onions, bell peppers and cumin seeds in the olive oil in a large saucepan for 10 minutes or until the onions and bell peppers are tender and golden brown. Add the chipotle chiles and mix well. Stir in the beans, undrained tomatoes and broth. Bring to a boil and reduce the heat to medium.

Simmer for 30 minutes or until the liquid is reduced by half, stirring occasionally. Process 2 to 4 cups of the chili in a blender until smooth and return the processed chili to the saucepan. Cook just until heated through and season with salt and pepper. Ladle into soup bowls. You may substitute a mixture of one can mild tomatoes with green chiles and three cans diced tomatoes for the diced tomatoes with roasted garlic.

Distance learning advanced when UAMC began using video tape in teaching.

1966

Beefy Vegetable Soup

Yield: 6 servings

Nutrients per serving

Calories 227

Protein 22 g

Carbo 22 g

Total Fat 6 g

Saturated Fat 2 g

Cholesterol 55 mg

Fiber 5 g

Sodium 195 mg

1 pound lean stew meat, cut into bite-size pieces

1 (16-ounce) can whole or chopped tomatoes

1 1/2 cups chopped peeled red potatoes

1 onion, chopped

1/2 (16-ounce) package frozen cut green beans

1/2 (16-ounce) package frozen cut okra

1 cup chopped celery

1 cup sliced carrots

2 teaspoons parsley flakes

1 1/2 teaspoons Worcestershire sauce

1/8 teaspoon pepper

1 (8-ounce) soup bone shank

Combine the stew meat, tomatoes, potatoes, onion, green beans, okra, celery, carrots, parsley flakes, Worcestershire sauce and pepper in a slow cooker. Add enough water to cover the ingredients and mix well. Place the shank on top of the ingredients.

Cook, covered, on High for 6 to 7 hours to the desired consistency, or on Low for 12 to 18 hours. Remove the shank to a platter. Remove the meat from the bone and cut into bite-size pieces, discarding the bone. Stir the meat into the soup. Ladle into soup bowls.

76

A lettuce leaf dropped onto the top of a stockpot of homemade soup will absorb the excess fat. If you prepare soup in advance, press a sheet of waxed paper over the top of the soup before storing in the refrigerator. Discard the waxed paper along with the hardened fat before reheating the soup.

1968

The Arkansas Legislature authorized School of Medicine's clinical faculty to accept fee-for-service patients.

Taco Soup

Soup

1   pound ground chuck
1   large onion, chopped
3   (15-ounce) cans Mexican-style
       chili beans
1   (15-ounce) can whole
       kernel corn
1   (15-ounce) can tomato sauce
1   (14-ounce) can diced tomatoes
1   (4-ounce) can chopped
       green chiles
1   envelope taco seasoning mix

1   envelope ranch salad
       dressing mix
1¹/₂ cups water

Toppings (Optional)

~   Corn chips
~   Shredded lettuce
~   Chopped tomato
~   Chopped onions
~   Sour cream
~   Shredded Cheddar cheese
~   Taco sauce or salsa

Yield: 6 servings

Nutrients per serving
Calories 446
Protein 27 g
Carbo 57 g
Total Fat 10 g
Saturated Fat 4 g
Cholesterol 47 mg
Fiber 14 g
Sodium 2319 mg

To prepare the soup, brown the ground chuck with the onion in a Dutch oven over medium-high heat until the ground chuck is crumbly and the onion is tender; drain. Stir in the undrained beans, undrained corn, tomato sauce, undrained tomatoes, green chiles, seasoning mix, salad dressing mix and water. Reduce the heat to medium.

Simmer for 15 minutes, stirring occasionally. Ladle into soup bowls and top with corn chips, shredded lettuce, chopped tomato, chopped onions, sour cream, cheese and/or taco sauce or salsa.

Brunswick Stew

1   (2¹/₂- to 3-pound) chicken
1   pound beef stew meat
1   (17-ounce) can cream-style corn
1   (16-ounce) can white whole
       kernel corn
1   (16-ounce) can tomatoes
1   green bell pepper, chopped

1   (6-ounce) can tomato paste
3   small onions, chopped
1   garlic clove, crushed
8   ounces fresh or
       canned mushrooms
1   (16-ounce) can lima beans
~   Salt and pepper to taste

Yield: 8 servings

Nutrients per serving
Calories 366
Protein 37 g
Carbo 34 g
Total Fat 10 g
Saturated Fat 3 g
Cholesterol 92 mg
Fiber 8 g
Sodium 858 mg

Combine the chicken and stew meat in a stockpot and add enough water to cover. Bring to a boil and reduce the heat to medium. Simmer for 2 hours or until the chicken and stew meat are tender. Remove the chicken to a platter and cool slightly. Chop the chicken into bite-size pieces, discarding the skin and bones. Chill, covered, until ready to use.

Add the corn, tomatoes, bell pepper, tomato paste, onions and garlic to the broth and simmer for 2³/₄ hours. Mix in the chicken, mushrooms and lima beans. Simmer just until heated through and season with salt and pepper. Ladle into soup bowls.

The million-dollar Child Study Center opened.   1969

Chicken and Andouille Filé Gumbo

Yield: 15 servings

Nutrients per serving
Calories 540
Protein 30 g
Carbo 37 g
Total Fat 31 g
Saturated Fat 7 g
Cholesterol 83 mg
Fiber 2 g
Sodium 451 mg

2¹/₂ to 3 pounds boneless skinless chicken thighs
1 cup vegetable oil
1 cup all-purpose flour
4 cups chopped onions
1 cup chopped green bell pepper
4 ribs celery, chopped
12 cups low-sodium chicken stock, heated
6 (or more) garlic cloves, chopped
6 (or more) bay leaves
~ Cayenne pepper (optional)
~ Salt and black pepper to taste

3 pounds andouille or other smoked sausage, casings removed and sausage cut into bite-size pieces
1 or 2 (16-ounce) cans diced tomatoes (optional)
2 tablespoons filé powder
7¹/₂ cups hot cooked white rice
~ Chopped green onions for garnish
~ Chopped fresh parsley for garnish

Brown the chicken on all sides in a Dutch oven. Cool slightly and cut into bite-size pieces. Heat the oil in a cast-iron skillet over medium heat until hot and gradually stir in the flour. Cook for 15 to 25 minutes or until the roux begins to thicken and turns a dark brown color and emits a smoky fragrance, stirring constantly.

Spoon the roux into a large stockpot and heat until hot. Stir in the onions, bell pepper and celery and cook for 5 minutes or until the vegetables are tender, stirring constantly. Add the hot stock, garlic, bay leaves, cayenne pepper, salt and black pepper gradually and mix well. Stir in the chicken, sausage and tomatoes.

Simmer for 3 hours or to the desired consistency, stirring occasionally. Discard the bay leaves. If you decide to go whole-hog and add seafood, add at this point. Skim the fat from the top and stir in the filé powder. Ladle over the rice in bowls. Garnish with green onions and parsley. Freeze, if desired, for future use.

Roux is a mixture of wheat flour and fat. It is used as a base for gravy, sauces, soups, and stews. To prepare a roux, the fat is heated first; then the flour is incorporated gradually and cooked to the desired color. Roux ranges in color from white (for rich flavor) to chocolate (for nutty flavor), depending on the use.

1970

The School of Health Related Professions was approved by the University of Arkansas Board of Trustees.

Slow-Cooker Chicken Mexican Soup

4	(5-ounce) boneless skinless chicken breasts, frozen
1	(16-ounce) can whole kernel corn
1	(15-ounce) can black beans
1	(15-ounce) can red kidney beans
1	(15-ounce) can white beans
1	(14-ounce) can fat-free beef broth
1	(14-ounce) can diced or crushed tomatoes
1	(6-ounce) can tomato paste
1	(4-ounce) can diced green chiles
1	envelope taco seasoning mix
1	envelope ranch salad dressing mix
~	Tortilla chips (optional)
~	Shredded Cheddar cheese (optional)

Yield: 8 servings

Nutrients per serving
Calories 307
Protein 26 g
Carbo 47 g
Total Fat 3 g
Saturated Fat 1 g
Cholesterol 39 mg
Fiber 11 g
Sodium 1572 mg

79

Mix the chicken, undrained corn, undrained beans, broth, tomatoes, tomato paste, green chiles, seasoning mix and salad dressing mix in a slow cooker. Cook on Low for about 11 hours or to the desired consistency, stirring occasionally. Break the chicken into bite-size pieces before serving. Ladle the soup over tortilla chips in soup bowls and sprinkle with cheese.

Step into the Neonatal Intensive Care Unit at UAMS and you will step into a world where staff members share a passionate commitment to provide world-class care to our tiny patients. Our NICU is composed of three separate units. Because of our high success rate with extremely premature infants, the NICU at UAMS has become the High Risk Delivery Center for the region. A premature baby born at UAMS and cared for in our NICU has a very high chance of not only going home, but going home healthy.

In mid-2005, the NICU Unit Council decided to put together a cookbook in order to raise funds for equipment for the nurseries. Recipes were gathered from staff members and their families, the youngest being three years old and the oldest ninety-five years old, and *Out of the Mouths of Babes* was born.

The artwork for the cookbook cover and chapter openers was designed by the daughter of one of our nurses. The cookbook went to press in October 2005 with books being pre-sold the first two weeks of November. More than 1,000 cookbooks were sold in November and December with the remaining 134 books sold over the course of 2006. More than $9,000 worth of equipment—including a weight scale, radiometer, crib toys, bouncers, swings, educational books, high back stools, and overbed tables—was purchased with the proceeds. Thanks to our UAMS family for supporting our project and making it such a success.

Dietetic Internship moved to the School of Health Related Professions. 1971

Minestrone

Yield: 8 servings

Nutrients per serving
Calories 238
Protein 11 g
Carbo 40 g
Total Fat 4 g
Saturated Fat 1 g
Cholesterol <1 mg
Fiber 9 g
Sodium 1693 mg

80

1	(10-ounce) package frozen chopped spinach, thawed and drained
4	chicken bouillon cubes
4	cups hot water
1	tablespoon olive oil
1	onion, chopped
2	garlic cloves, finely chopped
1	(28-ounce) can crushed tomatoes
4	cups tomato juice
1	(16-ounce) can kidney beans, drained and rinsed
1	(15-ounce) can garbanzo beans, drained and rinsed
1	cup dry red wine
2	carrots, sliced
2	small zucchini, chopped
1	tablespoon dried basil
1	teaspoon salt
1/2	teaspoon dried oregano
1/4	teaspoon pepper
~	Grated Parmesan cheese (optional)

Press the excess moisture from the spinach. Dissolve the bouillon in the hot water in a measuring cup. Heat the olive oil in an 8-quart Dutch oven over medium heat and add the onion and garlic. Cook for 2 minutes or until the onion is tender, stirring occasionally. Stir in the tomatoes, tomato juice, beans, wine, carrots, zucchini, basil, salt, oregano and pepper.

Bring to a boil and reduce the heat. Simmer, covered, for 1 hour or longer or until of the desired consistency. Ladle into soup bowls and serve with the cheese.

If you have over-salted soup or vegetables, try adding a mixture of one teaspoon of sugar and one teaspoon of cider vinegar. You can also minimize the salty flavor by adding uncooked potatoes to the soup or vegetables. Discard them after they have cooked.

1971

The School of Health Related Professions offered programs in Biomedical Instrumentation Technology, Dental Hygiene, Medical Technology, Operating Room Technology, Radiologic Technology, and Respiratory Therapy.

Potato Corn Chowder

3	baking potatoes, coarsely chopped
8	ounces sliced bacon, chopped
2	(17-ounce) cans cream-style corn
2	(16-ounce) cans whole kernel corn
1	quart (4 cups) half-and-half
1	tablespoon salt
1	tablespoon white pepper
1	cup (4 ounces) finely shredded Cheddar cheese
1	bunch green onions, trimmed and chopped

Yield: 8 servings

Nutrients per serving
Calories 454
Protein 16 g
Carbo 45 g
Total Fat 24 g
Saturated Fat 13 g
Cholesterol 70 mg
Fiber 7 g
Sodium 1905 mg

Cook the potatoes with enough water to cover in a saucepan until tender; drain. Cook the bacon in a skillet until brown and crisp; drain.

Combine the corn, half-and-half, salt and white pepper in a saucepan and mix well. Cook until hot; do not boil. Add the cheese to the half-and-half mixture and whisk until blended. Add the potatoes, bacon and green onions and mix gently. Cook just until heated through; do not boil. Ladle into soup bowls.

81

Specialty Tomato Soup

2	(10-ounce) cans tomato soup
3	ounces cream cheese or reduced-fat cream cheese, cubed
1	cup milk
2	(15-ounce) cans diced tomatoes
2	(15-ounce) cans kidney beans, drained
1/2	to 1 onion, finely chopped, or dried onion flakes (optional)
1	teaspoon paprika (optional)
~	Crushed dried basil to taste

Yield: 6 servings

Nutrients per serving
Calories 289
Protein 13 g
Carbo 45 g
Total Fat 8 g
Saturated Fat 4 g
Cholesterol 20 mg
Fiber 10 g
Sodium 1219 mg

Combine the soup and cream cheese in a saucepan and cook over low heat until blended, stirring frequently. Add the milk gradually, stirring constantly. Stir in the tomatoes, beans, onion, paprika and basil. Cook over low to medium heat until hot. Ladle into soup bowls.

Groundbreaking work by researchers from UAMC, the Little Rock Veterans Hospital, and the Arkansas Department of Health changed the way patients with tuberculosis were treated.

1972

Arugula Salad with Pear, Blue Cheese and Walnuts

Yield: 8 servings

Nutrients per serving

Calories 231

Protein 7 g

Carbo 9 g

Total Fat 19 g

Saturated Fat 6 g

Cholesterol 16 mg

Fiber 2 g

Sodium 307 mg

82

Apricot Dressing

2 tablespoons white wine vinegar

2 tablespoons all-fruit apricot spread

1/8 teaspoon lemon juice

1/3 cup olive oil

~ Salt and pepper to taste

Salad

3 bunches arugula, stems removed

~ Juice of 1/2 lemon

1 pear, julienned

6 ounces blue cheese, crumbled

2 ounces walnuts, chopped

To prepare the dressing, whisk the vinegar, apricot spread and lemon juice in a bowl until combined. Add the olive oil gradually, whisking constantly until incorporated. Season with salt and pepper.

To prepare the salad, toss the arugula in a salad bowl. Drizzle the lemon juice over the pear to prevent browning and arrange on top of the arugula. Sprinkle with the blue cheese and walnuts. Pour the dressing over the salad just before serving and toss to coat. You may substitute two 5-ounce packages of arugula or baby salad greens or a combination of the two for the 3 bunches arugula.

Pregnancy is typically a happy time, and women do not expect problems to occur. Luckily, only a small percentage of pregnancies are high risk. Dr. Curtis Lowery, the Arkansas Department of Health and Human Services, and UAMS founded a groundbreaking program in 2002 to better serve Arkansas women with high-risk pregnancies. Antenatal and Neonatal Guidelines, Education, and Learning Systems (ANGELS) provides support for women and health care providers in Arkansas. Evidence-based guidelines are continually being developed and revised in conjunction with rural providers. ANGELS also has a 24/7 phone line, staffed by obstetrical nurses, which providers or pregnant women can call. With ANGELS, high-risk pregnancies have a chance at a healthier outcome.

—Tina Benton, RN, and Curtis Lowery, MD

1973

The Area Health Education Centers (AHEC) program developed to educate family physicians and provide health education throughout the state.

Cranberry Spinach Salad

Poppy Seed Dressing

1/4	cup sugar
1	teaspoon dried minced onion
3/4	teaspoon poppy seeds
1/8	teaspoon paprika
2	tablespoons white wine vinegar
2	tablespoons apple cider vinegar
1/4	cup vegetable oil

Salad

10	ounces spinach, stems removed
3/4	cup dried cranberries
1	cup sliced orange, or 1 (11-ounce) can mandarin oranges, drained
3/4	cup sliced almonds, toasted
4	to 6 strawberries, sliced lengthwise
2	green onions, sliced
2	tablespoons chopped red onion (optional)

To prepare the dressing, mix the sugar, onion, poppy seeds and paprika in a bowl. Add the wine vinegar, cider vinegar and oil gradually, whisking constantly until incorporated.

To prepare the salad, toss the spinach, cranberries, orange, almonds, strawberries, green onions and red onion in a salad bowl. Drizzle the dressing over the salad 30 minutes before serving and toss until coated.

Yield: 8 servings

Nutrients per serving
Calories 199
Protein 4 g
Carbo 21 g
Total Fat 12 g
Saturated Fat 1 g
Cholesterol 0 mg
Fiber 3 g
Sodium 32 mg

83

Create a delicious applesauce by cooking sliced apples with a can of Fresca until of the desired consistency. Sugar is not required.

Special Strawberry Spinach Salad

Yield: 8 servings

Nutrients per serving

Calories 151

Protein 3 g

Carbo 9 g

Total Fat 12 g

Saturated Fat 1 g

Cholesterol 0 mg

Fiber 3 g

Sodium 29 mg

Poppy Sesame Dressing

1/4 cup vegetable oil

2 tablespoons sugar

2 tablespoons cider vinegar

1 tablespoon chopped onion

1 tablespoon poppy seeds

1 teaspoon sesame seeds

1/4 teaspoon paprika

1/8 teaspoon Worcestershire sauce

Salad

9 cups torn spinach

1 pint strawberries, cut into halves

1/2 cup slivered almonds, toasted

To prepare the dressing, combine the oil, sugar, vinegar, onion, poppy seeds, sesame seeds, paprika and Worcestershire sauce in a blender and process until combined.

To prepare the salad, toss the spinach, strawberries and almonds in a salad bowl. Add the dressing just before serving and toss to coat. Serve immediately.

USDA food guidelines were revised in 2005 to include better nutrition for Americans with an additional emphasis on physical activity. Based on these new guidelines, Americans need the following serving recommendations:

1. **Fruits:** 4 servings/day
2. **Vegetables:** 5 servings/day
3. **Grains:** 6 ounce equivalent (1 ounce equivalent = 1 slice bread, 1 cup dry cereal, 1/2 cup cooked rice/pasta/cereal)
4. **Meat and Beans:** 5.5 ounce equivalent (1 ounce equivalent = 1 ounce cooked lean meats/poultry/fish, 1 egg, 1/4 cup dried beans/tofu, 1 tablespoon peanut butter)
5. **Milk:** 3 cups/day
6. **Oils:** 6 teaspoons/day

More information is available at http://www.health.gov/dietaryguidelines/dga2005/document/

1974

The Arkansas Poison Control Center (state's only poison control center) and the Drug Information Center were established in School of Pharmacy.

Mango Mousse

1   (29-ounce) jar mangoes
3   (3-ounce) packages
    lemon gelatin
8   ounces cream cheese, cubed
~   Juice of 1 lime
~   Lettuce leaves

~   Sour cream for topping
    (optional)
~   Brown sugar for topping
    (optional)
~   Shredded coconut for topping
    (optional)
~   Sprigs of mint for garnish

Yield: 12 servings

Nutrients per serving
Calories 197
Protein 4 g
Carbo 34 g
Total Fat 7 g
Saturated Fat 4 g
Cholesterol 21 mg
Fiber 1 g
Sodium 174 mg

Drain the mangoes, reserving the liquid. Combine the reserved liquid with enough water to measure 3 cups in a microwave-safe measuring cup. Microwave until the liquid boils. Pour the boiling liquid over the gelatin in a heatproof bowl and stir until the gelatin dissolves.

Process the mangoes and cream cheese in a blender until creamy. Stir the mango mixture and lime juice into the gelatin. Pour into a ring mold, individual molds or a 9×13-inch dish. Chill for 4 to 10 hours or until set. Invert the mousse onto a lettuce-lined platter and top with sour cream, brown sugar and/or coconut. Garnish with sprigs of mint. This light refreshing salad is the perfect complement to a Mexican food buffet.

85

Orange Sherbet Salad

1   (20-ounce) can juice-pack
    crushed pineapple
2   (3-ounce) packages
    orange gelatin
1   pint orange sherbet

1   (11-ounce) can mandarin
    oranges, drained
1   cup sour cream
1   to 2 cups miniature
    marshmallows

Yield: 12 servings

Nutrients per serving
Calories 199
Protein 3 g
Carbo 39 g
Total Fat 5 g
Saturated Fat 3 g
Cholesterol 8 mg
Fiber 1 g
Sodium 82 mg

Drain the pineapple, reserving the juice. Combine the reserved juice with enough water to measure 2 cups in a microwave-safe measuring cup. Microwave until the liquid boils. Pour the boiling liquid over the gelatin in a heatproof bowl and stir until the gelatin dissolves. Add the sherbet and stir until blended. Stir in the pineapple and mandarin oranges.

Pour the gelatin mixture into a shallow dish and chill until set. Mix the sour cream and marshmallows in a bowl and spread the over the top of the gelatin. Cut into squares to serve.

The Department of Communicative Disorders (renamed Audiology and Speech Pathology) and its master's degree program were established in School of Health Related Professions.

1974

Rocky Mountain Salad

Yield: 6 servings

Nutrients per serving
Calories 511
Protein 16 g
Carbo 15 g
Total Fat 44 g
Saturated Fat 10 g
Cholesterol 30 mg
Fiber 6 g
Sodium 1201 mg

Spicy Mustard Dressing

1/3	cup chopped onion
3	tablespoons apple cider vinegar
2	teaspoons spicy brown mustard (do not substitute)
1/2	teaspoon sugar
1/2	teaspoon salt
1/4	teaspoon freshly ground pepper
3/4	cup olive oil

Salad

2	heads romaine, trimmed and torn into bite-size pieces
1	(14-ounce) can water-pack artichoke hearts, drained and quartered
1	large avocado, cut into bite-size pieces
8	ounces bacon, crisp-cooked and crumbled
4	ounces Parmesan cheese, grated

To prepare the dressing, process the onion and vinegar in a food processor or blender until puréed. Pour the onion purée into a bowl and whisk in the brown mustard, sugar, salt and pepper. Add the olive oil gradually, whisking constantly until thickened.

To prepare the salad, combine the romaine, artichokes, avocado, bacon and cheese in a bowl and mix well. Add enough of the dressing to coat and mix well. Serve immediately. When not serving immediately, place all of the prepared ingredients in separate sealable plastic bags and store in the refrigerator. Toss the salad ingredients and add the dressing just before serving.

Nutritional profile includes all of the dressing.

You will shed fewer tears if you remove the root end of the onion last. You can also place onions in the freezer for 4 to 5 minutes before slicing to reduce the number of tears.

1974

Construction began on the Education II Building, which would include two amphitheaters, classrooms, a library, and multi-media/audio-visual support units.

Baked Pineapple Salad

| 1 | (20-ounce) can juice-pack pineapple chunks |
| 1 | cup (4 ounces) shredded Cheddar cheese |

3/4	cup sugar
2	tablespoons all-purpose flour
1 1/2	cups butter crackers, crumbled
3/4	cup (1 1/2 sticks) butter, melted

Drain the pineapple, reserving 3 tablespoons of the juice. Combine the reserved juice, pineapple, cheese, sugar and flour in a bowl and mix well. Spread in an 8×8-inch baking dish.

Toss the cracker crumbs and butter in a bowl and sprinkle over the top of the prepared layer. Bake in a preheated 350-degree oven for 10 to 15 minutes or until light brown and bubbly. Serve warm.

Yield: 6 servings

Nutrients per serving
Calories 534
Protein 7 g
Carbo 54 g
Total Fat 33 g
Saturated Fat 19 g
Cholesterol 80 mg
Fiber 1 g
Sodium 428 mg

Warm Winter Fruit Salad

1	(17-ounce) can apricot halves, drained
1	(16-ounce) can sliced peaches, drained
1	(15-ounce) can pineapple chunks, drained

1	(15-ounce) can pears, drained
2/3	cup packed brown sugar
1/3	cup butter, melted
1/4	teaspoon ground nutmeg
1/4	teaspoon ground cinnamon
1/3	cup instant oats

Combine the apricots, peaches, pineapple and pears in a 9×13-inch baking dish and mix well. Mix the brown sugar, butter, nutmeg and cinnamon in a bowl and spread over the prepared layer. Sprinkle with the oats and bake in a preheated 325-degree oven for 20 minutes or until bubbly. Serve warm.

Yield: 12 servings

Nutrients per serving
Calories 185
Protein 1 g
Carbo 36 g
Total Fat 5 g
Saturated Fat 3 g
Cholesterol 13 mg
Fiber 2 g
Sodium 46 mg

Use the syrup from canned fruit to make a delicious coffee cake topping. Combine 2 cups syrup with 1 tablespoon lemon juice and 1 tablespoon butter and heat until bubbly. Whisk in 2 tablespoons all-purpose flour or cornstarch and cook until thickened. Drizzle over your favorite coffee cake.

The name of the campus changed to University of Arkansas Medical Sciences Campus (UAMSC) and the executive officer's title of UAMSC changed to chancellor. Dr. James Dennis was named as the first chancellor. All four schools became colleges.

1975

Chutney Chicken Salad

Yield: 8 servings

Nutrients per serving

Calories 504

Protein 31 g

Carbo 24 g

Total Fat 31 g

Saturated Fat 5 g

Cholesterol 88 mg

Fiber 3 g

Sodium 233 mg

1 cup mayonnaise

1/2 cup chutney

~ Lemon juice to taste

1 Granny Smith apple, coarsely chopped (see below)

8 (5-ounce) boneless skinless chicken breasts, cooked and cut into bite-size pieces

2 cups cooked brown rice

2 ribs celery, coarsely chopped

4 green onions, coarsely chopped

1/2 cup red seedless grape halves

1/2 cup chopped pecans, toasted (see below)

Combine the mayonnaise and chutney in a bowl and mix well. Drizzle lemon juice over the apple in a bowl. Stir the apple, chicken, rice, celery, green onions, grapes and pecans into the mayonnaise mixture. Chill, covered, until serving time.

88

Rather than using lemon juice to keep apples and other fruits from turning brown, try drizzling fresh fruits with lemon-lime soda. It contains enough citric acid to keep fruit from turning dark, but it does not have a strong flavor that can alter the taste of the fruit and/or the recipe.

Toasting nuts brings out the flavor. Arrange nuts in a single layer on a microwave-safe plate. Microwave on High for 3 to 4 minutes or until fragrant, or place on a baking sheet and toast in a preheated 375-degree oven for 5 to 10 minutes or until light brown, stirring every 2 to 3 minutes.

1975

First-year students were no longer required to live in the student dormitory. The Emergency Medical Sciences paramedic program was established in the College of Health Related Professions (CHRP) in its own department.

Tropical Curried Chicken Salad

3   or 4 (5-ounce) boneless skinless
      chicken breasts, cooked, chilled
      and coarsely chopped
1   (6-ounce) package dried diced
      tropical fruit, cooked and chilled
2   tablespoons shredded coconut
1/2   to 1 tablespoon curry powder
1/2   teaspoon salt

1/2   teaspoon pepper
1/4   cup mayonnaise-type
      salad dressing
1   to 2 tablespoons
      balsamic vinegar
~   Chopped green onions
      (optional)
~   Toasted almonds (optional)

Yield: 6 servings

Nutrients per serving
Calories 253
Protein 19 g
Carbo 27 g
Total Fat 7 g
Saturated Fat 2 g
Cholesterol 55 mg
Fiber 2 g
Sodium 346 mg

Combine the chicken, tropical fruit, coconut, curry powder, salt and pepper in a bowl and mix well. Mix the salad dressing and vinegar in a bowl. Add to the chicken mixture and mix well.

Chill, covered, for several hours to allow the flavors to blend. Sprinkle with green onions and almonds before serving.

89

Broccoli Tortellini Salad

7   ounces cheese tortellini
1   cup broccoli florets
1   (6-ounce) jar marinated
      artichoke hearts
1   (5-ounce) can sliced black
      olives, drained
1/2   cup chopped fresh parsley, or
      2 to 3 tablespoons parsley
      flakes
2   green onions, trimmed
      and sliced

1   tablespoon chopped pimento
2 1/2 teaspoons chopped fresh basil,
      or 1/4 teaspoon dried basil
      leaves
1/2   teaspoon garlic powder
1/2   cup Italian salad dressing
5   or 6 cherry tomatoes,
      cut into halves
1/2   cup (2 ounces) freshly grated
      Parmesan cheese

Yield: 6 servings

Nutrients per serving
Calories 288
Protein 9 g
Carbo 24 g
Total Fat 19 g
Saturated Fat 4 g
Cholesterol 20 mg
Fiber 4 g
Sodium 735 mg

Cook the pasta using package directions until the desired degree of doneness. Drain and rinse with cold water. Combine the pasta, broccoli, undrained artichokes, olives, parsley, green onions, pimento, basil and garlic powder in a bowl and mix well. Add the salad dressing and toss until coated.

Chill, covered, for 4 to 6 hours to allow the flavors to blend. Add the tomatoes just before serving and mix gently. Sprinkle with the cheese. You may prepare up to one day in advance and store, covered, in the refrigerator. Add the broccoli and tomatoes just before serving to avoid discoloration. Double the recipe for a larger crowd.

The Department of Pathology acquired first electron microscope to provide scanning, scanning transmission, and X-ray microanalysis capability in the country.

1976

Frog Eye Salad

Yield: 8 servings

Nutrients per serving
Calories 351
Protein 6 g
Carbo 65 g
Total Fat 7 g
Saturated Fat 6 g
Cholesterol 27 mg
Fiber 2 g
Sodium 381 mg

8 ounces acini di pepe
1/2 cup sugar
1 tablespoon all-purpose flour
1 1/4 teaspoons salt
7 ounces pineapple juice
1 egg, beaten
1 1/2 teaspoons lemon juice

1 1/2 (11-ounce) cans mandarin oranges, drained
1 (15-ounce) can pineapple chunks, drained
8 ounces whipped topping
1/2 cup miniature marshmallows
1/2 cup flaked coconut

Cook the pasta using package directions; drain. Combine the sugar, flour and salt in a saucepan and mix well. Stir in the pineapple juice, egg and lemon juice. Cook until the mixture thickens and turns a creamy color, stirring frequently.

Combine the pasta and egg mixture in a bowl and mix well. Stir in the mandarin oranges, pineapple, whipped topping, marshmallows and coconut. Chill, covered, until serving time.

90

Italian Pasta Salad

Yield: 8 servings

Nutrients per serving
Calories 319
Protein 10 g
Carbo 51 g
Total Fat 9 g
Saturated Fat 1 g
Cholesterol 2 mg
Fiber 4 g
Sodium 478 mg

16 ounces cavatappi (corkscrew)
1 (3-ounce) jar green olives, drained
2 or 3 ripe tomatoes, cut into quarters or coarsely chopped
1 large onion, chopped
1 cucumber, sliced
1 red bell pepper, sliced

1 green bell pepper, sliced
2 garlic cloves, minced
~ Italian spices (oregano, basil, Italian seasoning mix, etc.) to taste
1/2 cup zesty Italian salad dressing
1/4 cup (1 ounce) freshly grated Parmesan cheese

Cook the pasta using package directions; drain. Combine the pasta, olives, tomatoes, onion, cucumber, bell peppers, garlic and desired spices in a bowl and mix gently. Add the dressing and toss to coat.

Chill, covered, in the refrigerator until serving time. Sprinkle with the cheese just before serving. Add chopped cooked chicken to turn this salad into a main dish summer salad.

1977 *The Education II Building was completed.*

Black Bean Salad

Lime Vinaigrette

3   to 4 tablespoons fresh lime juice
2   tablespoons extra-virgin olive oil
1   tablespoon red wine vinegar
1   teaspoon salt
1/2   teaspoon freshly ground pepper

Salad

2   (15-ounce) cans black beans, drained and rinsed
1   (10-ounce) package frozen sweet corn, cooked and drained
2   large tomatoes, peeled, seeded and chopped
1   avocado, chopped
1/4   cup chopped fresh cilantro
2   jalapeño chiles, seeded and minced

Yield: 8 servings

Nutrients per serving
Calories 172
Protein 6 g
Carbo 29 g
Total Fat 9 g
Saturated Fat 1 g
Cholesterol 0 mg
Fiber 9 g
Sodium 824 mg

To prepare the vinaigrette, combine the lime juice, olive oil, vinegar, salt and pepper in a jar with a tight-fitting lid and seal tightly. Shake to mix.

To prepare the salad, combine the beans, corn, tomatoes, avocado, cilantro and jalapeño chiles in a bowl and mix gently. Add the vinaigrette and toss to coat. Serve immediately. If there is a delay between preparation and serving, add the avocado just before serving.

Broccoli Salad

Creamy Dressing

3/4   cup mayonnaise
2   tablespoons sugar
2   tablespoons vinegar

Salad

1   large bunch broccoli, trimmed and cut into bite-size pieces
8   ounces bacon, crisp-cooked and crumbled
1   red onion, chopped
1   cup sunflower kernels
1/2   cup raisins (optional)

Yield: 8 servings

Nutrients per serving
Calories 346
Protein 10 g
Carbo 13 g
Total Fat 29 g
Saturated Fat 5 g
Cholesterol 18 mg
Fiber 5 g
Sodium 356 mg

To prepare the dressing, mix the mayonnaise, sugar and vinegar in a large bowl.

To prepare the salad, stir the broccoli into the dressing mixture. Add the bacon, onion, sunflower kernels and raisins and mix well. Chill, covered, for up to 24 hours.

A microwave dish was installed to provide two-way visual and audio communications between UAMSC and Arkansas Children's Hospital.

1977

Grinnin' Greek Salad

Yield: 8 servings

Nutrients per serving

Calories 355

Protein 11 g

Carbo 16 g

Total Fat 28 g

Saturated Fat 8 g

Cholesterol 40 mg

Fiber 2 g

Sodium 1517 mg

92

Red Wine Vinaigrette

2/3　cup water

1/2　cup extra-virgin olive oil

1/2　cup red wine vinegar or balsamic vinegar

2　envelopes Caesar or Italian salad dressing mix

2　tablespoons sugar, or 2 packets Splenda

Salad

10　ounces mixed salad greens

4　to 8 ounces hard salami or smoked ham,
　　sliced and cut into quarters

1/2　large red onion, sliced and separated into rings

1　red or yellow bell pepper, sliced into rings

1　cucumber, peeled, seeded and sliced

10　to 12 cherry tomatoes, cut into halves

4　ounces feta cheese, drained and crumbled

1　(6-ounce) can black olives, drained

~　Banana peppers for garnish

~　Artichoke hearts for garnish

To prepare the vinaigrette, combine the water, olive oil, vinegar, salad dressing mix and sugar in a jar with a tight-fitting lid and seal tightly. Shake to mix.

To prepare the salad, toss the salad greens, salami, onion, bell pepper, cucumber, tomatoes, cheese and olives in a salad bowl. Add the vinaigrette and mix until coated. Top with the banana peppers and artichoke hearts. Chill, covered, for 1 to 2 hours before serving. Serve with grilled steak or chicken and garlic bread. Omit the salami to reduce the fat calories.

To speed up the ripening of tomatoes and avocados, place the fruits in a brown paper bag and seal tightly. Let stand at room temperature for a few days.

1979

Dr. Harry P. Ward was appointed second chancellor of UAMSC. The UAMSC Department of Pediatrics moved to Arkansas Children's Hospital, a longtime teaching affiliate of the medical school.

R
Breads and Breakfast

Make Cooking a Family Tradition

Many of us can remember helping our parents or grandparents in the kitchen when we were growing up. We have family recipes and secrets for delicious home cooking, but we rarely find the time to cook a three-course meal, much less let our kids help us. However, in 2005 the American Obesity Association found that nearly 15.3 percent of kids ages six through eleven are obese, and this terrifying fact has been blamed on the abundance of over-processed, nutrient-deficient food that has become the staple of American diets.

We can make delicious home-cooked meals with kids, and teach them about nutrition labels, following directions, proper use of equipment, and healthy eating. Not only can you share all of these skills with your children through cooking, you can share with them some of your own cooking stories and favorite recipes.

To help get you started, we compiled easy recipes on page 94 for your children to enjoy with you. Start a tradition of healthy eating and quality time with your kids.

Toffee Chip Bars, from *The Purple Cow*
(reprinted with permission)

Yield: 36 bars

2 cups all-purpose flour
2/3 cup firmly packed light brown sugar
1/2 cup (1 stick) butter (cold)
1 egg, lightly beaten
1 cup chopped pecans
1 (12-ounce) package semisweet chocolate chips
1 (14-ounce) can sweetened condensed milk
1 (10-ounce) package toffee chips

Preheat the oven to 350 degrees. Mix the flour and brown sugar in a large bowl and cut in the butter with a pastry blender or fork until crumbly. Add the egg and mix well. Stir in the pecans and half the chocolate chips. Reserve 1 1/2 cups of the chocolate chip mixture and press the remaining mixture over the bottom of a lightly greased 9x13-inch baking pan; do not use a glass baking dish. Bake for 10 minutes. Maintain the oven temperature.

Pour the condensed milk over the baked layer. Sprinkle with 1 1/2 cups of the toffee chips, the remaining chocolate chip mixture and the remaining chocolate chips. Bake for 25 to 30 minutes or until golden brown. Remove from the oven and sprinkle with the remaining toffee chips. Let stand until cool and cut into bars.

Cinnamon-Honey Oatmeal Pancakes, from *Wild Oats Natural Market*
(reprinted with permission)

Prep Time: 10 minutes,
Cook Time: 20 minutes,
Yield: 12 pancakes

1 1/2 cups organic rolled oats
1/2 cup unbleached, all-purpose flour
1 teaspoon baking soda
1 teaspoon salt
2 teaspoons cinnamon
2 cups organic buttermilk
2 tablespoons canola oil, plus more for cooking
3 tablespoons honey
1 teaspoon vanilla extract
2 organic eggs, beaten

Mix the oats, flour, baking soda, salt, cinnamon and buttermilk in a bowl. Mix in the canola oil, honey, vanilla and eggs. Heat a nonstick pan or griddle over medium heat. Drizzle the pan with a little oil. Spoon the batter into the skillet, making 3-inch round pancakes. Cook until the edges begin to brown and bubbles appear in the middle of the pancake. Turn and cook for about 30 seconds longer on the second side. Serve with organic maple syrup.

Anne Fruge, Little Rock Family Staff, reprinted with permission

Green Chile French Bread

1	(16-ounce) loaf French bread	16	ounces Monterey Jack cheese or Swiss cheese, shredded
1/2	cup (1 stick) butter or margarine, softened	1/2	cup mayonnaise
1	(4-ounce) can chopped green chiles, drained	1/8	teaspoon garlic powder

Yield: 20 slices

Nutrients per slice
Calories 231
Protein 8 g
Carbo 13 g
Total Fat 16 g
Saturated Fat 8 g
Cholesterol 34 mg
Fiber 1 g
Sodium 398 mg

Cut the loaf horizontally into halves. Mix the butter and green chiles in a bowl until combined and spread over the cut sides of the bread halves. Combine the cheese, mayonnaise and garlic powder in a bowl and mix well. Spread over the butter mixture.

Arrange the halves cut side up on a baking sheet and bake in a preheated 350-degree oven for 20 minutes. Slice and serve warm with soups and salads.

Mexican Corn Bread

1/4	cup vegetable oil	1	(17-ounce) can cream-style corn
1 1/2	pounds ground chuck	1	cup milk
1	cup yellow cornmeal	1	onion, finely chopped
1/2	teaspoon salt	2	jalapeño chiles, chopped
1/4	teaspoon baking soda	12	ounces Cheddar cheese, shredded
1/4	teaspoon baking powder		

Yield: 8 servings

Nutrients per serving
Calories 499
Protein 30 g
Carbo 25 g
Total Fat 32 g
Saturated Fat 14 g
Cholesterol 98 mg
Fiber 2 g
Sodium 706 mg

Coat an 8-inch cast-iron skillet with some of the oil. Heat the skillet in a preheated 350-degree oven until hot. Maintain the oven temperature. Brown the ground chuck in a skillet, stirring until crumbly; drain. Mix the cornmeal, salt, baking soda and baking powder in a bowl and stir in the corn and milk. Add the remaining oil to the batter and mix well.

Spoon half the batter into the hot skillet. Layer with the ground chuck, onion, jalapeño chiles and cheese. Spread with the remaining batter and bake for 55 minutes. Serve hot.

The name of the campus changed to University of Arkansas for Medical Sciences (UAMS). The first annual fund-raising campaign for UAMS began. The Ambulatory Care Center was completed.

1980

Almost Fat-Free Mexican Corn Bread

Yield: 10 servings

Nutrients per serving

Calories 162

Protein 6 g

Carbo 24 g

Total Fat 5 g

Saturated Fat 2 g

Cholesterol 9 mg

Fiber 2 g

Sodium 390 mg

1 tablespoon vegetable oil
1 cup cornmeal
1 cup all-purpose flour
4 teaspoons baking powder
1/2 teaspoon salt
1 cup skim milk
1/4 cup egg substitute or egg whites

1/4 cup no-salt-added applesauce
1/2 to 3/4 cup (2 to 3 ounces) shredded Cheddar cheese or low-fat Cheddar cheese
1/2 cup frozen or canned whole kernel corn
~ Sliced fresh or canned jalapeño chiles to taste

Coat a 10×10-inch nonstick baking pan with the oil and heat the pan in a preheated 425-degree oven for 5 minutes; this will make the cornbread crunchy on the bottom. Maintain the oven temperature.

Combine the cornmeal, flour, baking powder and salt in a bowl and mix well. Mix the milk, egg substitute and applesauce in a bowl and stir into the cornmeal mixture. Add the cheese, corn and jalapeño chiles and mix well. Spoon the batter into the hot baking pan and bake for 20 to 25 minutes or until a wooden pick inserted in the center comes out dry and the top is brown.

96

Banana Blueberry Bread

Yield: 12 slices

Nutrients per slice

Calories 195

Protein 3 g

Carbo 31 g

Total Fat 7 g

Saturated Fat 2 g

Cholesterol 35 mg

Fiber 1 g

Sodium 221 mg

1 3/4 cups all-purpose flour
2 3/4 teaspoons baking powder
1/2 teaspoon salt
2/3 cup sugar
1/3 cup shortening

1 cup mashed bananas (3 to 4 very ripe bananas)
2 eggs
1 cup frozen blueberries (do not thaw)

Grease the bottom of a 5×9-inch loaf pan. Mix the flour, baking powder and salt together. Beat the sugar and shortening in a mixing bowl until creamy. Add the bananas and eggs and beat until blended. Add the dry ingredients and stir just until moistened. Fold in the frozen blueberries; overmixing will cause the bread to turn blue.

Spoon the batter into the prepared pan. Bake in a preheated 350-degree oven for 1 hour. Cool in the pan for 10 minutes and remove to a wire rack. Cool for 30 minutes before slicing. Serve warm with butter.

1981

The Ambulatory Care Center was officially designated as the Isaac Folsom Clinic but later became known as the Outpatient Center.

Cranberry Sweet Potato Bread

1 1/2 cups all-purpose flour
1 1/3 cups sugar
2 eggs
1/3 cup canola oil
1 teaspoon vanilla extract
1 teaspoon baking soda

1 teaspoon ground cinnamon
1/2 teaspoon salt
1 cup mashed cooked sweet potato
1 cup chopped dried cranberries

Yield: 12 slices

Nutrients per slice
Calories 266
Protein 3 g
Carbo 48 g
Total Fat 7 g
Saturated Fat 1 g
Cholesterol 35 mg
Fiber 2 g
Sodium 221 mg

Mix the flour and sugar in a bowl. Whisk the eggs in a bowl until blended and stir in the canola oil. Add the vanilla, baking soda, cinnamon and salt and mix well. Stir in the mashed sweet potato and mix in the flour mixture. Fold in the cranberries.

Spoon the batter into a 5×9-inch loaf pan sprayed with nonstick cooking spray and bake in a preheated 350-degree oven for 1 hour. Cool in the pan for 10 minutes and remove to a wire rack to cool completely.

Irish Soda Bread

2 1/2 cups light and dark raisins
5 cups sifted all-purpose unbleached flour
3/4 cup sugar
2 teaspoons baking powder
1 1/2 teaspoons salt

1 teaspoon baking soda
1/2 cup (1 stick) butter
3 tablespoons caraway seeds
2 1/2 cups buttermilk
1 egg, lightly beaten

Yield: 24 slices

Nutrients per slice
Calories 195
Protein 4 g
Carbo 36 g
Total Fat 5 g
Saturated Fat 3 g
Cholesterol 20 mg
Fiber 1 g
Sodium 297 mg

Soak the raisins in enough water to generously cover in a bowl for 15 to 20 minutes; drain. Mix the flour, sugar, baking powder, salt and baking soda in a bowl. Cut the butter into the flour mixture until crumbly. Stir in the raisins and caraway seeds. Add the buttermilk and egg and mix until well moistened.

Shape the dough into two loaves on a lightly floured surface. Place each loaf in a generously buttered 5×9-inch bread pan. Bake in a preheated 350-degree oven for 1 hour; test with a wooden pick for doneness. Cool in the pans for 3 to 5 minutes and remove to a wire rack to cool completely.

The Education I Building was renamed the Winston K. Shorey building, honoring Shorey's 14 years as the College of Medicine dean.

1981

Pumpkin Bread

Yield: 18 slices

Nutrients per slice

Calories 349

Protein 4 g

Carbo 54 g

Total Fat 14 g

Saturated Fat 2 g

Cholesterol 47 mg

Fiber 2 g

Sodium 442 mg

3¹/₂	cups all-purpose flour
2	teaspoons baking soda
2	teaspoons salt
1	teaspoon baking powder
1	teaspoon ground nutmeg
1	teaspoon ground cinnamon
1	teaspoon ground allspice
¹/₂	teaspoon ground cloves
3	cups sugar or Splenda
1	cup vegetable oil or unsweetened applesauce
4	eggs, beaten, or equivalent amount of egg substitute
1	(16-ounce) can pumpkin
²/₃	cup water
~	Raisins (optional)
~	Chopped nuts (optional)

Sift the flour, baking soda, salt, baking powder, nutmeg, cinnamon, allspice and cloves into a bowl and mix well. Mix the sugar, oil and eggs in a bowl and stir in the pumpkin. Add the flour mixture and mix well. Stir in the water, raisins and nuts.

Spoon the batter into three miniature loaf pans and bake in a preheated 350-degree oven for 1 hour or until the tops are slightly cracked and a wooden pick inserted in the centers comes out clean. Cool in the pans for 10 minutes and remove to a wire rack to cool completely.

If you need a quick glaze for cinnamon rolls, quick breads, or a bundt cake, heat a small amount of vanilla frosting in the microwave until of the desired consistency, stirring frequently.

1981 *The Cytotechnology program moved to the College of Health Related Professions.*

Zucchini Bread

3   eggs
1 3/4 cups sugar
1   cup vegetable oil
1   tablespoon vanilla extract
1   tablespoon ground cinnamon
1   teaspoon baking soda
1   teaspoon salt
1/4 teaspoon baking powder
3   cups all-purpose flour
2   cups raisins (optional)
2   cups chopped walnuts or pecans (optional)
2   cups grated zucchini (1 large zucchini)
1   tablespoon sugar

Yield: 24 slices

Nutrients per slice
Calories 209
Protein 3 g
Carbo 28 g
Total Fat 10 g
Saturated Fat 1 g
Cholesterol 26 mg
Fiber 1 g
Sodium 165 mg

Beat the eggs in a mixing bowl until foamy. Add 1 3/4 cups sugar, the oil and vanilla and beat until blended. Add the cinnamon, baking soda, salt and baking powder, beating constantly until combined. Blend in the flour. Fold in the raisins, walnuts and zucchini.

Spoon the batter into two greased 5×9-inch loaf pans and sprinkle the tops with 1 tablespoon sugar. Bake in a preheated 325-degree oven for 1 hour. Cool in the pans for 10 minutes and remove to a wire rack to cool completely.

99

Take a glimpse at some of the Arkansas Health Care milestones accomplished at UAMS:
* First open-heart surgery
* First bypass heart surgery
* First bone marrow transplant
* First high-risk nursery
* First kidney transplant
* First to treat sickle cell disease
* First to treat hemophiliacs
* First ophthalmic laser
* First eye bank
* First corneal transplant
* First breast reconstruction surgery
* First cryosurgery for liver tumors
* First to perform balloon dilatation of coronary arteries
* First outpatient chemotherapy
* First comprehensive eye institute
* First gene therapy for multiple myeloma in the United States

Fresh Apple Muffins

Yield: 18 muffins

Nutrients per muffin
Calories 381
Protein 3 g
Carbo 42 g
Total Fat 24 g
Saturated Fat 3 g
Cholesterol 24 mg
Fiber 1 g
Sodium 143 mg

3	cups all-purpose flour	2	eggs
1	teaspoon ground cinnamon	2	teaspoons vanilla extract
1	teaspoon baking soda	3	cups chopped peeled Granny Smith apples
1/2	teaspoon salt	1	cup pecans, chopped
2	cups sugar		
1 1/2	cups vegetable oil		

Mix the flour, cinnamon, baking soda and salt together. Beat the sugar, oil, eggs and vanilla in a mixing bowl until blended. Add the flour mixture and mix just until moistened. Stir in the apples and pecans.

Spoon the batter into muffin cups sprayed with nonstick cooking spray. Bake in a preheated 350-degree oven for 30 minutes. Cool in the pan for 2 minutes and remove to a wire rack. Serve warm or at room temperature.

100

Focaccia

Yield: 12 servings

Nutrients per serving
Calories 138
Protein 5 g
Carbo 26 g
Total Fat 2 g
Saturated Fat <1 g
Cholesterol 0 mg
Fiber 1 g
Sodium 388 mg

1	envelope fast-rising yeast		Olive oil to taste
1 1/4	cups lukewarm water		Chopped fresh rosemary to taste
2	tablespoons olive oil		Coarse sea salt to taste
2	teaspoons salt		
3	to 3 1/2 cups unbleached bread flour		

Dissolve the yeast in the lukewarm water in a mixing bowl. Stir in 2 tablespoons olive oil and 2 teaspoons salt. Add 3 cups of the flour gradually, beating constantly until a soft dough that holds its shape forms. Knead the dough with a dough hook for 6 to 7 minutes, adding the remaining 1/2 cup flour as needed until the dough pulls from the side of the bowl.

Shape the dough into a ball and place in a greased bowl, turning to coat the surface. Let rise, covered with plastic wrap, in a warm place for 1 hour or until doubled in bulk. Turn onto a lightly floured surface and press flat.

Shape the dough into a ball and arrange on an oiled baking sheet. Let rest for 5 minutes and then stretch the dough to roughly fit the pan. Cover with a tea towel and let rise for 30 minutes or until puffy.

Make a pattern of dimples at 2-inch intervals over the surface of the dough using your fingertips. Brush with olive oil to taste and sprinkle lightly with rosemary and sea salt. Bake in a preheated 400-degree oven for 15 to 20 minutes or until golden brown.

1985

University Hospital and ACH initiated University Careflight to transport patients to University Hospital by ambulance after flown by helicopter to nearby Rick's Armory.

Doughnuts—The Best in Town

Doughnuts

2	envelopes dry yeast
1/2	cup lukewarm water
2	cups scalded milk, cooled
1/2	cup sugar
2	teaspoons salt
2	eggs, beaten
6	cups all-purpose flour
1/2	cup shortening, melted and cooled
~	Vegetable oil for frying

Confectioners' Sugar Glaze

1 1/2	(1-pound) packages confectioners' sugar
3/4	cup hot water
1	teaspoon vanilla extract
1/4	teaspoon ground cinnamon

Yield:

24 doughnuts

Nutrients per doughnut

Calories 297
Protein 5 g
Carbo 57 g
Total Fat 5 g
Saturated Fat 2 g
Cholesterol 20 mg
Fiber 1 g
Sodium 209 mg

101

To prepare the doughnuts, dissolve the yeast in the lukewarm water in a bowl. Mix the scalded milk, sugar and salt in a mixing bowl and stir until the sugar and salt dissolve. Stir in the yeast mixture. Beat in the eggs. Add 3 cups of the flour and beat until blended. Mix in the shortening. Add the remaining 3 cups flour and beat until blended.

Place the dough on a sheet of waxed paper and let rest for 10 minutes. Knead for 1 minute and place the dough in a large greased bowl, turning to coat the surface. Let rise, covered with a damp tea towel, for 2 hours. Punch the dough down and roll 1/4 inch thick on a lightly floured surface. Cut the dough using a doughnut cutter and arrange the doughnuts on a sheet of waxed paper. Let rise for 1 hour. Fry in hot oil in a deep skillet until brown on all sides; drain.

To prepare the glaze, mix the confectioners' sugar, hot water, vanilla and cinnamon in a large bowl until of a glaze consistency. Dip the warm doughnuts in the glaze and drain on a sheet of waxed paper.

Nutritional profile does not include vegetable oil for frying.

Rinse a saucepan with cold water before scalding milk to prevent the milk from sticking to the pan. To prevent sticky liquids from adhering to measuring cups or spoons, lightly coat with vegetable oil. Rinse in hot water.

The Family Medical Center completed and the Women's Health Center opened at Freeway Medical Center.

1986

100% Whole Wheat Bread

Yield: 48 slices

Nutrients per slice

Calories 134

Protein 4 g

Carbo 26 g

Total Fat 2 g

Saturated Fat <1 g

Cholesterol 0 mg

Fiber 4 g

Sodium 291 mg

5¹/3 cups warm water

¹/2 cup honey

¹/3 cup olive oil

2 tablespoons salt

1 envelope dry yeast or fast-rising yeast

12 cups stone-ground whole wheat flour

Combine the warm water, honey, olive oil, salt and yeast in a large bowl and mix well. Add enough of the whole wheat flour to reach the desired consistency and stir until moistened. Let stand for 20 to 40 minutes.

Knead the dough on a lightly floured surface for about 10 minutes or until blistered. Shape into a ball and place in a greased bowl, turning to coat the surface. Cover with a tea towel that has been moistened with hot water and let rise for 2 hours or until doubled in bulk. Punch the dough down and shape into loaves in four greased 5×9-inch loaf pans.

Let rise, covered, until the dough reaches the tops of the pans. Bake at 325 degrees for 45 minutes or until the loaves sound hollow when lightly thumped; do not preheat the oven. Remove the loaves to a wire rack and lay on their sides. Let stand until cool.

For easy slicing, slice the loaves on their sides with a serrated knife. Freeze the loaves, if desired, for future use. Arrowhead Mills or King Arthur flour is preferred, or if buying in bulk, confirm that the flour is hard, red, winter wheat.

The nutritional profile includes all of the whole wheat flour.

102

The UAMS Office of Research and Sponsored Programs (ORSP) is the facilitator of the pre-award grants, contracts, subcontracts, and industry-sponsored agreements process. Funding is often contingent on approval of research protocols overseen by the UAMS Institutional Review Board, a division of ORSP. The office also works with persons engaged in nonresearch projects and programs—functions such as outreach programs, training, and fellowships—which have an equally important impact on funding within the medical community at UAMS. In addition, the office serves as a conduit of information on grant programs, sponsored programs, the latest funding and research news, medical fellowships, and governmental and non-governmental agencies.

Over the last twenty years, extramural funding activity on the UAMS campus alone has grown from approximately $10 million to almost $90 million.

1987

The UAMS Helipad officially opened at the north end of Education II Building, where the College of Public Health is now located.

Oven-Baked Dutch Apple Pancake

2	(21-ounce) cans apple pie filling	1/2	cup all-purpose flour
2	tablespoons butter, softened	1	tablespoon sour cream
1	teaspoon ground cinnamon	1	teaspoon grated lemon zest
3	eggs	1/4	teaspoon salt
1/2	cup milk	1	tablespoon confectioners' sugar

Yield: 8 servings

Nutrients per serving

Calories 247

Protein 4 g

Carbo 47 g

Total Fat 6 g

Saturated Fat 3 g

Cholesterol 89 mg

Fiber 2 g

Sodium 192 mg

Mix the pie filling, butter and cinnamon in a 10-inch cast-iron skillet. Heat in a preheated 350-degree oven until warm. Maintain the oven temperature. Beat the eggs in a mixing bowl until frothy. Add the milk, flour, sour cream, lemon zest and salt and beat just until combined. Immediately pour the batter over the hot pie filling mixture and bake for 20 to 25 minutes or until the pancake is puffed and golden brown. Lightly dust with the confectioners' sugar and cut into wedges. Serve warm.

Buttermilk and Walnut Pancakes

Pancakes

1 1/4 cups all-purpose flour

3/4 cup whole wheat flour

1 tablespoon sugar

1 teaspoon baking soda

1/2 teaspoon salt

1/2 cup chopped walnuts

2 cups buttermilk

2 tablespoons vegetable oil

1 egg

Apple Cinnamon Topping

2 large apples, peeled and chopped

1 cup raisins

1/3 to 1/2 cup maple syrup (do not use pancake syrup)

1 teaspoon ground cinnamon

Yield: 10 pancakes

Nutrients per pancake

Calories 282

Protein 7 g

Carbo 49 g

Total Fat 8 g

Saturated Fat 1 g

Cholesterol 23 mg

Fiber 3 g

Sodium 304 mg

To prepare the pancakes, mix the all-purpose flour, whole wheat flour, sugar, baking soda and salt in a bowl. Stir in the walnuts. Whisk the buttermilk, oil and egg in a bowl until blended. Add to the flour mixture and mix just until moistened, adding additional buttermilk if needed for a thinner batter. Pour approximately 1/4 cup of the batter for each pancake onto a hot lightly greased griddle. Cook until bubbles appear on the surface and the underside is golden brown. Turn and cook until golden brown on the remaining side. Keep warm in a 200-degree oven.

To prepare the apple cinnamon topping, combine the apples, raisins, syrup and cinnamon in a microwave-safe bowl and mix well. Microwave, covered, on High for 3 minutes, stirring halfway through the process. Let stand, covered, for 5 minutes before serving. Serve warm with the pancakes.

Breakfast Burrito Casserole

Yield: 20 servings

Nutritional profile
for this recipe is
not available.

12 to 16 frozen egg and sausage breakfast burritos or tacos
2 (10-ounce) cans cream of mushroom soup
1 (11-ounce) can tomatoes with green chiles
2 cups (8 ounces) shredded Cheddar cheese

Cut the tacos into thirds and evenly cover the bottoms of two greased 9×13-inch baking dishes with the tacos. Mix the soup and tomatoes with green chiles in a bowl and spread evenly over the prepared layers. Sprinkle 1 cup of the cheese over the top of each.

Bake in a preheated 325-degree oven until bubbly. Serve with salsa. Microwave for 12 minutes instead of baking, if desired.

The Breakfast Burrito Casserole is served annually at the ACRC Staff Breakfast, which is prepared and hosted by the ACRC Auxiliary. It treats five hundred-plus employees and volunteers to breakfast to honor everyone at ACRC for the work they do throughout the year. This event takes the place of celebrating isolated events throughout the year. It is enjoyed by all. After the Breakfast Burrito Casserole was served the first year, the employees said this was the breakfast entrée they wanted each year.

1989

The Arkansas Cancer Research Center opened. The kidney transplant program celebrated its 25th anniversary.

Brunch Eggs

Cheese Sauce
2 tablespoons margarine or butter
2 tablespoons all-purpose flour
1/8 teaspoon salt
1/8 teaspoon pepper
2 cups milk
4 ounces Velveeta cheese, cubed

Eggs
4 ounces Canadian bacon or honey-roasted ham, chopped
1 bunch green onions, trimmed and chopped
2 teaspoons margarine
1 (4-ounce) can mushroom pieces, drained
12 eggs, beaten
3 1/2 slices bread, crumbled
3 tablespoons butter, melted
~ Paprika to taste

Yield: 10 servings

Nutrients per serving
Calories 262
Protein 15 g
Carbo 12 g
Total Fat 18 g
Saturated Fat 7 g
Cholesterol 280 mg
Fiber 1 g
Sodium 570 mg

105

To prepare the sauce, melt the margarine in a saucepan and stir in the flour, salt and pepper. Cook until bubbly, stirring constantly. Add the milk and cook until thickened, stirring frequently. Stir in the cheese and cook until blended.

To prepare the eggs, sauté the bacon and green onions in 2 teaspoons margarine in a nonstick skillet. Add the mushrooms and sauté for several minutes. Soft-scramble the eggs in a skillet and add to the bacon mixture. Fold in the sauce and spoon into a buttered 8×12-inch baking dish. Sprinkle with the bread crumbs and drizzle with 3 tablespoons butter. Dust with paprika. Chill, covered, for 8 to 10 hours. Bake, uncovered, in a preheated 350-degree oven for 30 minutes. Serve immediately.

Sausage Grits Casserole

3 cups beef bouillon
1 cup quick-cooking grits
1/2 teaspoon salt
1 pound mild, medium or hot bulk sausage

1 cup (2 sticks) butter
1 cup milk
4 eggs, beaten
1/2 cup (2 ounces) shredded sharp Cheddar cheese

Yield: 8 servings

Nutrients per serving
Calories 460
Protein 14 g
Carbo 18 g
Total Fat 37 g
Saturated Fat 20 g
Cholesterol 199 mg
Fiber <1 g
Sodium 1036 mg

Combine the bouillon, grits and salt in a saucepan and mix well. Bring to a boil and cook for 3 to 4 minutes or until thickened. Brown the sausage in a skillet, stirring until crumbly. Drain on paper towels. Stir the sausage into the grits. Add the butter, milk, eggs and 1/4 cup of the cheese and mix well. Spoon into a greased baking dish and sprinkle with the remaining 1/4 cup cheese. Bake in a preheated 350-degree oven for 30 to 40 minutes or until brown and bubbly.

The UAMS Continuing Medical Education Outreach program began and the outpatient surgery center opened. The Medical Application of Science for Health (MASH) program went statewide to all six AHECs.

1990

Sausage and Cheese Strata

Yield: 10 servings

Nutrients per serving
Calories 526
Protein 25 g
Carbo 18 g
Total Fat 39 g
Saturated Fat 21 g
Cholesterol 262 mg
Fiber 1 g
Sodium 879 mg

2   tablespoons butter
1/2 (16-ounce) loaf French bread, torn into bite-size pieces
1/4 cup (1/2 stick) butter, melted
1   pound cocktail franks, sliced
11/2 cups (6 ounces) shredded Swiss cheese
1   cup (4 ounces) shredded Monterey Jack cheese
13/4 cups milk
8   eggs
2   green onions, chopped
2   tablespoons Dijon mustard
1/4 teaspoon pepper
1   cup sour cream
1/2 cup (2 ounces) freshly grated Parmesan cheese

Coat a 9×13-inch baking dish with 2 tablespoons butter. Arrange the bread pieces over the bottom of the prepared baking dish and drizzle with 1/4 cup butter. Mix the franks, Swiss cheese and Monterey Jack cheese in a bowl and sprinkle over the prepared layer. Beat the milk, eggs, green onions, Dijon mustard and pepper in a bowl until foamy and pour over the top. Chill, covered, for 8 to 10 hours.

Remove from the refrigerator 30 minutes before baking. Bake, covered, in a preheated 325-degree oven for 1 hour. Remove the cover and spread with the sour cream. Sprinkle with the Parmesan cheese and bake for 10 minutes longer or until crusty and light brown. You may bake one day in advance and store, covered, in the refrigerator. Reheat, covered, spreading with the sour cream and sprinkling with the Parmesan cheese during the last 10 minutes of the reheating process.

106

Hash Brown Potato Quiche

Yield: 10 servings

Nutrients per serving
Calories 393
Protein 24 g
Carbo 10 g
Total Fat 28 g
Saturated Fat 17 g
Cholesterol 194 mg
Fiber 1 g
Sodium 861 mg

1   (16-ounce) package frozen diced hash brown potatoes, thawed
1/2 cup (1 stick) butter or margarine, melted
    Salt and pepper to taste
21/2 cups chopped cooked ham
8   ounces Monterey Jack cheese with jalapeño chiles, shredded
8   ounces Monterey Jack and Cheddar cheese blend, shredded
1   cup milk
5   eggs

Pat the potatoes over the bottom of a 9×13-inch baking dish and drizzle with the butter. Sprinkle with salt and pepper. Bake in a preheated 425-degree oven for 25 minutes. Reduce the oven temperature to 375 degrees.

Top the baked layer with the ham and cheeses. Whisk the milk and eggs in a bowl until blended and pour over the top. Bake for 40 minutes or until set. Substitute your favorite topping for the ham, if desired.

1991

The Rural Hospital Program was established, and the Internet was installed at UAMS.

Rx

International Cuisine

American Heart Association
2006 Diet and Lifestyle Recommendations

reprinted from the American Heart Association Web site

A healthy diet and lifestyle are the best weapons you have to fight cardiovascular disease. It's not as hard as you may think! Remember, it is the overall pattern of the choices you make that counts.

Make the simple steps below part of your life for long-term benefits to your health and your heart.

Use up at least as many calories as you take in.

Start by knowing how many calories you should be eating and drinking to maintain your weight. Don't eat more calories than you know you can burn up every day. Increase the amount and intensity of your physical activity to match the number of calories you take in. Aim for at least thirty minutes of moderate physical activity on most days of the week or—best of all—at least thirty minutes every day.

Regular physical activity can help you maintain your weight, keep off weight that you lose, and reach physical and cardiovascular fitness. If you can't do at least thirty minutes at one time, you can add up ten minute sessions throughout the day. Eat a variety of nutritious foods from all the food groups.

You may be eating plenty of food, but your body may not be getting the nutrients it needs to be healthy. Nutrient-rich foods have vitamins, minerals, fiber, and other nutrients but are lower in calories. To get the nutrients you need, choose foods like vegetables, fruits, whole-grain products, and fat-free or low-fat dairy products most often.

• Vegetables and fruits are high in vitamins, minerals, and fiber—and they're low in calories. Eating a variety of fruits and vegetables may help you control your weight and your blood pressure.

- Eat fish at least twice a week. Recent research shows that eating oily fish containing omega-3 fatty acids (for example, salmon, trout, and herring) may help lower your risk of death from coronary artery disease.

Eat less of the nutrient-poor foods. There is a right number of calories to eat each day based on your age and physical activity level and whether you are trying to gain, lose, or maintain your weight. You could use your daily allotment of calories on a few high-calorie foods and beverages, but you probably wouldn't get the nutrients your body needs to be healthy. Limit foods and beverages that are high in calories but low in nutrients, and limit how much saturated fat, trans fat, cholesterol, and sodium you eat. Read labels carefully—the Nutrition Facts panel will tell you how much of those nutrients each food or beverage contains.

As you make daily food choices, base your eating pattern on these recommendations

- Choose lean meats and poultry without skin, and prepare them without added saturated and trans fat.

- Select fat-free, 1 percent fat, and low-fat dairy products.

- Cut back on foods containing partially hydrogenated vegetable oils to reduce trans fat in your diet.

- Cut back on foods high in dietary cholesterol. Aim to eat less than 300 milligrams of cholesterol each day.

- Cut back on beverages and foods with added sugars.

- Choose and prepare foods with little or no salt. Aim to eat less than 2,300 milligrams of sodium per day.

- If you drink alcohol, do so in moderation. That means one drink per day if you're a woman and two drinks per day if you're a man.

- Follow the American Heart Association recommendations when you eat out, and keep an eye on your portion sizes.

Also, don't smoke tobacco—and stay away from tobacco smoke.

See the American Heart Association's Web site for more information on this topic and many others: http://www.americanheart.org

Maast-o-Khiar (Persian)

17.5 ounces (500 grams) plain low-fat or fat-free yogurt
1 cucumber, chopped
1 small onion, chopped
2 teaspoons finely chopped mint

~ Salt and black or red pepper to taste
~ Chopped garlic to taste (optional)

Stir the yogurt in a bowl until it flows smoothly, adding a little water if the yogurt appears too thick. Stir in the cucumber, onion, mint, salt, pepper and garlic. Chill, covered, for 2 hours. Serve as a side dish or appetizer.

Yield: 4 servings

Nutrients per serving
Calories 106
Protein 9 g
Carbo 15 g
Total Fat 1 g
Saturated Fat 1 g
Cholesterol 8 mg
Fiber 1 g
Sodium 105 mg

Chicken Satay

3 tablespoons soy sauce
2 tablespoons rice wine vinegar
1 tablespoon sesame oil
1 tablespoon dark brown sugar
1 tablespoon honey

2 garlic cloves, minced
1/2 teaspoon red chili pepper flakes
1 pound boneless skinless chicken breasts, cut into 1×5-inch strips

Combine the soy sauce, vinegar, sesame oil, brown sugar, honey, garlic and red pepper flakes in a bowl and mix well. Add the chicken and toss to coat. Marinate in the refrigerator for 30 minutes, stirring occasionally.

Thread the chicken on skewers and grill on a preheated grill for 2 minutes on each side or until the chicken is cooked through and slightly charred. Serve immediately with peanut dipping sauce.

Yield: 8 servings

Nutrients per serving
Calories 97
Protein 12 g
Carbo 5 g
Total Fat 3 g
Saturated Fat 1 g
Cholesterol 31 mg
Fiber <1 g
Sodium 522 mg

In 2006, a 4,000-square-foot bookstore was built across from the College of Public Health. In addition to offering students the necessary educational materials, the bookstore stocks PDA software, lab coats, scrubs, a large selection of medical equipment, and the latest editions of popular medical books. More than just a bookstore, the UAMS bookstore also carries gift items, apparel, and backpacks with the UAMS logo.

The Arkansas Heart Transplant Program formed a consortium between UAMS, Arkansas Children's Hospital, and Baptist Medical Center.

1991

Kishik Soup

Yield: 2 servings

Nutritional profile
for this recipe is
not available.

1	onion, chopped
~	Chopped cabbage (optional)
1	to 2 tablespoons vegetable oil
1	cup kishik
3	cups water

Sauté the onion and cabbage in the oil in a saucepan until tender. Stir in the kishik and simmer for 1 minute. Mix in the water and cook until thickened, stirring occasionally.

Ladle into soup bowls or spoon over steamed rice. Kishik is a powdered mixture of leban, wheat and spices that can be purchased at any Middle Eastern market.

Italian Vegetable Soup

Yield: 8 servings

Nutrients per serving
Calories 367
Protein 18 g
Carbo 47 g
Total Fat 13 g
Saturated Fat 3 g
Cholesterol 19 mg
Fiber 9 g
Sodium 1200 mg

16	ounces Italian sausage, casings removed and sausage crumbled
2	or 3 zucchini, chopped
1	cup chopped onion
1/2	bell pepper, chopped
2	to 4 garlic cloves, minced
2	tablespoons olive oil
2	(14-ounce) cans chicken broth
1	(15-ounce) can diced tomatoes
1	(16-ounce) can sliced carrots
1	(15-ounce) can kidney beans
1	(15-ounce) can Great Northern beans
1 1/2	teaspoons Italian seasoning
1/2	teaspoon hot red pepper sauce
1/4	teaspoon pepper
6	ounces pasta of choice
1 3/4	cups water
~	Grated Parmesan cheese for garnish

Sauté the sausage, zucchini, onion, bell pepper and garlic in the olive oil in a stockpot until the sausage is brown and the vegetables are tender; drain. Add the broth, tomatoes, carrots, beans, Italian seasoning, hot sauce and pepper and mix well.

Bring to a boil and add the pasta and water. Cook until the pasta is tender, stirring occasionally. Ladle into soup bowls and sprinkle with Parmesan cheese. Serve with garlic bread and a mixed green salad.

1991

The first Mini-Medical School was sponsored by the College of Medicine. The State Health Department and UAMS purchased Freeway Medical Building.

Tabouli

Salad

1/2	cup fine bulgur
1	cup water
1	bunch parsley tops, chopped
2	tomatoes, chopped
1/2	cucumber, chopped
1/2	head lettuce, torn into bite-size pieces
2	tablespoons dried mint

Lemon Dressing

~	Juice of 1 lemon
3	tablespoons olive oil
~	Salt and pepper to taste

Yield: 4 servings

Nutrients per serving
Calories 193
Protein 5 g
Carbo 22 g
Total Fat 11 g
Saturated Fat 1 g
Cholesterol 0 mg
Fiber 6 g
Sodium 29 mg

To prepare the salad, soak the bulgur in the water in a bowl for 20 to 30 minutes or until softened; drain. Combine the bulgur, parsley tops, tomatoes, cucumber, lettuce and mint in a bowl and mix well.

To prepare the dressing, whisk the lemon juice and olive oil in a bowl. Season with salt and pepper. Pour the dressing over the salad and toss to coat.

111

Huevos Rancheros

1/2	cup chopped onion
2	or 3 garlic cloves, minced
1	to 2 tablespoons vegetable oil
2	large tomatoes, chopped
1/4	cup fresh cilantro leaves, or 1 1/2 teaspoons dried cilantro

1 1/2	to 2 teaspoons ground cumin
4	eggs
~	Salt and pepper to taste
2	(6-inch) flour tortillas
1/2	cup (2 ounces) shredded Pepper Jack cheese

Yield: 2 servings

Nutrients per serving
Calories 530
Protein 24 g
Carbo 31 g
Total Fat 36 g
Saturated Fat 10 g
Cholesterol 453 mg
Fiber 4 g
Sodium 528 mg

Brown the onion and garlic in the oil in a large skillet until the onion is tender. Stir in the tomatoes, cilantro and cumin. Cook over low to medium heat for 5 minutes or until the tomato is cooked through but not mushy. Break the eggs over the tomato mixture, spacing them evenly so that you can serve each egg individually with the tomato mixture. Sprinkle with salt and pepper.

Cook, covered, over low heat for 5 minutes or until the eggs are the desired degree of doneness. Microwave each tortilla on a microwave-safe plate until warm. Divide the tomato mixture into four portions so that each portion contains one egg. Arrange two portions on each tortilla. Sprinkle 1/4 cup of the cheese on each serving. Heat in a preheated 200-degree oven until the cheese melts. Serve immediately.

The Arkansas CARES formed in the Department of Psychiatry to help break cycle of maternal drug addiction.

1992

Balsamic-Glazed Pot Roast

Yield: 10 servings

Nutrients per serving
Calories 431
Protein 46 g
Carbo 2 g
Total Fat 25 g
Saturated Fat 8 g
Cholesterol 156 mg
Fiber <1 g
Sodium 113 mg

1/4	cup olive oil	3	whole cloves
1	(4- to 5-pound) beef chuck roast or round roast	3	sprigs of thyme
1	yellow onion, sliced	3	sprigs of parsley
1	carrot, sliced	2	tablespoons balsamic vinegar
1	rib celery, sliced	1	cup water
1	bay leaf	~	Salt and pepper to taste

Heat the olive oil in a Dutch oven over medium-high heat and add the roast. Cook for 8 to 10 minutes or until brown on all sides. Remove the roast to a platter, reserving the pan drippings. Add the onion, carrot and celery to the reserved pan drippings and sauté for 5 to 7 minutes. Stir in the bay leaf, cloves, thyme and parsley. Return the roast to the Dutch oven and drizzle with the vinegar. Stir in the water.

Reduce the heat to low and simmer, covered, for 2 hours, turning the roast after 1 hour. Season the roast with salt and pepper and cook, covered, for 30 minutes. Remove the roast to a platter and tent with foil.

Strain the pan juices through a fine mesh sieve into a saucepan and skim the fat, discarding the solids. Cook over high heat for 3 to 5 minutes or until reduced by half. Taste and adjust the seasonings and serve the gravy with the roast.

Korean Barbecued Beef (Pul-Kogi)

Yield: 4 servings

Nutrients per serving
Calories 240
Protein 24 g
Carbo 12 g
Total Fat 10 g
Saturated Fat 2 g
Cholesterol 42 mg
Fiber 1 g
Sodium 1364 mg

1	pound beef top sirloin, thinly sliced	1	tablespoon sesame oil
6	garlic cloves, minced	1	tablespoon rice wine
1/2	Asian pear, peeled and minced (optional)	1	tablespoon sesame seeds (optional)
2	green onions, trimmed and thinly sliced	1	teaspoon minced fresh ginger
1/4	cup soy sauce	~	Freshly ground pepper to taste
2	tablespoons sugar	2	teaspoons vegetable oil

Combine the beef, garlic, pear and green onions in a sealable plastic bag. Mix the soy sauce, sugar, sesame oil, wine, sesame seeds, ginger and pepper in a bowl and pour over the beef; seal tightly. Shake to coat. Marinate in the refrigerator for 2 to 10 hours, turning occasionally. Preheat a grill pan over high heat and brush with the vegetable oil. Add the beef and cook for 3 to 6 minutes or to the desired degree of doneness, turning frequently to ensure even browning. Cook the beef in a skillet, if desired.

1993

The Community Women's Clinic, a joint project of UAMS Medical Center, the Arkansas Department of Health, and Pulaski County, officially opened.

Gamuzz's Johnny Marzetti

2	cups chopped celery
1	cup chopped onion
2	green bell peppers, chopped
1/4	cup olive oil
1 1/2	pounds ground beef
1	(10-ounce) can tomato soup
1	(8-ounce) can tomato sauce
1	(6-ounce) can tomato paste
2	teaspoons salt
1/4	teaspoon pepper
2	(4-ounce) cans sliced mushrooms
2	cups (8 ounces) shredded mild or sharp Cheddar cheese
8	ounces wide noodles, cooked and drained
1/2	cup sliced pimento-stuffed green olives
1/2	cup (2 ounces) shredded mild or sharp Cheddar cheese

Yield: 8 servings

Nutrients per serving
Calories 538
Protein 32 g
Carbo 37 g
Total Fat 30 g
Saturated Fat 12 g
Cholesterol 115 mg
Fiber 5 g
Sodium 1749 mg

113

Sauté the celery, onion and bell peppers in the olive oil in a deep skillet for 5 minutes or until the vegetables are tender. Remove the celery mixture to a bowl using a slotted spoon, reserving the pan drippings. Brown the ground beef in the reserved pan drippings, stirring until crumbly; drain. Stir in the celery mixture, soup, tomato sauce, tomato paste, salt and pepper.

Simmer for 30 minutes, stirring occasionally. Stir in the mushrooms, 2 cups cheese, the pasta and olives. Spoon the ground beef mixture into an 11×14-inch baking dish and sprinkle with 1/2 cup cheese. Bake in a preheated 350-degree oven for 30 to 45 minutes or until brown and bubbly. Freeze, if desired, for future use.

Rinse cooked pasta under hot water to prevent stickiness. Rubbing a small amount of vegetable oil inside the saucepan before adding water and pasta will prevent boil overs.

Pierogi

Yield: 4 servings

Nutrients per serving
Calories 988
Protein 42 g
Carbo 107 g
Total Fat 42 g
Saturated Fat 21 g
Cholesterol 239 mg
Fiber 8 g
Sodium 1463 mg

114

Filling
1	pound ground beef
1/2	cup chopped onion
4	potatoes
1/2	cup (1 stick) butter or margarine, softened
~	Salt and pepper to taste
1/2	to 1 cup milk

Pastry
4	cups all-purpose flour
2	teaspoons salt
2	eggs, lightly beaten
2	teaspoons vegetable oil

To prepare the filling, brown the ground beef with the onion in a skillet, stirring until the ground beef is crumbly; drain. Cook the potatoes in boiling water in a saucepan until tender but not mushy; drain. Mash the potatoes in a bowl and mix in the butter, salt and pepper. Add milk to the potato mixture until the consistency of mashed potatoes and mix well. Stir in the ground beef mixture.

To prepare the pastry, mix the flour and salt in a bowl and stir in the eggs and oil. Add water until a stiff dough forms and mix well. Roll the dough 1/8 to 1/4 inch thick on a lightly floured surface. Cut into 3-inch rounds.

Spoon some of the potato filling over half of each round and fold the pastry over the filling to enclose. Crimp the edges with a fork to seal. Drop the pierogi in a stockpot of boiling water and boil until they rise to the top. Remove to a platter using a slotted spoon and serve with butter and sour cream.

Approximately seventy-six million cases of food-borne infections occur annually in the United States. Most cases are mild, but serious, life-threatening illness and death can occur. To address this public health concern and ensure the world's food supply is safe, scientists at the UAMS College of Pharmacy and the University of Arkansas, Fayetteville, discovered that cetylpyridinium chloride (Cecure), the active ingredient in several over-the-counter mouthwashes and throat lozenges, is very effective in eliminating germs (Salmonella, E. coli, Listeria, Campylobacter) from food. Cecure minimizes the bacteria on food without affecting its color, odor, taste, or texture and is used by food processors worldwide.

1994

The Harvey and Bernice Jones Eye Institute opened. ACRC expanded to 11 floors. University's Women's Health Center opened at Freeway Medical Building.

Rolled Grape Leaves (Wadadish)

Grape Leaf Filling
1   (16-ounce) jar grape leaves
1 1/2   pounds lean ground beef
1   cup rice
1   tablespoon dried mint
2   teaspoons ground cinnamon
2   teaspoons minced garlic
3   lamb shanks (18 ounces)
2   cups water
~   Juice of 2 lemons
~   Salt and pepper to taste

Leban
1/2   cucumber, minced
~   Salt to taste
1   cup plain yogurt
1   teaspoon minced garlic
1   teaspoon dried mint
~   Pepper to taste

Yield: 12 servings

Nutrients per serving
Calories 213
Protein 17 g
Carbo 19 g
Total Fat 8 g
Saturated Fat 3 g
Cholesterol 48 mg
Fiber 1 g
Sodium 1122 mg

To prepare the filling, drain the grape leaves, discarding the brine. Rinse the grape leaves and remove the stems. Combine the ground beef, rice, mint, cinnamon and garlic in a bowl and mix well. Lay the grape leaves flat on a hard surface. Place 1 to 2 tablespoons of the ground beef mixture at the base of each leaf. Fold the sides of the leaves over the filling and roll to enclose.

Arrange the lamb shanks in a stockpot and place the filled grape leaves on top of the shanks, alternating the direction of layers. Pour the water and lemon juice over the prepared layers and simmer on low heat for 30 minutes. Let stand until cool and season with salt and pepper.

To prepare the leban, sprinkle the cucumber with salt in a colander and drain for 15 to 20 minutes. Mix the cucumber, yogurt, garlic and mint in a bowl. Season with salt and pepper and chill. Top the rolled grape leaves with the sauce. Traditionally, this sauce is used as a topping for many meats and vegetables.

115

The Arkansas Poison Control Center provides potentially lifesaving aid to anyone in the state. One of only sixty certified poison control centers in North America, the center is accessible with its 24-hour-a-day, 365-day-a-year service that can be reached by calling toll free 1-800-3Poison (1-800-376-4766) or 1-800-222-1222. The center also provides professional and public education services throughout the state.

The Drug Information Center is a consulting service for health care professionals seeking information and consultation on drugs and medicines.

The Arkansas Poison Control Center and the Drug Information Center have been operated by the UAMS College of Pharmacy since 1973. In 2005, these centers provided 30,296 callers with vital poison and drug information.

Stuffed Bell Peppers (Dolmeh-yeh Felfel)

Yield: 4 servings

Nutrients per serving

Calories 297
Protein 15 g
Carbo 40 g
Total Fat 9 g
Saturated Fat 4 g
Cholesterol 41 mg
Fiber 5 g
Sodium 1254 mg

2	onions, finely chopped
~	Vegetable oil for sautéing
8³/4	ounces (250 grams) ground lamb or ground beef
1/2	cup water
3	to 4 teaspoons tomato paste
~	Salt and pepper to taste
1/2	cup finely chopped spring onions
1/3	cup parsley, finely chopped
1/3	cup mint, finely chopped
1/3	cup finely chopped garlic chives
1/3	cup tarragon, finely chopped (optional)
2	cups water
3¹/2	ounces (100 grams) long grain or basmati rice
1	teaspoon salt
4	large green or red bell peppers
2	cups water
1	teaspoon salt
3	to 4 tablespoons fresh lime juice
2	to 3 teaspoons sugar
1/2	cup hot water

Sauté the onions in oil in a nonstick skillet over medium heat until golden brown. Add the ground lamb and cook until the lamb is crumbly and no longer pink. Stir in 1/2 cup water and most of the tomato paste. Season with salt and pepper. Cook until the water evaporates, stirring occasionally.

Sauté the spring onions, parsley, mint, garlic chives and tarragon in oil in a nonstick skillet over medium heat until wilted. Bring 2 cups water to a boil in a saucepan and stir in the rice and 1 teaspoon salt. Boil until the rice is tender. Drain and cool slightly.

Remove the tops from the bell peppers and discard the seeds, reserving the tops. Bring 2 cups water to a boil in a stockpot and add 1 teaspoon salt. Arrange the bell peppers side by side in the boiling water; do not stack. Cook until slightly softened; do not overcook. Drain and let stand until cool.

Combine the ground lamb mixture, spring onion mixture, rice, most of the lime juice and most of the sugar in a bowl and mix well. Sprinkle the inside of the bell peppers lightly with salt to taste and fill evenly with the lamb mixture; replace the tops.

Arrange the stuffed bell peppers side by side in a large stockpot. Mix 1/2 cup hot water, the remaining tomato paste, remaining lime juice and remaining sugar in a bowl and pour over the bell peppers. Simmer for 5 to 10 minutes or until heated through.

Nutritional profile does not include vegetable oil for sautéing.

Szechuan Chicken

3	(5-ounce) boneless skinless chicken breasts
3	to 5 tablespoons teriyaki sauce
2	bunches green onions, trimmed and chopped
3	to 5 garlic cloves, minced
1	tablespoon olive oil
1	red bell pepper, chopped
1	green bell pepper, chopped
1/4	cup peanuts
~	Szechuan sauce to taste
2	cups cooked white rice

Yield: 4 servings

Nutrients per serving
Calories 356
Protein 29 g
Carbo 36 g
Total Fat 11 g
Saturated Fat 2 g
Cholesterol 59 mg
Fiber 4 g
Sodium 928 mg

Cut the chicken into bite-size pieces. Combine the chicken and teriyaki sauce in a sealable plastic bag and seal tightly. Shake to coat. Marinate in the refrigerator for 1 hour, turning occasionally.

Stir-fry the chicken, green onions and garlic in the olive oil in a wok or skillet until the chicken is cooked through. Stir in the bell peppers and any other vegetables you desire (such as baby corn, water chestnuts, onions and/or broccoli) and stir-fry until the desired degree of doneness. Add the peanuts and Szechuan sauce and mix well. Serve over hot cooked white rice.

117

Listed below are New Year's food traditions from around the world.
* Eating noodles at midnight is customary at Buddhist temples in Japan.
* A German/Pennsylvania Dutch tradition is to eat pork and sauerkraut on New Year's day for good luck.
* It is the tradition of Bosnia & Croatia (both of former Yugoslavia) to eat what is called "Sarma" or beef wrapped tightly in cabbage to bring good luck in health and wealth for the upcoming year.
* It is a Cuban tradition to eat twelve grapes at the stroke of midnight. The twelve grapes signify the last twelve months of the year.
* German folklore says that eating herring at the stroke of midnight will bring luck for the next year.
* From the South comes the custom of eating greens such as cabbage, collard greens, mustard greens, kale, or spinach to bring money.
* Also from the Southerners is that eating corn bread will bring wealth.
* The Southern custom of eating greens can be found in other cultures as well, although the cabbage can take many forms, such as sauerkraut or even kimchi.

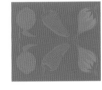

Asian Maple Salmon

Yield: 4 servings

Nutrients per serving
Calories 635
Protein 53 g
Carbo 56 g
Total Fat 21 g
Saturated Fat 4 g
Cholesterol 164 mg
Fiber 0 g
Sodium 1884 mg

4	(8-ounce) salmon steaks
1	cup maple syrup
1/3	cup soy sauce
2	teaspoons chopped fresh ginger (optional)
1/2	teaspoon sesame oil

Arrange the steaks in a single layer in a shallow dish. Mix the syrup, soy sauce, ginger and sesame oil in a bowl and pour over the salmon, turning to coat. Marinate, covered, in the refrigerator for 3 to 6 hours, turning occasionally.

Grill on a preheated grill over medium heat for 5 minutes per side or until the salmon flakes easily when tested with a fork, turning once. You may substitute pancake syrup for the maple syrup but the flavor is compromised.

118

South-of-the-Border Pinto Beans

Yield: 6 servings

Nutrients per serving
Calories 518
Protein 26 g
Carbo 49 g
Total Fat 23 g
Saturated Fat 8 g
Cholesterol 42 mg
Fiber 18 g
Sodium 553 mg

2 1/2	cups dried pinto beans
1	pound chorizo, beef or pork, crumbled or chopped
1	onion, chopped
4	slices bacon, chopped
2	to 3 tablespoons (heaping) ground cumin, or to taste
3	or 4 garlic cloves, minced
1	jalapeño chile, finely chopped (optional)
2	teaspoons dried cilantro, or 2 tablespoons fresh cilantro leaves
~	Salt and pepper to taste

Combine the beans with enough water to cover by 2 to 4 inches in a bowl and soak for 8 to 10 hours; drain. Combine the beans with just enough water to cover in a Dutch oven. Stir in the sausage, onion, bacon, cumin, garlic, jalapeño chile, cilantro, salt and pepper.

Bring to a boil over high heat and reduce the heat to low. Simmer, covered, for 2 hours or until the beans are tender, stirring occasionally and adding additional water as needed.

1995

The UAMS Graduate School was granted independent status from the Graduate School at the University of Arkansas, Fayetteville.

Lentils and Rice (Imjundra)

1	cup medium grain rice
1	small onion, chopped
1	tablespoon butter
1	cup dried lentils, sorted
2	cups water
2	tablespoons butter
~	Salt and pepper to taste

Yield: 4 servings

Nutrients per serving
Calories 434
Protein 18 g
Carbo 72 g
Total Fat 9 g
Saturated Fat 5 g
Cholesterol 23 mg
Fiber 7 g
Sodium 62 mg

Lightly sauté the rice and onion in 1 tablespoon butter in a saucepan over medium heat for about 5 minutes. Stir in the lentils and water. Bring to a boil and reduce the heat to low.

Simmer for 20 to 25 minutes or until the lentils are tender, stirring occasionally. Add 2 tablespoons butter, salt and pepper and mix well. Serve immediately.

119

Armenian Rice Fluff

2	cups very fine noodles
1/2	cup (1 stick) butter
2	cups chicken broth
1	cup long grain rice

Yield: 4 servings

Nutrients per serving
Calories 449
Protein 7 g
Carbo 51 g
Total Fat 24 g
Saturated Fat 15 g
Cholesterol 81 mg
Fiber 1 g
Sodium 658 mg

Brown the noodles in the butter in a saucepan. Stir in the broth and bring to a boil. Add the rice and mix well. Simmer, covered, for 25 minutes.

Rub hands with lemon, then salt, and rinse with cold water to remove garlic, onion, and other cooking odors from your hands. This also works on wooden cutting boards.

"Here's to Your Health," a radio information show sponsored by UAMS, went on air on KUAR-FM. The Education III Building was completed.

1995

Traditional Scottish Shortbread

Yield: 48 servings

Nutrients per square

Calories 139
Protein 1 g
Carbo 17 g
Total Fat 8 g
Saturated Fat 5 g
Cholesterol 20 mg
Fiber <1 g
Sodium 54 mg

2	cups (4 sticks) butter, softened
1	cup superfine sugar
2	teaspoons cold water
3	cups all-purpose flour
1	cup cornstarch
1	cup rice flour
1/3	cup sugar

Combine the butter, 1 cup sugar and the cold water in a mixing bowl and beat for 7 to 10 minutes, scraping the bowl occasionally. Add the all-purpose flour, cornstarch and rice flour to the butter mixture gradually, one ingredient at a time, and beat until blended.

Press the dough into a 3/4-inch-thick oval on a baking sheet that nearly fills the entire sheet. Place a sheet of waxed paper over the top of the oval and roll flat with a rolling pin. Remove the waxed paper and prick the top of the dough with a fork. Using a knife, loosen the edge of the dough from the baking sheet. Bake in a preheated 325-degree oven for 45 minutes. Cut into squares while hot and sprinkle with 1/3 cup sugar.

Take a glimpse at some of the Arkansas Health Care milestones accomplished at UAMS.

* First articular knee cartilage transplant
* First in-vitro fertilization (IVF) program
* First in-vitro pregnancy occurred
* First frozen embryo pregnancy by IVF program
* First and only skull-base surgery
* First intracytoplasmic sperm injection (ICSI) program
* First and only combined kidney/pancreas transplant
* First and only fetal blood transfusion in the womb
* First pallidotomy for Parkinson's disease
* First lymph node preservation program for breast cancer and melanoma
* First and only gamma knife
* First laser lumpectomey for breast tumors
* First laparoscopic gastric bypass surgery performed at UAMS
* First laparoscopically implanted stomach pacemaker
* First endoscopic spinal surgery
* First liver transplant

1995

The Arkansas Heart Transplant Program team performed the 100th heart transplant. UAMS Medical Center became the first Arkansas hospital to be named to U.S. News & World Report *list of "America's Best Hospitals."*

R_x

Main Dishes

Eating and Exercising Right

Recently, an international conference released recommendations to stem the worldwide epidemic of obesity. It advised a restricted intake of fats, sugars, and salt. When reviewing the findings, I noted with some irony that virtually every member of the congress was overweight. At lunch today, as I browsed around the restaurant serving burgers, meat loaf sandwiches, and cheese omelets, I felt quite at home amongst the pleasantly plump. I struggled to find even one person at ideal body weight.

Obesity has become not only a problem but an industry. Most of us are on or have been on a diet. And virtually all of us have failed. Sadly to say, I must include myself amongst the losers. It is the rare person who remains sufficiently motivated not to regain the weight loss. Most studies suggest that failure rates from diets approach 99 percent.

Now comes the new diet revolution. The increase in weight has been ascribed to excessive intake of carbohydrates. Now, we all follow the Atkins Diet or the South Beach Diet, consuming low-carbohydrate, high-protein, and high-fat diets. Despite the widely reported successes of the low-carbohydrate craze, failure rates remain as high as ever.

So, what do we know about these diets?

We know that total calories consumed remains the major predictor of weight gain or loss. A high-fat diet rapidly causes satiety, and total calorie intake is reduced. Restricting carbohydrates causes accumulation of molecules called ketones that are also known to restrict appetite. By contrast, replacing fat with more carbohydrate can lead to an even greater increase in caloric intake and weight gain. High-carbohydrate intake alters metabolism, leading to an increased risk of diabetes.

The problem is clouded by the fact that careful research studies show that a low-fat, low-calorie diet leads to as much weight loss as the current trendy low-carbohydrate diet.

Let me use a little history to put things into perspective. In the 1950s, our diet was rich in saturated (animal) fat, and there was an epidemic of sudden deaths from heart attack, primarily affecting men between the ages of forty and sixty. Around that time the dangers of bacon, red meat, and eggs received national attention. Thanks to modern medicine, medication and (surprise, surprise) a low-fat diet, death rates from heart attacks have halved.

Does it make sense to go back to the era of our predecessors and consume a high-fat diet? What will the risks be five to ten years from now? Will the current twenty-somethings start dying in their forties from heart disease? And what about the well-known connection between dietary fat intake and cancer?

A year ago, a friend of mine proudly told me he had lost 100 pounds on the Atkins Diet. This week I saw him again. Virtually all of the weight had returned. He was still consuming a high-fat, high-protein diet, but like most of us, his weakness for the good life had led him to once again enjoy desserts, bread, and pastas. Now he was consuming the worst diet possible, high-fat and high-carbohydrate.

Few, if any of us, have the willpower to consume a diet that restricts fats and carbohydrates. Furthermore, losing and gaining weight (called yo-yo dieting) is far more dangerous than maintaining a constant weight. The answer for me is simple. Eat right, be prudent, watch portion sizes, and, most importantly, remember that weight is only a minor predictor of ill health.

Our goal is to live a long and independent life, and this requires that we be happy and healthy. Happiness is a more powerful predictor of health than being 10 to 15 percent overweight. The key elements of happiness are to have love in your life, to have faith, to control stress, to have a purpose, and to have high self-esteem. To be healthy, exercise first and foremost—the more the better. Make sure that you have regular medical checkups, and screen for the common illnesses that lead to poor health. And, if you eat right and prudently, guess what: the weight loss will follow, and you will live happily ever after.

Reprinted with permission of Dr. David Lipschitz

Texas Brisket

1	(6-pound) beef brisket	1/4	cup salt	
1	tablespoon prepared yellow mustard	2	tablespoons chipotle chili powder	
3/4	cup paprika	2	tablespoons onion powder	
1/4	cup packed dark brown sugar	2	tablespoons garlic powder	
1/4	cup black pepper	1	tablespoon cayenne pepper	

Trim the fat cap on the brisket to 1/8 to 1/4 inch. Coat the brisket with the prepared mustard. Mix the paprika, brown sugar, black pepper, salt, chili powder, onion powder, garlic powder and cayenne pepper in a bowl. Pat the paprika mixture over the surface of the brisket.

Arrange the brisket on a rack in a smoker preheated to 194 to 205 degrees. Smoke the brisket for 1 1/2 hours per pound or until a meat thermometer registers 185 to 195 degrees. Remove the brisket from the smoker and let stand for 30 minutes before slicing.

Yield: 12 servings

Nutrients per serving
Calories 345
Protein 48 g
Carbo 12 g
Total Fat 11 g
Saturated Fat 4 g
Cholesterol 97 mg
Fiber 3 g
Sodium 2453 mg

123

Pot Roast Dijon

1/3	cup olive oil	1	(4-pound) beef pot roast or rump roast	
3	tablespoons wine vinegar			
1	onion, thinly sliced	2	tablespoons vegetable oil	
2	garlic cloves, chopped	2	cups water	
2	teaspoons seasoned salt	1	tablespoon Dijon mustard	
1/4	teaspoon pepper			

Combine the olive oil, vinegar, onion, garlic, seasoned salt and pepper in a bowl and mix well. Pour the olive oil mixture over the roast in a shallow dish, turning to coat. Marinate, covered, in the refrigerator for 2 to 10 hours, turning occasionally. Drain, reserving the marinade.

Heat the vegetable oil in a Dutch oven and add the roast. Brown the roast on all sides in the hot oil. Add the reserved marinade and 1 cup of the water and simmer, tightly covered, for 3 hours or until the roast is tender. Stir a mixture of the remaining 1 cup water and Dijon mustard into the pan drippings and cook until the liquid is reduced and of a sauce consistency. Remove the roast to a platter and cut into thin slices. Drizzle with the sauce.

Yield: 8 servings

Nutrients per serving
Calories 457
Protein 37 g
Carbo 3 g
Total Fat 33 g
Saturated Fat 10 g
Cholesterol 108 mg
Fiber <1 g
Sodium 375 mg

Red Apple Inn Five-Peppercorn Fillets with Sun-Dried Cherry Sauce

Yield: 4 servings

Nutrients per serving

Calories 555

Protein 29 g

Carbo 81 g

Total Fat 10 g

Saturated Fat 4 g

Cholesterol 84 mg

Fiber 5 g

Sodium 189 mg

Sun-Dried Cherry Sauce

1/2	cup dried cherries
1/4	cup granulated sugar
1/2	cup red wine
1	tablespoon balsamic vinegar
1	cup packed brown sugar
1	sprig of rosemary
1	bay leaf
2	juniper berries

Beef Fillets

1/4	cup peppercorn mélange, ground
4	(6-ounce) beef fillets

To prepare the sauce, plump the cherries in hot water in a heatproof bowl; drain. Caramelize the granulated sugar in a saucepan until deep golden brown. Mix in the wine and vinegar and stir until the sugar dissolves.

Cook until the mixture is reduced by half. Stir in the brown sugar, rosemary, bay leaf and juniper berries. Simmer for 10 minutes, stirring occasionally. Discard the sprig of rosemary, bay leaf and juniper berries.

To prepare the fillets, rub the peppercorn mixture over the surface of the fillets. Grill or bake the fillets to the desired degree of doneness. Serve with the sauce.

UAMS employees, visitors, guests, and patients often frequent surrounding points of interest in Central Arkansas. The Red Apple Inn is a popular bed and breakfast in Eden Isle, Arkansas. It is located on 160 acres of what was originally natural Ozark forests and farmland, overlooking Greers Ferry Lake.

The Inn, built in 1963, was designed by a Dallas architect who had studied under Frank Lloyd Wright. It has a distinctive Mediterranean look with furnishings from Spain, Italy, and Mexico. Patti and Dick Upton, strong UAMS supporters, purchased the Inn in 1995. The Red Apple Dining Room has been featured in *Southern Living* magazine several times and is known for its contemporary American cuisine.

1996

Phase II expansion of the ACRC building was completed.

Mom's Meat Loaf

2	sleeves saltine crackers
2	pounds ground beef
8	ounces medium bulk pork sausage (optional)
1	large bell pepper, chopped
1	white onion, chopped
1¹/₂	(8 ounce) cans tomato sauce
3	eggs, beaten
~	Salt and pepper to taste
¹/₃	cup ketchup

Yield: 8 servings

Nutrients per serving
Calories 376
Protein 27 g
Carbo 28 g
Total Fat 17 g
Saturated Fat 5 g
Cholesterol 147 mg
Fiber 2 g
Sodium 750 mg

Process the crackers in a food processor until of the consistency of bread crumbs. Combine the ground beef, sausage, bell pepper, onion, tomato sauce, eggs, salt and pepper in a bowl and mix well. Add the cracker crumbs gradually, mixing constantly until the mixture is firm enough to hold its shape. The amount of cracker crumbs required will vary according to taste and the amount of moisture in the ground beef.

Shape the ground beef mixture into a loaf in a large baking dish. Bake in a preheated 400-degree oven for 45 minutes. Drain the pan drippings and spread with the ketchup. Bake for 10 minutes longer.

125

You can make individual servings of meat loaf by using muffin tins. Remember that the cooking time will have to be adjusted. Meat loaf will not stick to the loaf pan if you place a slice of uncooked bacon in the bottom of the pan before adding the meat loaf mixture.

The Diagnostic Medical Sonography program was established in CHRP.

1996

Very Lazy Lasagna

Yield: 10 servings

Nutrients per serving

Calories 516

Protein 37 g

Carbo 34 g

Total Fat 26 g

Saturated Fat 13 g

Cholesterol 107 mg

Fiber 4 g

Sodium 1267 mg

126

2 pounds ground beef
1 cup chopped onion, or 1/4 cup dried onion flakes
3 garlic cloves, minced
4 cups vegetable juice cocktail
1 (14-ounce) can crushed tomatoes,
  or equivalent amount of crushed peeled fresh tomatoes
1 (8-ounce) can mushrooms, drained (optional)
1 (6-ounce) can tomato paste
1/4 cup lemon juice
1 tablespoon Worcestershire sauce
1 teaspoon oregano
1 teaspoon salt
1/4 teaspoon pepper, or to taste
1 (6-ounce) can whole black olives, drained and sliced
2 cups ricotta cheese or cottage cheese
2 cups (8 ounces) shredded mozzarella cheese
  or Italian six-cheese blend
1 1/2 cups (6 ounces) grated Parmesan cheese
1 tablespoon parsley flakes
8 ounces uncooked lasagna noodles

Brown the ground beef with the onion and garlic in a large skillet, stirring until the ground beef is crumbly; drain. Stir in the vegetable juice cocktail, tomatoes, mushrooms, tomato paste, lemon juice, Worcestershire sauce, oregano, salt and pepper. Simmer for 30 minutes, stirring occasionally. Remove from the heat. Stir in the olives just before assembling the lasagna.

Mix the ricotta cheese, mozzarella cheese, Parmesan cheese and parsley flakes in a bowl. Layer the noodles, ground beef mixture and ricotta cheese mixture half at a time in a deep-dish 9×13-inch baking dish, 3- to 4-quart baking dish or lasagna pan.

Bake, covered with foil, in a preheated 350-degree oven for 30 minutes. Remove the foil and bake for 15 minutes longer. Let stand for 15 to 20 minutes before serving. You may prepare in advance and store, covered, in the refrigerator. Bake, covered, for 45 minutes and then uncover and bake for 15 minutes longer. Freeze the unbaked lasagna for future use, if desired, allowing extra baking time.

1997

The Biomedical Biotechnology Center established UAMS BioVentures program, Arkansas' first biotechnology business incubator.

Stuffed Pasta Shells

6	ounces jumbo pasta shells	1	egg, beaten
1	pound ground beef	1/4	teaspoon pepper
1	cup chopped onion	1	(27- to 30-ounce) jar
1	garlic clove, minced		spaghetti sauce
2	cups (8 ounces) shredded	1/4	cup (1 ounce) grated
	mozzarella cheese		Parmesan cheese
1/2	cup seasoned bread crumbs		

Yield: 5 servings

Nutrients per serving
Calories 688
Protein 39 g
Carbo 65 g
Total Fat 31 g
Saturated Fat 12 g
Cholesterol 135 mg
Fiber 8 g
Sodium 1467 mg

Cook the pasta using package directions. Drain and rinse with cold water; drain. Brown the ground beef with the onion and garlic in a skillet, stirring until the ground beef is crumbly; drain. Stir in the mozzarella cheese, bread crumbs, egg and pepper. Stuff the pasta shells evenly with the ground beef mixture. Spread three-fourths of the sauce over the bottom of a 9×13-inch baking dish. Arrange the stuffed shells in a single layer in the prepared baking dish. Pour the remaining sauce over the top and sprinkle with the Parmesan cheese.

Bake, loosely covered with foil, in a preheated 400-degree oven for 20 to 25 minutes or until heated through. You may prepare in advance and store, covered, in the refrigerator. Bake, covered, in a preheated 375-degree oven for 35 to 40 minutes. Remove the foil and bake for 15 to 20 minutes longer or until heated through.

127

Pork Medallions with Blackberry Sauce

2	(1-pound) pork tenderloins	2/3	cup dry white wine or white
1	teaspoon salt		grape juice
1	teaspoon coarsely	3	tablespoons seedless
	ground pepper		blackberry fruit spread
1	teaspoon coarsely ground	2	tablespoons butter
	allspice	~	Sprigs of thyme for garnish
2	tablespoons butter	~	Fresh blackberries for garnish
1/2	cup chopped shallots		

Yield: 8 servings

Nutrients per serving
Calories 220
Protein 23 g
Carbo 6 g
Total Fat 10 g
Saturated Fat 5 g
Cholesterol 78 mg
Fiber <1 g
Sodium 378 mg

Sprinkle the tenderloins evenly with the salt, pepper and allspice. Chill, covered, for 30 minutes. Grill the tenderloins over medium-high heat (350 to 400 degrees) for 20 minutes or until a meat thermometer registers 160 degrees, turning once. Remove to a platter and let stand for 10 minutes.

Melt 2 tablespoons butter in a small saucepan over medium-high heat and add the shallots. Sauté for 5 minutes or until tender and stir in the wine. Cook for 13 minutes or until the liquid is reduced by half. Reduce the heat to low and whisk in the fruit spread and 2 tablespoons butter. Cook for 2 minutes longer or until slightly thickened. Cut the tenderloins into 1/4-inch slices and drizzle with the sauce. Garnish with thyme and blackberries.

The Donald W. Reynolds Center on Aging, now the Institute on Aging, opened. 1997

Pork Piccata

Yield: 6 servings

Nutrients per serving
Calories 528
Protein 32 g
Carbo 53 g
Total Fat 19 g
Saturated Fat 6 g
Cholesterol 78 mg
Fiber 2 g
Sodium 364 mg

128

12	ounces fettuccini
1/2	cup all-purpose flour
1/2	teaspoon salt
1/4	teaspoon pepper
1 1/2	pounds pork tenderloin, cut into 12 medallions
3	to 4 tablespoons olive oil
1/2	cup dry white wine
1/2	cup lemon juice
3	tablespoons butter or margarine
1/4	cup chopped fresh parsley
1 1/2	tablespoons capers

Cook the pasta using package directions; drain. Cover to keep warm. Mix the flour, salt and pepper in a shallow dish. Pound the pork medallions 1/4 inch thick between sheets of waxed paper. Coat the pork with the flour mixture.

Heat the olive oil in a skillet over medium heat. Add the pork in batches to the hot oil and cook for 2 minutes per side or until light brown and cooked through. Remove the pork to a platter using a slotted spoon, reserving the pan drippings. Cover to keep warm.

Deglaze the skillet with the wine and lemon juice, scraping the bottom of the skillet with a wooden spoon to loosen any browned bits. Cook until heated through and stir in the butter, parsley and capers. Cook until the butter melts. Arrange the pork over the pasta on a serving platter and drizzle with the wine mixture. Serve immediately.

Barbecued Spareribs

Yield: 4 servings

Nutrients per serving
Calories 932
Protein 63 g
Carbo 25 g
Total Fat 64 g
Saturated Fat 24 g
Cholesterol 255 mg
Fiber 1 g
Sodium 1687 mg

3	to 4 pounds pork spareribs, cut into serving portions
1	large onion, thinly sliced
1	lemon, thinly sliced
2	cups water
1	cup ketchup
1/3	cup Worcestershire sauce
1	teaspoon chili powder
1	teaspoon salt
1/4	teaspoon Tabasco sauce

Arrange the spareribs in a shallow roasting pan, meat side up. Place one onion slice and one lemon slice on each portion. Roast in a preheated 450-degree oven for 30 minutes. Reduce the oven temperature to 350 degrees.

Mix the water, ketchup, Worcestershire sauce, chili powder, salt and Tabasco sauce in a saucepan and bring to a boil. Pour over the spareribs. Bake for 45 minutes or until tender, basting the spareribs with the sauce every 15 minutes. If the sauce becomes too thick, thin with additional water.

1997

Internet-based distance learning began in the College of Nursing.

Spaghetti alla Carbonara

~	Salt (for water)
16	ounces spaghetti
2	tablespoons extra-virgin olive oil
4	ounces pancetta or slab bacon, chopped or cut into small strips
4	garlic cloves, finely chopped
2	eggs
1	cup (4 ounces) freshly grated Parmigiano-Reggiano cheese
~	Freshly ground pepper to taste
1	handful fresh flat-leaf parsley, chopped, for garnish

Yield: 8 servings

Nutrients per serving
Calories 318
Protein 14 g
Carbo 44 g
Total Fat 10 g
Saturated Fat 3 g
Cholesterol 62 mg
Fiber 2 g
Sodium 245 mg

Bring a large stockpot of salted water to a boil and add the pasta. Cook for 8 to 10 minutes or until the pasta is al dente. Drain, reserving 1/2 cup of the cooking liquid. Cover the pasta to keep warm.

Heat the olive oil in a deep skillet over medium heat and add the pancetta. Sauté for 3 minutes or until the fat is rendered and the pancetta is crisp. Add the garlic and sauté for less than 1 minute to soften. Add the hot pasta to the pancetta mixture and cook for 2 minutes, stirring constantly to coat the pasta.

Whisk the eggs and cheese in a bowl until the mixture is lump-free. Remove the pancetta mixture from the heat and add the egg mixture, whisking constantly until the eggs thicken but do not scramble. Thin the sauce with some of the reserved cooking liquid until of the desired consistency. Season with salt and pepper to taste. Mound the pasta mixture in heated individual bowls and garnish with the parsley. Serve with additional Parmigiano-Reggiano cheese.

Prepare the sauce while the pasta is cooking to ensure that the pasta will be hot and ready to add when needed. It is very important that the pasta is hot when adding the egg mixture, so that the heat of the pasta cooks the raw eggs in the sauce.

Add a small amount of vegetable oil to the water before adding pasta. It reduces the amount of pasta sticking together.

The Hospital's Harry P. Ward Tower was dedicated. 1997

Chicken Curry

Yield: 5 servings

Nutrients per serving

Calories 338

Protein 32 g

Carbo 6 g

Total Fat 20 g

Saturated Fat 4 g

Cholesterol 96 mg

Fiber 1 g

Sodium 803 mg

1/4   cup vegetable oil
1   large onion, chopped
2   teaspoons garlic paste or crushed garlic
1 1/2 teaspoons salt
1   teaspoon crushed ginger or ginger paste
3/4   teaspoon red pepper
1/2   teaspoon black pepper
1/3   teaspoon ground coriander
1/3   teaspoon turmeric
2   tomatoes, chopped
1   (2 1/2- to 3-pound) chicken, cut into 10 pieces
1/2   cup plain yogurt, beaten
1   green chile, chopped (optional)

Heat the oil in a skillet over medium heat and add the onion. Sauté for 3 to 4 minutes or until the onion is light brown. Stir in the garlic paste, salt, ginger, red pepper, black pepper, coriander and turmeric. Cook for 2 minutes, stirring constantly. Add the tomatoes and cook for 2 to 3 minutes. Mix in the chicken and yogurt.

Bring to a boil and reduce the heat to low. Simmer, covered, for 20 to 30 minutes or until the chicken is cooked through and the sauce is reduced and slightly thickened, stirring occasionally.

130

Established in 1976, the Center for Diversity Affairs (CDA), formerly the Office of Minority Affairs, was developed under the auspices of the College of Medicine to serve the traditionally underrepresented students (African Americans, Hispanics, Native Americans, and Pacific Islanders) in medicine. The fundamental principle that guides the CDA is the development of a diversified health care system and is carried out by ensuring that underrepresented minorities are adequately prepared for a career in health care.

The CDA is also responsible for recruiting and encouraging admission, successful matriculation, retention, and graduation of underrepresented candidates interested in pursuing a career in medicine at UAMS. Overall the goal of CDA is to:

* develop pipeline programs to ensure adequate educational preparation of underrepresented students;
* assist students in their personal development by providing programs and initiatives that are educational, motivational, and challenging; and
* foster an environment conducive to the recruitment, training, and success of an ethnically, socially, and culturally diverse health care workforce.

1998

UAMS assumed responsibility for the Pulaski County Head Start Program. The Society of the Double Helix was established to honor major donors.

Chicken Waikiki Beach

Chicken

2   (8-ounce) whole chicken breasts, split
1/2   cup all-purpose flour
1/3   cup vegetable oil
1   teaspoon salt
1/4   teaspoon pepper

Pineapple Sauce and Assembly

1   (20-ounce) can sliced pineapple in heavy syrup
1   cup sugar
2   tablespoons cornstarch
1/4   teaspoon ginger
3/4   cup cider vinegar
1   tablespoon soy sauce
1   chicken bouillon cube
1   large green bell pepper, cut into 1/4-inch rounds

Yield: 4 servings

Nutrients per serving
Calories 680
Protein 26 g
Carbo 97 g
Total Fat 22 g
Saturated Fat 3 g
Cholesterol 63 mg
Fiber 2 g
Sodium 1258 mg

131

To prepare the chicken, coat the chicken with the flour. Heat the oil in a large skillet and add the chicken in batches. Cook until brown on all sides; drain. Arrange the chicken skin side up in a shallow roasting pan and sprinkle with the salt and pepper.

To prepare the sauce, drain the pineapple, reserving the syrup. Combine the reserved syrup with enough water to measure 1 1/4 cups. Mix the sugar, cornstarch and ginger in a saucepan. Stir in the reserved syrup mixture, the vinegar, soy sauce and bouillon cube. Bring to a boil, stirring constantly.

Boil for 2 minutes and pour the sauce over the chicken. Bake in a preheated 350-degree oven for 30 minutes. Add the pineapple slices and bell pepper and bake for 30 minutes longer or until the chicken is tender. Serve with hot cooked fluffy white rice.

Chill chicken for one hour after coating. The coating will adhere better when cooking.

Chicken Superb

Yield: 10 servings

Nutrients per serving
Calories 500
Protein 26 g
Carbo 20 g
Total Fat 35 g
Saturated Fat 19 g
Cholesterol 163 mg
Fiber 2 g
Sodium 594 mg

4	(8-ounce) boneless skinless chicken breasts
6	tablespoons butter
6	tablespoons all-purpose flour
2	cups chicken broth
3	tablespoons chopped fresh parsley
1¹/₂	teaspoons celery salt
1/2	teaspoon ground marjoram
1/8	teaspoon Beau Monde seasoning
2	cups whipping cream
2	tablespoons dry sherry
10	ounces mushrooms, trimmed and sliced
2	tablespoons butter
1/2	cup slivered almonds, toasted
6	ounces medium egg noodles, cooked and drained
1/2	cup (2 ounces) shredded Cheddar cheese

Wrap each chicken breast in foil and bake in a preheated 350-degree oven for 1 hour. Let the chicken cool and cut into large strips. Maintain the oven temperature.

Melt 6 tablespoons butter in a large skillet and stir in the flour. Cook over low heat until bubbly but not brown. Stir in the broth, parsley, celery salt, marjoram and Beau Monde seasoning. Cook until thickened and of a sauce consistency, stirring constantly. Add the cream and sherry and mix well.

Sauté the mushrooms in 2 tablespoons butter in a small skillet. Stir the mushrooms and almonds into the sauce. Add the chicken and noodles and mix well. Spoon the chicken mixture into a baking dish and sprinkle with the cheese. Bake for 35 to 40 minutes or until brown and bubbly.

Double the amount of your favorite casserole recipes when you cook. Place half in a freezer container for dinner on a busy day.

1999

Arkansas' only Gamma Knife Center opened at UAMS. The Arkansas AHEC program named best in the nation by National AHEC Organization.

Lost Chicken

4   (5-ounce) boneless skinless chicken breasts
1/4   cup fresh lime juice (2 limes)
1   envelope Italian salad dressing mix
1/4   cup (1/2 stick) butter or margarine, melted

Arrange the chicken in a single layer in a baking dish. Mix the lime juice, dressing mix and butter in a bowl and pour over the chicken.

Bake, covered with foil, in a preheated 350-degree oven for 1 hour. Remove the foil and bake for 15 minutes longer. Serve the pan drippings over hot cooked rice, if desired.

Yield: 4 servings

Nutrients per serving
Calories 500
Protein 26 g
Carbo 20 g
Total Fat 35 g
Saturated Fat 19 g
Cholesterol 163 mg
Fiber 2 g
Sodium 594 mg

Easy Poppy Seed Chicken

133

3   or 4 (5-ounce) boneless skinless chicken breasts, cooked and chopped
2   (10-ounce) cans cream of chicken soup
1   cup sour cream
1/2   cup sliced almonds, toasted
3   tablespoons poppy seeds
3   cups hot cooked rice

Combine the chicken, soup, sour cream, almonds and poppy seeds in a bowl and mix well. Spoon into a slow cooker and cook on Low until heated through. Serve over the hot cooked rice.

Yield: 8 servings

Nutrients per serving
Calories 260
Protein 29 g
Carbo 2 g
Total Fat 15 g
Saturated Fat 8 g
Cholesterol 108 mg
Fiber <1 g
Sodium 389 mg

The Schmieding Center for Senior Health and Education of Northwest Arkansas established in Springdale as the first satellite Center on Aging affiliated with Arkansas Aging Initiative.

1999

Chicken Marinara

Yield: 8 servings

Nutrients per serving
Calories 374
Protein 23 g
Carbo 59 g
Total Fat 6 g
Saturated Fat 1 g
Cholesterol 31 mg
Fiber 6 g
Sodium 342 mg

5	garlic cloves, chopped
2	tablespoons olive oil
1	pound boneless skinless chicken breasts, cut into bite-size pieces
1	cup sliced mushrooms (optional)
1	large yellow onion, sliced (optional)
~	Salt and pepper to taste
3	tablespoons tomato paste
2	(28-ounce) cans crushed tomatoes
1 3/4	cups water
1	tablespoon dried basil
1/4	cup red wine (optional)
16	ounces spaghetti, angel hair pasta, penne or favorite pasta
~	Grated Parmesan cheese (optional)
1	teaspoon sugar (optional)

Sauté the garlic in 1 tablespoon of the olive oil in a skillet until light brown. Remove the garlic to a bowl using a slotted spoon, reserving the pan drippings. Heat the remaining 1 tablespoon olive oil with the reserved pan drippings until hot and stir in the chicken, mushrooms and onion.

Cook until the chicken is no longer pink and season with salt and pepper. Stir in the sautéed garlic and tomato paste. Add the tomatoes, water and basil and bring to a boil. Reduce the heat to low and simmer, covered, for 30 minutes, stirring occasionally. Stir in the wine and cook, covered, for 30 minutes longer. Season with salt and pepper.

Cook the pasta using package directions; drain. Spoon into a large pasta bowl. Pour the marinara sauce over the pasta and sprinkle with cheese. Serve immediately.

Chicken Marinara cooks much quicker than the traditional sausage/meatball marinara.

1999

"Aging Successfully with Dr. David," starring Dr. David Lipschitz, debuted on Arkansas Educational Television Network (AETN).

Makeover Greek Spaghetti

2 (10-ounce) packages frozen chopped spinach, thawed and drained
16 ounces spaghetti, broken into 2-inch pieces
4 cups chopped cooked chicken breasts
~ Salt and pepper to taste
1 (10-ounce) can reduced-fat reduced-sodium cream of chicken soup
3/4 cup reduced-fat mayonnaise
3/4 cup reduced-fat sour cream
3 ribs celery, chopped
1 small onion, chopped
1/2 cup chopped green and/or red bell pepper

1 (2-ounce) jar diced pimento, drained
1/2 teaspoon salt-free lemon pepper seasoning
1 1/3 cups skim milk
2 to 3 tablespoons all-purpose flour
1 teaspoon chicken bouillon granules
1 cup (4 ounces) shredded part-skim mozzarella cheese
1/2 cup soft bread crumbs or crushed croutons
1/4 cup (1 ounce) shredded Parmesan cheese

Yield: 10 servings

Nutrients per serving
Calories 450
Protein 32 g
Carbo 49 g
Total Fat 14 g
Saturated Fat 5 g
Cholesterol 71 mg
Fiber 4 g
Sodium 512 mg

135

Press the excess moisture from the spinach. Cook the pasta using package directions; drain. Season the chicken with salt and pepper and add to the pasta. Stir in the spinach, soup, mayonnaise, sour cream, celery, onion, bell pepper, pimento and lemon pepper seasoning.

Whisk the skim milk and flour in a saucepan until smooth. Bring to a boil over medium heat and cook for 2 minutes or until thickened, stirring constantly. Add the bouillon granules and stir until blended. Add to the chicken mixture and mix well.

Spoon into a 9□13-inch baking dish coated with nonstick cooking spray. Sprinkle with the mozzarella cheese, bread crumbs and Parmesan cheese. Bake in a preheated 350-degree oven for 25 to 30 minutes or until heated through.

Established in 1974, the UAMS Police Department has forty full-time police officers, who are certified by the state of Arkansas, serving the campus. Responsible for the protection of both life and property on the UAMS campus, as well as the enforcement of local and state laws, the mission of the UAMS Police Department is to provide a crime-free environment through the efforts of a team of professional law enforcement officers working together with the campus community. Accomplishing this goal and ensuring a safe and healthy environment creates an ideal atmosphere for the promotion of learning, fosters high standards of research, and encourages the highest quality health care. The UAMS Police Department consists of different divisions, which work together to fulfill our mission of providing a safe and secure environment and delivering police services to our community.

Dr. M. Gazi Yasargil was named "Neurosurgeon of the Century" by the Congress of Neurological Surgeons.

1999

Turkey, Black Bean and Spinach Enchiladas

Yield: 10 enchiladas

Nutrients per enchilada

Calories 531

Protein 28 g

Carbo 47 g

Total Fat 24 g

Saturated Fat 11 g

Cholesterol 88 mg

Fiber 11 g

Sodium 1306 mg

1	(10-ounce) package frozen chopped spinach, thawed and drained
1	to 1¹/₂ pounds ground turkey, browned and drained
1	(15-ounce) can black beans, drained and rinsed
1	(8-ounce) can corn, drained
1	(4-ounce) can chopped green chiles
8	ounces cream cheese, softened
6	to 8 green onions, chopped
2	teaspoons ground cumin
~	Salt and pepper to taste
10	(8- to 10-inch) flour tortillas
1	(10-ounce) can enchilada sauce
1¹/₃	cups shredded Mexican cheese blend

136

Press the excess moisture from the spinach. Combine the spinach, ground turkey, beans, corn, green chiles, cream cheese, green onions and cumin in a bowl and mix well. Season with salt and pepper.

Coat the tortillas with the enchilada sauce. Spoon the turkey mixture evenly down the centers of the tortillas and roll to enclose the filling. Arrange the filled tortillas seam side down in a lightly greased 9×13-inch baking pan. Drizzle with the remaining enchilada sauce and sprinkle with the Mexican cheese blend. Bake in a preheated 350-degree oven for 30 minutes.

UAMS takes steps to prepare employees and students for disasters. Faculty have traveled throughout the state educating citizens about how to prepare for and respond to disasters. Many staff, faculty, and students volunteered to help Hurricane Katrina and Rita Evacuees in 2005. National organizations such as the American Red Cross (www.redcross.org) and the Federal Emergency Management Agency (www.fema.gov) provide extensive information about how to store food and water to survive for at least three days after a disaster. Listed below are a few helpful tips.

* Store one gallon of water per person per day.
* Have non-perishable foods that require no refrigeration, cooking, water, or special preparation. Examples include dried fruit, canned fruit or vegetables, canned meat, poultry, or fish, peanut butter and jelly, small packages of cereal, granola bars, crackers, nonfat dry milk, and small boxes of juice drinks. Store small containers to avoid storing leftovers.
* Remember food for infants, pets, or family members with special dietary needs.
* Be sure to include a manual can opener.
* Do not forget to periodically use and replace your supplies

1999

Dr. Milton Warner held first UAMS International Telemedicine consultation with 5-year-old patient and her doctors in Israel.

Grilled Rock Cornish Game Hens with Merlot Sauce

Game Hens
1/4 cup merlot
1/4 cup lemon juice
2 tablespoons grated fresh ginger
1 garlic clove, minced
2 (1¹/2-pound) Rock Cornish game hens, split lengthwise into halves

Glaze and Assembly
1/2 cup raspberry jelly
1/4 cup merlot
2 tablespoons butter
2 tablespoons lemon juice
~ Salt and pepper to taste

Yield: 4 servings

Nutrients per serving
Calories 369
Protein 32 g
Carbo 30 g
Total Fat 11 g
Saturated Fat 5 g
Cholesterol 161 mg
Fiber <1 g
Sodium 129 mg

To prepare the game hens, combine the wine, lemon juice, ginger and garlic in a bowl and mix well. Pour the marinade over the game hens in a shallow dish, turning to coat. Marinate, covered, in the refrigerator for 30 minutes, turning occasionally.

To prepare the glaze, bring the jelly, wine, butter, lemon juice, salt and pepper to a boil in a small saucepan and boil until reduced and slightly thickened.

Drain the game hens and arrange on a grill rack coated with nonstick cooking spray. Grill over medium heat for 15 minutes per side or until the juices run clear, basting frequently with the glaze.

Nutritional profile includes the entire amount of the marinade.

137

In 1965, chicken mogul Donald John Tyson created the Rock Cornish game hen by cross-breeding White Rock and Cornish hens. His intent was to create a specialty item at a higher price to appeal to foodies. In addition to commanding a higher price, the game hens have a shorter growing span. In spite of the marketing ploy, Cornish game hens are still quite affordable. Helen Gurley Brown's *Single Girl's Cookbook* advised that Rock Cornish game hens were always in good taste—far more impressive than mundane chicken but not as daunting to prepare as duck or goose. Rock Cornish game hens look just like miniature chickens, and the flavor is the same, but they are all white meat. Of Cornish game hens sold in the United States, 67 percent come from Tyson Foods, Inc., of Northwest Arkansas.

The Central Arkansas Radiation Therapy Institute (CARTI) was completed. 2000

Grilled Mahi Mahi with Jerk Spice

Yield: 4 servings

Nutritional profile for this recipe is not available due to variable amount of jerk sauce.

Jerk Spice

1	red onion, coarsely chopped
~	Green tops of 2 scallions, chopped
1	jalapeño chile, chopped
2	tablespoons olive oil
1	tablespoon sea salt
1	tablespoon white pepper
1 1/2	teaspoons dried thyme
1	teaspoon ground allspice
1/2	teaspoon ground cinnamon
1/4	teaspoon ground nutmeg

Mahi Mahi

4	(5-ounce) mahi mahi fillets
~	Salt to taste

To prepare the spice, combine the onion, scallion tops, jalapeño chile, olive oil, salt, white pepper, thyme, allspice, cinnamon and nutmeg in a food processor and process for 15 seconds. Store the leftover spice in the refrigerator for up to 1 week or freeze for up to 2 months.

To prepare the mahi mahi, season the fillets with salt. Coat each side of each fillet with 2 teaspoons of the jerk spice. Arrange the fillets on a grill rack in a grill preheated on high and reduce the heat to medium. Grill for 2 minutes or until brown and turn. Grill for 3 to 5 minutes longer or until the fillets flake easily. Or, grill in a preheated grill pan.

Thaw frozen fish fillets in milk in the refrigerator. The milk absorbs the "frozen" taste and adds a "fresh-caught" taste. Place a layer of celery and onions under fish fillets when baking. Besides adding flavor, this will prevent the fillets from sticking to the baking pan.

138

2000 *The Endoscopy and General Clinical Research Centers opened.*

Red Apple Inn Tuna Napoleon with Asian Greens and Wasabi Cream

2	cups soy sauce
1	cup honey
3	tablespoons sesame seeds, toasted
2	tablespoons dark sesame oil
3	tablespoons cornstarch
2	tablespoons water
4	(6-ounce) tuna steaks
~	Salt and pepper to taste
2	tablespoons olive oil

4	bunches kale, stemmed
2	tablespoons chopped garlic
2	pounds spinach, stemmed
1	cup teriyaki sauce
1/2	cup rice vinegar
1	cup heavy cream
2	tablespoons wasabi paste
8	won ton wrappers, fried

Yield: 4 servings

Nutrients per serving
Calories 1199
Protein 70 g
Carbo 137 g
Total Fat 47 g
Saturated Fat 18 g
Cholesterol 157 mg
Fiber 9 g
Sodium 13838 mg

139

Combine the soy sauce, honey, sesame seeds and sesame oil in a saucepan and bring to a simmer. Mix the cornstarch and water in a small bowl and stir into the soy sauce mixture. Simmer until thickened, stirring occasionally.

Season the tuna with salt and pepper or your choice of seasonings. Grill the tuna over hot coals until medium-rare. Remove to a platter.

Heat the olive oil in a large skillet and add the kale and garlic. Cook until the kale is almost cooked and stir in the spinach, teriyaki sauce and vinegar. Cook until the kale and spinach have wilted. Mix the cream and wasabi paste in a saucepan and cook until thickened and of a sauce consistency, stirring occasionally.

Cut each tuna fillet into several slices. Arrange one-fourth of the kale mixture on each of four serving plates. Top each serving with half of one tuna fillet. Brush the tuna liberally with the soy sauce mixture and top each with one won ton wrapper. Spoon the remaining kale mixture evenly over the prepared layers and top with the remaining tuna and remaining won ton wrappers. Spoon the wasabi cream sauce around the edge of the Napoleon. Serve immediately.

Nutritional profile includes all of the soy sauce mixture.

Another favorite recipe from the Red Apple Inn. Refer to page 124 for further details about the Red Apple Inn.

University Hospital was named one of "100 Most Wired" hospitals and health systems by Hospitals and Health Networks.

2000

Crab Cakes

Yield: 12
crab cakes

Nutrients per crab cake

Calories 225
Protein 3 g
Carbo 6 g
Total Fat 21 g
Saturated Fat 6 g
Cholesterol 63 mg
Fiber 1 g
Sodium 340 mg

2	tablespoons unsalted butter
2	tablespoons olive oil
1 1/2	cups finely chopped celery
3/4	cup finely chopped red onion
1/2	cup finely chopped yellow bell pepper
1/2	cup finely chopped red bell pepper
1/4	cup minced fresh flat-leaf parsley
1	tablespoon capers, drained
1/2	teaspoon Worcestershire sauce
1 1/2	teaspoons Old Bay seasoning
1/2	teaspoon kosher salt
1/2	teaspoon freshly ground pepper
1/4	teaspoon Tabasco sauce
8	ounces lump crab meat, drained and shells removed
1/2	cup plain dry bread crumbs
1/2	cup mayonnaise
2	teaspoons Dijon mustard
2	extra-large eggs, lightly beaten
1/4	cup (1/2 stick) unsalted butter
1/4	cup olive oil

Heat 2 tablespoons butter and 2 tablespoons olive oil in a large sauté pan until the butter melts. Stir in the celery, onion, bell peppers, parsley, capers, Worcestershire sauce, Old Bay seasoning, salt, pepper and Tabasco sauce. Cook over medium-low heat for 15 to 20 minutes or until the vegetables are tender. Cool to room temperature.

Separate the crab meat into small pieces and place in a bowl. Add the bread crumbs, mayonnaise, Dijon mustard and eggs and mix gently until combined. Stir in the celery mixture. Chill, covered, for 30 minutes.

Shape the crab meat mixture into bite-size crab cakes. Heat 1/4 cup butter and 1/4 cup olive oil in a large sauté pan over medium heat until the butter melts. Fry the crab cakes in batches in the butter mixture for 4 to 5 minutes per side or until brown. Drain on paper towels. Keep warm in a 250-degree oven. Serve hot.

2000

The Department of Ophthalmic Technologies and its Ophthalmic Medical Technology program, as well as the Radiation Therapy program, were established in CHRP.

Louisiana Barbecued Shrimp

4	pounds large shrimp, heads removed
1/2	cup (1 stick) butter or margarine
1/4	cup olive oil
3	tablespoons Worcestershire sauce
2	tablespoons lemon juice, or 1 lemon, sliced
2	tablespoons pepper
4	to 6 bay leaves
1	teaspoon salt
1/4	teaspoon oregano
1/4	teaspoon ground rosemary
1/4	teaspoon Tabasco sauce
1/2	garlic clove, pressed or finely chopped

Yield: 4 servings

Nutrients per serving
Calories 680
Protein 73 g
Carbo 5 g
Total Fat 40 g
Saturated Fat 17 g
Cholesterol 732 mg
Fiber 1 g
Sodium 1643 mg

Arrange the shrimp in a shallow baking dish. Melt the butter in a saucepan and stir in the olive oil, Worcestershire sauce, lemon juice, pepper, bay leaves, salt, oregano, rosemary, Tabasco sauce and garlic. Pour over the shrimp, turning to coat.

Bake in a preheated 350-degree oven for 10 minutes. Turn the shrimp and bake for 10 minutes longer or until the shrimp turn pink; do not overcook. Discard the bay leaves. Serve the shrimp and pan juices with sliced French bread for dipping. Bibs are optional when peeling and eating barbecued shrimp.

141

The Student Activities and Housing Office (SAHO) serves to bridge communication between UAMS administration and the Associate Student Government (ASG). The SAHO staff:

* provides housing for students and guests of UAMS;
* plans and organizes activities for UAMS students; and
* oversees and coordinates the ASG, intramural sports, Student Wellness program, and student insurance at UAMS.

The Jeff Banks Student Union and Dormitory opened in 1959. In 2005, all students and guests had vacated the existing dormitory as preparation began for clearing the site for the UAMS hospital expansion. Furniture and equipment were removed from the facility. By January 2006, offices located in the Jeff Banks Student Union were relocated. Then on February 19, 2006, the forty-seven-year-old dormitory was imploded. A new UAMS Residence Hall opened in the fall of 2006 with 177 units. Students and guests of UAMS are invited to "Live Where Medicine Lives" at the UAMS Residence Hall. Executive suites are available at the Residence Hall for guests of UAMS.

The world's first Myeloma Institute for Research and Therapy was established.

2001

Louisiana Red Beans and Rice

Yield: 6 servings

Nutrients per serving
Calories 697
Protein 43 g
Carbo 97 g
Total Fat 14 g
Saturated Fat 5 g
Cholesterol 57 mg
Fiber 20 g
Sodium 933 mg

1 (16-ounce) package dried red beans
1 (1-pound) meaty ham bone, cut into several large pieces
3 cups water
1 onion, chopped
1 rib celery, chopped
1 garlic clove, chopped
1 bay leaf, crushed
1 pound smoked bulk pork sausage, cut into 2-inch pieces
~ Salt to taste
~ Chopped parsley to taste
2 cups long grain rice, cooked
~ Chopped green onions to taste

Rinse and sort the beans. Combine the beans with enough water to cover by at least 1 inch in a bowl and soak for 8 to 10 hours; drain.

Combine the beans, ham bone, 3 cups water, the onion, celery, garlic and bay leaf in a stockpot and bring to a boil. Reduce the heat and cook for 1 1/2 to 2 hours or until the beans are tender, adding additional water as needed to prevent sticking.

Remove the ham bone to a platter and cut off the ham. Chop the ham into bite-size pieces and return the ham to the stockpot. Stir in the sausage, salt and parsley. Cook for 30 minutes longer, stirring occasionally and adding hot water if needed if the beans become too dry. Spoon the beans over the rice in bowls and sprinkle with green onions.

Baked Herb Rice with Pecans

Yield: 6 servings

Nutrients per serving
Calories 299
Protein 4 g
Carbo 30 g
Total Fat 19 g
Saturated Fat 8 g
Cholesterol 31 mg
Fiber 2 g
Sodium 317 mg

6 tablespoons butter
1 cup sliced mushrooms
1/2 cup chopped shallots
1 cup long grain rice
1/2 cup chopped pecans, toasted
1 1/4 cups chicken broth
1 1/4 cups water
2 bay leaves
2 tablespoons chopped fresh parsley
1 tablespoon Worcestershire sauce
1 teaspoon thyme
1 teaspoon rosemary
~ Tabasco sauce to taste
~ Salt and pepper to taste
~ Toasted pecan pieces for garnish

Melt the butter in a heavy ovenproof skillet and add the mushrooms and shallots. Sauté until tender. Add the rice and 1/2 cup chopped pecans and stir until coated with the butter. Stir in the broth, water, bay leaves, parsley, Worcestershire sauce, thyme, rosemary, Tabasco sauce, salt and pepper and bring to a rolling boil.

Remove from the heat and bake, covered, in a preheated 350-oven for 1 hour or until the rice is tender. Discard the bay leaves and garnish with pecan pieces. Serve immediately.

2001

The College of Public Health was formed. Jones Eye Institute celebrated its tenth anniversary.

Rx

Vegetables

Healthy Eating

The holidays are all about fun, friends, festivities, and food. But somewhere between feasting and fasting there is a healthy level of eating that you should try to follow if you don't want the gift of an extra five or ten pounds this year. Betsy Day of UAMS' Weight Control Program says one solution is to plan ahead. If your goal is to make healthy food choices through the holidays, don't rely on other people to provide the healthy food. For instance, if you are going to Aunt Mabel's for dinner, and you know that she cooks only with bacon fat, offer to bring a healthy vegetable dish. And be a good guest; bring along your favorite lesser-calorie snacks, such as desserts, salad dressing, and so forth. It's a good idea to have a plan for food preparation and storage when it comes to leftovers. Consider purchasing small disposable containers to make sure everyone at your party goes home with some leftover goodies. And don't let stress, fatigue, or loneliness be emotional triggers for overeating.

With all the parties and extravagant meals associated with the holidays, it's not always easy to curtail your consumption. One way to avoid packing on those unwanted pounds is to continue on your normal exercise program during this time; it may not be as strenuous as your regular regimen but anything is better than nothing.

Clinic Coordinator Betsy Day of UAMS' Weight Control Program advises you to put the "active" in family activities. Instead of sitting around the table and visiting after a meal, why not get up and have a group walk to view local holiday decorations or play a friendly game of touch football? Cut back on your family's television viewing time, and limit the number of hours your children are allowed to spend playing video games. Holiday music is perfect for dancing or exercise; encourage some of the older members of your family to get up and enjoy some of the classic tunes. And remember, physical activity is a great way to relieve holiday stress and fatigue.

If you're like most people at this time of year, it's pretty difficult to pass up that tray of holiday cookies or that box of candy your favorite business associate left on your desk. You don't have to starve yourself or go on some ridiculous diet come New Year's Day if you remember to simply take control of your holiday eating habits. Don't arrive at parties hungry. Instead, focus on the people, not the food. Standing by the buffet table is a temptation to overeat. Try to limit your intake of foods high in fat or sugar. Drink at least five glasses of water per party, and alternate a glass of water with an alcoholic beverage, or skip the alcohol altogether. One 12-ounce beer or five ounces of wine can contribute about 100 calories as well as lowering your resistance to overeating. Take smaller portions. Just because the food is there does not mean that you have to eat it all. Wait twenty minutes before having a second helping, just to make sure that you are really, truly hungry.

Planning that special holiday meal? New research shows that you may want to include cranberry sauce on your table. Cranberries, which are already known to help thwart urinary tract infections, may also prevent tooth decay and cavities, according to a study done at the University of Rochester Medical Center in New York. The same sticky compounds in cranberries, a staple at American winter holiday meals, which help keep bacteria at bay in the bladder, also appear to help prevent bacteria from clinging to teeth, according to the study. The researcher also found it seemed to help ward off plaque,

a gooey substance formed from bits of food, saliva, and acid that can harbor bacteria and eventually irritate the gums. Consuming excessive amounts of cranberry products isn't recommended, however, as many of these items contain large amounts of sugar. The fruit is also loaded with a natural acid that can strip away essential minerals in teeth.

The best way to keep from being stressed about any pounds you are afraid you'll gain during the holidays is to be realistic about your weight, advises Betsy Day of UAMS' Weight Control Program. Even though you may be extremely busy with all that the holidays involve, take time for an attitude check. Maintaining your weight is more realistic than expecting to lose weight. Allow yourself some special treats on the holidays but have moderate servings. When there's a lot of food available, try an appetizer-size helping of each dish instead of dishing up a full serving. Get plenty of sleep. People who are sluggish or sleep-deprived are more likely to overeat. And avoid sources of temptation whenever you can. After visiting a buffet, leave the room that's filled with food. If there are sweets in the office break room, don't go there. If you're given unhealthy food as a gift, why not bring it to the office to share with co-workers. Remember, tis the season to be sensible.

Dr. T. Glenn Pait and "Here's to Your Health," produced by the UAMS Office of Communications and Marketing

Greek Green Bean Medley

3 (16-ounce) cans French-style green beans, drained and rinsed
1 pint cherry tomatoes, cut into halves
1 pint mushrooms, trimmed and sliced
1 (8-ounce) bottle Italian salad dressing
2 tablespoons Cavender's Greek seasoning
~ Salt and pepper to taste

Combine the beans, tomatoes, mushrooms, salad dressing, Greek seasoning, salt and pepper in a bowl and mix well. Serve at room temperature or chilled.

Yield: 12 servings

Nutrients per serving
Calories 116
Protein 2 g
Carbo 7 g
Total Fat 9 g
Saturated Fat 1 g
Cholesterol 0 mg
Fiber 2 g
Sodium 999 mg

Cauliflower Casserole

145

1 chicken bouillon cube
1 head cauliflower
1 tablespoon butter
2 tablespoons all-purpose flour
1 (10-ounce) can cream of mushroom soup
8 ounces Cheddar cheese, shredded or finely chopped
1/4 cup bread crumbs
1/2 teaspoon paprika
2 tablespoons butter

Bring the bouillon cube and enough water to cover the cauliflower by half to a boil in a saucepan. Add the cauliflower to the boiling water and cook, covered, for 15 minutes; drain. Place the cauliflower in an ungreased 1 1/2-quart baking dish.

Melt 1 tablespoon butter in a saucepan and whisk in the flour until blended. Stir in the soup and cook until thickened. Stir in the cheese and pour the soup mixture over the cauliflower. Sprinkle with the bread crumbs and paprika. Dot with 2 tablespoons butter. Bake in a preheated 375-degree oven for 20 minutes or until the top is brown.

Yield: 6 servings

Nutrients per serving
Calories 299
Protein 13 g
Carbo 14 g
Total Fat 22 g
Saturated Fat 12 g
Cholesterol 55 mg
Fiber 3 g
Sodium 856 mg

The Institutional Review Board (IRB) reviews research that involves human subjects. The IRB is the federally mandated peer review body for ensuring ethical treatment of humans in research on the UAMS campus. The IRB is accredited by the Association for the Accreditation of Human Research Protection Programs. The IRB maintains integrity in the research environment by acting as a central point of contact for expertise regarding human subjects research activity on the UAMS campus.

The Alzheimer's Disease Center was founded in the Department of Geriatrics—one of only twenty-nine such centers in the United States at the time.

2001

Hot Peas

Yield: 9 servings

Nutrients per serving
Calories 149
Protein 6 g
Carbo 19 g
Total Fat 6 g
Saturated Fat 3 g
Cholesterol 11 mg
Fiber 5 g
Sodium 766 mg

1	(10-ounce) can cream of mushroom soup
1	(5-ounce) roll garlic cheese, chopped
3	(15-ounce) cans tiny peas, drained
~	Cayenne pepper to taste

Combine the soup and cheese in a microwave-safe bowl. Microwave until the cheese melts, stirring occasionally. Stir in the peas.

Spoon into a baking dish and sprinkle with cayenne pepper. Bake in a preheated 350-degree oven for 30 minutes.

Mashed Potato Casserole

Yield: 10 servings

Nutrients per serving
Calories 164
Protein 5 g
Carbo 8 g
Total Fat 13 g
Saturated Fat 8 g
Cholesterol 36 mg
Fiber 4 g
Sodium 99 mg

10	potatoes
8	ounces cream cheese, softened and cubed
1/2	cup sour cream
~	Salt and pepper to taste
2	tablespoons butter, melted
~	Chopped green onions for garnish

Combine the potatoes with enough water to cover in a saucepan. Bring to a boil and boil until fork tender; drain. Mash the potatoes and stir in the cream cheese, sour cream, salt and pepper, adding additional sour cream if needed for the desired consistency.

Spread the potato mixture in a buttered baking dish and drizzle with 2 tablespoons butter. Bake in a preheated 350-degree oven for 45 minutes. Garnish with green onions.

Potatoes will bake more quickly if preboiled in salted water for 10 minutes. A thin slice taken off the ends of potatoes will also reduce baking time.

2001   *Dr. Harry P. Ward retired as chancellor at UAMS; Dr. I. Dodd Wilson was appointed as the third chancellor.*

Scalloped Potatoes

3	pounds potatoes, peeled and thinly sliced	1	teaspoon salt	
4	onions, thinly sliced	1/4	teaspoon pepper	
2	teaspoons salt	1/8	teaspoon paprika	
3	tablespoons butter	21/4	cups milk	
2	tablespoons all-purpose flour	2	tablespoons chopped parsley	

Yield: 8 servings

Nutrients per serving
Calories 243
Protein 7 g
Carbo 40 g
Total Fat 7 g
Saturated Fat 4 g
Cholesterol 18 mg
Fiber 4 g
Sodium 943 mg

Combine the potatoes, onion and 2 teaspoons salt with a small amount of boiling water in a saucepan. Cook, covered, for 5 minutes or until the potatoes and onions are slightly tender; drain.

Melt the butter in a saucepan and whisk in the flour, 1 teaspoon salt, the pepper and paprika until blended. Add the milk and cook until slightly thickened and of a sauce consistency, stirring frequently.

Layer one-third of the potato mixture, 1 tablespoon of the parsley and one-third of the sauce in a lightly greased 2-quart casserole. Layer the prepared layers with one-half of the remaining potato mixture, the remaining parsley and one-half of the remaining sauce. Top with the remaining potato mixture and the remaining sauce. Bake in a preheated 400-degree oven for 35 minutes or until the potatoes are fork tender and the top is brown.

Sweet Potato Puffs

1	cup mashed cooked sweet potato	1/8	teaspoon ground cinnamon
1	tablespoon brown sugar	10	marshmallows
11/4	teaspoons salt	1/3	cup graham cracker crumbs

Yield: 10 puffs

Nutrients per puff
Calories 65
Protein 1 g
Carbo 15 g
Total Fat <1 g
Saturated Fat 1 g
Cholesterol 0 mg
Fiber 1 g
Sodium 323 mg

Combine the sweet potato, brown sugar, salt and cinnamon in a bowl and mix well. Shape the sweet potato mixture evenly around the marshmallows until enclosed. Coat with the cracker crumbs.

Arrange the encrusted marshmallows in a single layer on a greased baking sheet. Bake in a preheated 350-degree oven for 6 minutes or until lightly puffed. Do not overbake as the marshmallows will melt.

The Russian-American Family Medicine Clinic opened in Volgograd, Russia, a result of educational exchange between AHEC and Volgograd Medical Academy.

2001

Disappearing Sweet Potato Strips

Yield: 4 servings

Nutrients per serving
Calories 62
Protein 1 g
Carbo 15 g
Total Fat <1 g
Saturated Fat <1 g
Cholesterol 0 mg
Fiber 3 g
Sodium 21 mg

2	sweet potatoes, peeled
1	tablespoon ground cinnamon or spice of choice
1/2	teaspoon sugar (optional)

Cut the sweet potatoes into 1/4- to 1/2-inch strips. Arrange the strips in a single layer on a baking sheet lined with foil. Spray the strips lightly with nonstick cooking spray and sprinkle with the cinnamon and sugar. Bake in a preheated 350-degree oven for 40 minutes or until light brown.

Spinach and Artichoke Casserole

Yield: 6 servings

Nutrients per serving
Calories 277
Protein 11 g
Carbo 25 g
Total Fat 16 g
Saturated Fat 9 g
Cholesterol 101 mg
Fiber 6 g
Sodium 349 mg

1	(10-ounce) package frozen spinach	2	tablespoons lemon juice
1/4	cup chopped onion	~	Salt and pepper to taste
2	eggs	~	Hot red pepper sauce or chopped jalapeño chiles (optional)
1	cup sour cream		
1	(14-ounce) can artichoke hearts, drained and chopped	1	cup dry bread crumbs
1/3	cup grated Parmesan cheese	2	tablespoons butter, melted

Combine the spinach and onion with a small amount of water in a saucepan and cook until the spinach thaws. Drain and press the excess moisture from the spinach mixture. Whisk the eggs in a bowl until blended and stir in the sour cream, artichokes, cheese, lemon juice, salt, pepper and hot sauce. Add the spinach mixture and mix well.

Spoon into a 2-quart baking dish and sprinkle with a mixture of the bread crumbs and butter. Bake in a preheated 350-degree oven for 25 to 30 minutes or until brown and bubbly. Serve as a side dish or as a dip with pita chips, bagel chips or melba toast rounds.

Reduce the fat grams by using low-fat or fat-free sour cream and egg whites and omitting the buttered bread crumbs. Serve with baked tortilla chips or pita chips.

2002

The College of Pharmacy celebrated its fiftieth anniversary.

Squash Casserole

1 pound cooked yellow squash, drained and mashed
1/2 onion, chopped
1/2 cup (scant) milk
2 tablespoons brown sugar
1 teaspoon salt
1 egg, lightly beaten
21/2 cups crumbled hush puppies
1 cup (4 ounces) shredded Cheddar cheese
1/4 cup (1/2 stick) butter

Combine the squash, onion, milk, brown sugar, salt and egg in a bowl and mix well.
Spoon one-third of the hush puppies into a buttered baking dish. Top with layers of the
squash mixture, cheese and remaining hush puppies one-half at a time. Dot with 1/4 cup
butter. Bake in a preheated 350-degree oven for 45 minutes.

Yield: 6 servings

Nutrients per serving
Calories 343
Protein 10 g
Carbo 29 g
Total Fat 21 g
Saturated Fat 10 g
Cholesterol 96 mg
Fiber 2 g
Sodium 859 mg

149

Frozen herbs require about twice the amount you would use of the fresh herb. If frozen
herbs are reconstituted or stored in liquid such as vinegar, use the same amount as fresh.
When substituting fresh herbs for dried herbs, use 1 tablespoon of the fresh for each 1/2 to
1 teaspoon of dried, or roughly two times the amount of the dried.

Save sprigs of fresh herbs to use as garnishes, or add to salad dressings for
extra flavor.

*Arkansas Department of Human Services (DHS) and UAMS launched
the ANGELS program, a first of its kind, designed to help reduce the number
of premature births in Arkansas.*

2003

Squash Patties

Yield: 30 (2-inch) patties

Nutrients per patty
Calories 40
Protein 1 g
Carbo 4 g
Total Fat 2 g
Saturated Fat <1 g
Cholesterol 7 mg
Fiber <1 g
Sodium 82 mg

1/2 cup all-purpose flour
1/2 cup cornmeal
1 teaspoon sugar
1 teaspoon salt
1/4 cup milk
1/4 cup vegetable oil
1 egg, lightly beaten

3 cups shredded yellow squash or zucchini
1 onion, finely chopped
3 tablespoons chopped jalapeño chiles
~ Vegetable oil for deep-frying

Combine the flour, cornmeal, sugar and salt in a bowl and mix well. Add the milk, oil and egg and stir until combined. Stir in the squash, onion and jalapeño chiles.

Drop the batter by spoonfuls into hot oil in a deep skillet and fry until brown on all sides; drain. Serve warm. The batter may be stored in the refrigerator for several days.

Nutritional profile does not include vegetable oil for deep-frying.

Tomato Pie

Yield: 6 serving

Nutrients per serving
Calories 353
Protein 4 g
Carbo 17 g
Total Fat 30 g
Saturated Fat 6 g
Cholesterol 10 mg
Fiber 1 g
Sodium 361 mg

2 tablespoons margarine
1 small onion, chopped
2 ripe tomatoes, peeled and sliced
1 baked (9-inch) pie shell

1/2 cup mayonnaise
1/4 cup (1 ounce) grated Parmesan cheese
2 teaspoons garlic powder
~ Salt and pepper to taste

Melt the margarine in a small skillet and stir in the onion. Sauté until the onion is tender. Arrange the tomato slices over the bottom of the pie shell and top with the sautéed onion.

Combine the mayonnaise, cheese, garlic powder, salt and pepper in a bowl and mix well. Spread over the prepared layers. Bake in a preheated 325-degree oven for 30 minutes.

The Research Support and Regulatory Affairs (RSRA) Department supports researchers on the UAMS, VA, and ACH campuses through education, project development, regulatory review and consultation, Investigational New Drugs and Device monitoring, and quality assurance activities for Good Manufacturing Practice, Good Laboratory Practice, and Good Tissue Practice studies.

2003 *The Walker Eye Research Center was dedicated at Jones Eye Institute, and the Jackson T. Stephens Spine & Neurosciences Institute opened.*

Desserts

Arkansas Children's Hospital Advises Safety First When Cooking

Arkansas Children's Hospital (ACH) in Little Rock warns that parents should be aware of hidden dangers in kitchens and food preparation and outlines precautions parents can take to have an enjoyable, safe cooking experience with their children.

When working together in the kitchen, parents should closely supervise their children at all times. They should also take time to store all hazardous substances out of the reach of children, including cleaning supplies and alcohol, the hospital said.

"Parents should make sure all alcoholic beverages and alcohol used for cooking cannot be easily reached by children and possibly ingested," Donna Parnell-Beasley, R.N., Trauma Program Coordinator at Arkansas Children's Hospital, said. "Parents should also be aware of the dangers of food sitting out, both in terms of the risk of food-borne illness and the risk to very young children who could help themselves and choke while others are distracted."

Parents should also keep a close eye on hot liquids, surfaces and steam. Burns in the kitchen are common injuries. Scald burns from hot liquid or steam are the most common type of burns among children 4 years old and under. A child can suffer a third-degree burn after just three seconds of exposure to 140-degree water.

"When cooking, keep pot handles turned toward the back of the stove," Parnell-Beasley said. "Keep electrical cords out of reach. Also be aware that children may venture into the kitchen while you are cooking. Be mindful of their presence to prevent inadvertent burns from hot food items."

Parnell also suggests using caution when placing hot liquids and foods on tablecloths. Curious children or those who just started walking may use the hanging edges to pull up on.

Safe Kids USA also recommends these precautions against kitchen burns:

• Never leave a hot stove unattended.

• Never hold a child while cooking or carrying hot items.

• Cook on back burners whenever possible, and turn all handles toward the back of the stove.

• Don't allow loose-fitting clothing in the kitchen.

• Keep hot foods and liquids away from the edges of counters and tables.

If you think your child may have ingested a poison or hazardous substance, Parnell-Beasley advises calling the Poison Control Center at 1-800-222-1222.

Nicole Boddington, Little Rock Family Staff

For more information, visit www.archildrens.org.

Reprinted with permission from Little Rock Family and Donna Parnell-Beasley, RN, in conjunction with Arkansas Children's Hospital

Cheesecake with Raspberry Sauce

Graham Cracker Crust
1¹/4 cups graham cracker crumbs
¹/4 cup sugar
¹/3 cup margarine, melted

Cream Cheese Filling
24 ounces cream cheese, softened
1 cup sugar
4 eggs
2 teaspoons vanilla extract

Sour Cream Topping
1 cup sour cream
3 tablespoons sugar
1 teaspoon vanilla extract

Raspberry Sauce
¹/4 cup sugar
2 teaspoons cornstarch
1 (10-ounce) package frozen raspberries
¹/2 cup red currant jelly

Yield: 12 servings

Nutrients per serving
Calories 501
Protein 8 g
Carbo 49 g
Total Fat 31 g
Saturated Fat 17 g
Cholesterol 141 mg
Fiber 1 g
Sodium 314 mg

153

To prepare the crust, mix the cracker crumbs and sugar in a bowl. Add the margarine and stir until crumbly. Pat the crumb mixture into a 9-inch springform pan sprayed lightly with nonstick cooking spray. Bake in a preheated 375-degree oven for 8 minutes or until light brown. Let stand until cool. Reduce the oven temperature to 325 degrees.

To prepare the filling, beat the cream cheese, sugar, eggs and vanilla in a mixing bowl until creamy. Spoon the filling into the prepared pan and bake for 40 minutes. Let cool on a wire rack for 30 minutes.

To prepare the topping, combine the sour cream, sugar and vanilla in a bowl and mix well. Spread the topping over the baked layers. Chill, covered with foil, for 8 to 10 hours.

To prepare the sauce, combine the sugar and cornstarch in a saucepan and mix well. Add the raspberries and jelly and cook over medium heat until thickened and clear, stirring frequently. Pour the sauce through a fine sieve into a bowl, discarding the seeds. Chill and serve with the cheesecake.

Soften frozen or extra-hard butter using a grater. Soften hard butter for spreading by inverting a heated bowl over the butter for a few minutes. Similarly, run measuring spoons under hot water before measuring shortening or tub butter. It will slide right out.

The College of Public Health opened as did the BioVentures and Biomedical Research Center II buildings.

2003

Nutty Pumpkin Cheesecake

Yield: 12 servings

Nutrients per serving
Calories 677
Protein 9 g
Carbo 58 g
Total Fat 48 g
Saturated Fat 25 g
Cholesterol 190 mg
Fiber 3 g
Sodium 318 mg

Graham Cracker Crust
1/2 cup graham cracker crumbs
1/4 cup packed light brown sugar
6 tablespoons butter or margarine, melted

Pumpkin Filling
24 ounces cream cheese, softened
1 cup packed brown sugar
1/2 cup granulated sugar
4 eggs

1 (16-ounce) can pumpkin
1 cup whipping cream
1 tablespoon ground cinnamon
1 1/2 teaspoons ground ginger
3/4 teaspoon ground cloves

Nutty Topping
1 cup packed light brown sugar
1 cup chopped pecans or walnuts
6 tablespoons butter, melted

To prepare the crust, combine the cracker crumbs, brown sugar and butter in a bowl and mix until crumbly. Pat the crumb mixture into a 10-inch springform pan. Bake in a preheated 350-degree oven for 5 to 7 minutes or until light brown. Maintain the oven temperature.

To prepare the filling, beat the cream cheese, brown sugar and granulated sugar in a mixing bowl until creamy. Add the eggs one at a time, mixing well after each addition. Add the pumpkin, cream, cinnamon, ginger and cloves and beat until combined. Spread the filling over the crust and bake for 1 hour and 20 minutes.

To prepare the topping, combine the brown sugar, pecans and butter in a bowl and mix well. Spread over the top of the cheesecake and bake for 20 minutes longer. Let stand until cool and store, covered, in the refrigerator.

If your brown sugar has hardened, grate the amount you need. Then place a slice of soft bread in a sealed container with the rock-hard brown sugar. The brown sugar should soften in a few hours. Remove the bread and seal the sugar in a sealable plastic bag.

2003

UAMS collaborated in the funding of the Clinton School of Public Service. The College of Nursing celebrated its fiftieth anniversary.

One-Cup Cobbler

1/2	cup (1 stick) butter	1	cup milk	
1	cup self-rising flour	1	(30-ounce) can freestone	
1	cup sugar		peaches	
1/8	teaspoon salt			

Melt the butter in a 9×11-inch baking dish in a preheated 350-degree oven. Maintain the oven temperature.

Mix the flour, sugar and salt in a bowl. Add the milk and stir until combined. Pour the batter into the prepared baking dish and top with the peaches; do not stir. Bake for about 1 hour or until the top is brown.

Yield: 8 servings

Nutrients per serving

Calories 349

Protein 3 g

Carbo 59 g

Total Fat 13 g

Saturated Fat 8 g

Cholesterol 33 mg

Fiber 2 g

Sodium 334 mg

155

Apple Crisp

2	pounds firm baking apples, peeled, cored and cut into 1/4-inch slices	1/2	cup all-purpose flour	
		6	tablespoons old-fashioned rolled oats	
2	tablespoons orange juice	1/2	cup granular Splenda	
1/4	cup granular Splenda	1	teaspoon ground cinnamon	
1	tablespoon all-purpose flour	1/4	cup (1/2 stick) light butter	
1/2	teaspoon ground cinnamon			

Toss the apples with the orange juice in a bowl. Mix 1/4 cup Splenda, 1 tablespoon flour and 1/2 teaspoon cinnamon in a bowl. Sprinkle the flour mixture over the apples and toss to coat. Spread the apple mixture in an 8×8-inch baking dish sprayed with nonstick cooking spray.

Combine 1/2 cup flour, the oats, 1/2 cup Splenda and 1 teaspoon cinnamon in a bowl and mix well. Cut the butter into the oats mixture with a pastry blender until crumbly. Sprinkle the crumb mixture over the prepared layer. Bake in a preheated 350-degree oven for 40 to 45 minutes or until the apples are tender and the top is brown and bubbly. Delicious served warm.

Yield: 8 servings

Nutrients per serving

Calories 135

Protein 2 g

Carbo 24 g

Total Fat 4 g

Saturated Fat 2 g

Cholesterol 7 mg

Fiber 2 g

Sodium 30 mg

The Department of Respiratory and Surgical Technologies formed in the College of Health Related Professions by combining the Departments of Respiratory Care and Surgical Technology.

2003

Dew the Dew Apple Dumplings

Yield: 16 dumplings

Nutrients per dumpling

Calories 402

Protein 5 g

Carbo 50 g

Total Fat 21 g

Saturated Fat 7 g

Cholesterol 15 mg

Fiber 1 g

Sodium 573 mg

2   (8-count) cans crescent rolls

3   cups (bite-size) pieces peeled apples

1¹/₄ cups sugar

2   teaspoons ground cinnamon

¹/₈ teaspoon salt

¹/₂ cup (1 stick) butter, melted

1   (12-ounce) can Mountain Dew (do not use diet)

Unroll the crescent roll dough and separate into 16 triangles. Toss the apples with 2 to 3 tablespoons of the sugar and 1 teaspoon of the cinnamon in a bowl. Wrap each dough triangle around some of the apple pieces to form a dumpling, sealing the edges. Arrange the dumplings in a 9×13-inch baking dish.

Mix the remaining sugar, the remaining 1 teaspoon cinnamon, the salt and butter in a bowl and drizzle over the dumplings. Pour the soda over the top and bake in a preheated 350-degree oven for 45 minutes. Great with vanilla ice cream.

156

Soak peeled apples in a mixture of cold water and a pinch of salt to prevent browning. Ripen green fruit in a perforated plastic bag. The bag allows the air to circulate but holds in the gases for ripening.

2003

The Department of Laboratory Sciences established in the College of Health Related Professions by combining the Departments of Medical Technology and Cytotechnology.

New Orleans Bread Pudding with White Chocolate Sauce

Bread Pudding

1	(16-ounce) loaf dry French bread, sliced
1/2	cup (1 stick) butter
4	cups milk
2	cups sugar
3	eggs, beaten
2	tablespoons ground cinnamon
2	teaspoons ground nutmeg
2	teaspoons vanilla extract

White Chocolate Sauce

12	ounces white chocolate, chopped
2	tablespoons water
1/2	cup (1 stick) butter, melted
1	cup confectioners' sugar
1	teaspoon vanilla extract

Yield: 15 servings

Nutrients per serving
Calories 514
Protein 9 g
Carbo 68 g
Total Fat 23 g
Saturated Fat 14 g
Cholesterol 89 mg
Fiber 1 g
Sodium 347 mg

To prepare the bread pudding, layer the bread slices in a 9×13-inch baking pan. Melt the butter in a saucepan and stir in the milk, sugar, eggs, cinnamon, nutmeg and vanilla. Pour over the bread slices. Bake in a preheated 350-degree oven for 1 hour.

To prepare the sauce, combine the chocolate and water in a saucepan and cook over low heat until blended, stirring frequently. Remove from the heat. Add the butter, confectioners' sugar and vanilla individually in the order listed, mixing until completely blended after each addition. Pour the sauce over the warm bread pudding and let stand for 10 minutes before serving, or serve the sauce on the side.

Nutritional profile does not include Whiskey or Rum Sauce or Pecan Praline Sauce (see below).

157

For variety, serve the Bread Pudding with one or both of the following sauces. To prepare **Whiskey or Rum Sauce**, combine 1/2 cup butter and 1 cup confectioners' sugar in a saucepan and cook over low heat until the butter melts. Add 1 beaten egg yolk and cook for several minutes. Add 1/2 cup whiskey or rum gradually and continue to cook over low heat until of the desired consistency, stirring constantly. Pour the sauce over the bread pudding and let stand for about 10 minutes before serving, or serve on the side. Or, try **Pecan Praline Sauce**. Combine 1 cup packed light brown sugar, 1/2 cup light cream or half-and-half, 1/4 cup light corn syrup and 2 tablespoons melted butter in a saucepan and mix well. Cook over low heat for 10 minutes or until thickened, stirring constantly. Remove from the heat and stir in 1 teaspoon vanilla extract and 1 cup chopped pecans. Pour the sauce over the bread pudding and let stand for 10 minutes before serving, or serve on the side.

Four-Layer Delight

Yield: 15 servings

Nutrients per serving

Calories 432

Protein 5 g

Carbo 37 g

Total Fat 31 g

Saturated Fat 19 g

Cholesterol 62 mg

Fiber 1 g

Sodium 345 mg

1   cup all-purpose flour
1   cup (2 sticks) butter or margarine, softened
1/2 cup chopped pecans
1   cup confectioners' sugar
12 ounces cream cheese, softened
16 ounces whipped topping
1   (4-ounce) package chocolate instant pudding mix
1   (4-ounce) package vanilla instant pudding mix
3   cups milk
1/4 cup chopped pecans

Combine the flour, butter and 1/2 cup pecans in a bowl and mix well. Pat the pecan mixture over the bottom of a baking dish. Bake in a preheated 350-degree oven for 15 minutes. Let stand until cool.

Combine the confectioners' sugar, cream cheese and 1 1/2 cups of the whipped topping in a mixing bowl and beat until blended. Spread over the baked layer.

Combine the pudding mixes and the milk in a mixing bowl and beat until thickened. Immediately pour the pudding over the prepared layers and chill until set. Spread with the remaining whipped topping and sprinkle with 1/4 cup pecans. Chill, covered, until serving time.

158

Whipping cream will whip more quickly if the bowl, beaters, and cream are chilled. To keep whipped cream from separating, add 1/4 teaspoon unflavored gelatin per cup of cream.

2004   *The plans were unveiled for the University Hospital expansion.*

Vanilla Ice Cream

6   cups milk
2   cups sugar
1   (12-ounce) can evaporated milk
8   ounces whipped topping
1   (4-ounce) package vanilla instant pudding mix

Combine the milk, sugar, evaporated milk, whipped topping and pudding mix
in a bowl and mix well. Pour into an ice cream freezer container and freeze using
manufacturer's directions.

Yield: 16 servings

Nutrients per serving
Calories 235
Protein 5 g
Carbo 40 g
Total Fat 7 g
Saturated Fat 5 g
Cholesterol 16 mg
Fiber <1 g
Sodium 143 mg

Ice Cream-in-a-Bag

2   cups milk
1/2 cup sugar
1/2 teaspoon vanilla extract

5   cups ice
3/4 cup rock salt
1/4 cup water

Combine the milk, sugar and vanilla in a bowl and stir until the sugar dissolves. Pour into a
1-quart sealable plastic freezer bag and seal tightly.

Combine the ice, rock salt and water in a 1-gallon sealable plastic freezer bag. Place the
1-quart freezer bag inside the 1-gallon freezer bag and seal tightly. Shake for 10 minutes for
soft-serve ice cream. For a richer flavor, substitute a mixture of 1 cup whole milk and 1 cup
evaporated milk for 2 cups whole milk.

Yield: 2 servings

Nutrients per serving
Calories 340
Protein 8 g
Carbo 61 g
Total Fat 8 g
Saturated Fat 5 g
Cholesterol 24 mg
Fiber 0 g
Sodium 98 mg

A light sherbet is often used to cleanse the palate in between courses of a meal. Try this
Fruit Sherbet. Bring 3 cups sugar and 3 cups water to a boil. Remove from the heat and
let stand until cool. Stir in 11/2 cups orange juice, the juice of 1 lemon, 1 mashed banana,
1 undrained 8-ounce can crushed pineapple and 1 undrained small bottle maraschino
cherries. Pour the mixture into an ice cream freezer container and add enough milk to reach
the 1 gallon mark. Freeze using manufacturer's directions.

*A new fitness center opened in the College of Public Health, and UAMS
became one of the first medical centers in the country and first in Arkansas
to adopt a campus-wide non-smoking policy.*

2004

Butter Pecan Fudge

Yield: 24 squares

Nutrients per square
Calories 154
Protein 1 g
Carbo 19 g
Total Fat 9 g
Saturated Fat 4 g
Cholesterol 17 mg
Fiber <1 g
Sodium 43 mg

1/2   cup (1 stick) butter
1/2   cup granulated sugar
1/2   cup packed brown sugar
1/2   cup heavy whipping cream
1/8   teaspoon salt
1   teaspoon vanilla extract
2   cups confectioners' sugar
1   cup pecan halves, chopped

Combine the butter, granulated sugar, brown sugar, cream and salt in a heavy saucepan. Bring to a boil over medium heat, stirring occasionally. Boil for 5 minutes, stirring constantly. Remove from the heat and stir in the vanilla. Add the confectioners' sugar and stir until smooth. Mix in the pecans.

Spread the fudge in a buttered 8×8-inch dish. Let stand until room temperature. Cut into squares and store in an airtight container in the refrigerator.

Rocky Road Fudge

Yield: variable

Nutrients per serving
Nutritional profile for this recipe is not available due to variable yield.

2   cups dry roasted peanuts
1   (10-ounce) package miniature marshmallows
2   cups (12 ounces) milk chocolate chips
1   (14-ounce) can sweetened condensed milk
2   tablespoons margarine

Toss the peanuts and marshmallows in a bowl. Combine the chocolate chips, condensed milk and margarine in a saucepan and cook over low heat until blended. Pour over the marshmallow mixture and mix well. Spread on waxed paper. Let stand until set. Cut into squares.

If you do not want to worry about remembering to take home a cake plate at a carry-in dinner, save the cardboard from frozen pizzas and wrap with foil.

2004

The Genetic Counseling and Medical Dosimetry programs were established in the College of Health Related Professions.

Chewy Pecan Pralines

1   cup sugar
1   cup light corn syrup
1/8 teaspoon salt
1/4 cup (1/2 stick) margarine

3/4 cup plus 2 tablespoons milk
2   cups pecan halves
1/2 teaspoon vanilla extract

Mix the sugar, corn syrup and salt in a saucepan and cook over medium heat until the sugar dissolves. Stir in the margarine, milk and pecan halves gradually. Cook over medium heat to 240 to 248 degrees on a candy thermometer, firm-ball stage, stirring frequently; the mixture will darken in color. Stir in the vanilla.

Let stand until the mixture stops bubbling. Drop by teaspoonfuls onto a greased baking sheet. Let stand until firm.

Yield: 30 (2-inch) pralines

Nutrients per praline
Calories 124
Protein 1 g
Carbo 16 g
Total Fat 7 g
Saturated Fat 1 g
Cholesterol 1 mg
Fiber 1 g
Sodium 37 mg

Almond Legend Cake

Cake
1/2 cup chopped almonds
1   (2-layer) package yellow cake mix with pudding
1/2 cup orange juice
1/2 cup water
1/3 cup vegetable oil
3   eggs
1/2 teaspoon almond extract
1   whole almond

Apricot Glaze
1/2 cup apricot preserves
2   to 3 teaspoons orange juice

Yield: 16 servings

Nutrients per serving
Calories 244
Protein 4 g
Carbo 34 g
Total Fat 11 g
Saturated Fat 2 g
Cholesterol 40 mg
Fiber 1 g
Sodium 242 mg

To prepare the cake, generously grease a bundt pan or 10-inch tube pan. Gently press the chopped almonds over the bottom and halfway up the side of the pan. Combine the cake mix, orange juice, water, oil, eggs and flavoring in a mixing bowl and beat at low speed just until moistened. Beat at high speed for 2 minutes. Stir in the whole almond.

Pour the batter into the prepared pan. Bake in a preheated 350-degree oven for 35 to 45 minutes or until a wooden pick inserted near the center comes out clean. Cool in the pan on a wire rack for 10 minutes. Invert onto a cake plate.

To prepare the glaze, mix the preserves and orange juice in a bowl until of a glaze consistency. Spoon the glaze over the warm cake. Let stand until cool.

The "Almond Legend"—whoever gets the whole almond is assured of good luck!

Construction began on the expansion of Jones Eye Institute, and construction was completed on the building housing the new PET (Positron Emission Tomography) scanner and cyclotron.

2005

Banana Nut Cake

Yield: 30 slices

Nutrients per slice
Calories 258
Protein 3 g
Carbo 35 g
Total Fat 13 g
Saturated Fat 2 g
Cholesterol 29 mg
Fiber 1 g
Sodium 173 mg

1 cup buttermilk	1 teaspoon vanilla extract
2 teaspoons baking soda	3 cups all-purpose flour
3 cups sugar	2 cups mashed bananas
1 cup (2 sticks) margarine	2 cups chopped pecans
4 eggs	

Mix the buttermilk and baking soda in a small bowl and let stand for 1 minute. Beat the sugar, margarine, eggs and vanilla in a mixing bowl until creamy. Add the flour and beat until blended. Mix in the buttermilk mixture and stir in the bananas and pecans.

Spoon the batter evenly into three 5×9-inch nonstick loaf pans. Bake in a preheated 350-degree oven for 1 hour. Cool in the pans for 10 minutes. Remove to a wire rack to cool completely.

Sour Cream Pound Cake

Yield: 12 servings

Nutrients per serving
Calories 518
Protein 7 g
Carbo 75 g
Total Fat 22 g
Saturated Fat 13 g
Cholesterol 151 mg
Fiber 1 g
Sodium 225 mg

3 cups all-purpose flour	6 egg yolks
1/4 teaspoon salt	1 cup sour cream
1/4 teaspoon baking soda	6 egg whites, stiffly beaten
3 cups sugar	2 teaspoons vanilla extract
1 cup (2 sticks) butter	

Sift the flour, salt and baking soda together three times. Beat the sugar, butter and egg yolks in a mixing bowl until creamy. Add the flour mixture alternately with the sour cream, mixing well after each addition. Blend in the egg whites and vanilla.

Spoon the batter into a greased 10-inch tube pan. Bake in a preheated 320-degree oven for 1 hour. Increase the oven temperature to 350 degrees and bake for 30 minutes longer. Cool in the pan for 10 minutes. Invert onto a cake plate.

Freeze overripe bananas for later use in cakes, coffee cakes, and breads.

2005

UAMS, the University of Arkansas at Fayetteville, the University of Arkansas at Little Rock, and seven partner institutions announced a five-year, $16.7 million federal grant from National Institutes of Health to expand and improve biomedical research in Arkansas.

Blondies with Brown Sugar Icing

Blondies

2²/3 cups all-purpose flour

2¹/2 teaspoons baking powder

¹/2 teaspoon salt

1 (1-pound) package light
brown sugar

²/3 cup butter

3 eggs

1 tablespoon vanilla extract

¹/2 cup pecans (optional)

Brown Sugar Icing

¹/2 cup (1 stick) butter

1 cup packed brown sugar

¹/4 cup milk

3¹/4 cups confectioners' sugar

Yield: 36 bars

Nutrients per bar

Calories 207

Protein 2 g

Carbo 36 g

Total Fat 6 g

Saturated Fat 4 g

Cholesterol 33 mg

Fiber <1 g

Sodium 122 mg

To prepare the blondies, mix the flour, baking powder and salt together. Beat the brown sugar and butter in a mixing bowl until creamy. Add the eggs and vanilla and beat until blended. Blend in the flour mixture and stir in the pecans. Spread the batter in a greased and floured 9×13-inch baking pan. Bake in a preheated 350-degree oven for 20 minutes.

To prepare the icing, melt the butter in a saucepan and stir in the brown sugar. Bring to a boil and boil for 1 to 2 minutes or until slightly thickened, stirring constantly. Cool slightly and pour into a mixing bowl. Add the milk and beat until smooth. Add the confectioners' sugar and beat until of a spreading consistency. Spread the icing over the blondies. Let stand until cool and cut into bars. Store in an airtight container.

163

Pecan Pie Squares

Crust

3 cups all-purpose flour

¹/4 cup plus 2 tablespoons sugar

³/4 teaspoon salt

³/4 cup (1¹/2 sticks)
margarine, softened

Pecan Filling

1¹/2 cups corn syrup

1¹/2 cups sugar

4 eggs, lightly beaten

3 tablespoons margarine, melted

1¹/2 teaspoons vanilla extract

2¹/2 cups chopped pecans

Yield: 48 squares

Nutrients per square

Calories 168

Protein 2 g

Carbo 23 g

Total Fat 9 g

Saturated Fat 1 g

Cholesterol 18 mg

Fiber 1 g

Sodium 90 mg

To prepare the crust, mix the flour, sugar and salt in a bowl. Cut in the margarine until crumbly; the mixture will be dry. Pat over the bottom of a greased 10×15-inch baking pan. Bake in a preheated 350-degree oven for 20 minutes. Maintain the oven temperature.

To prepare the filling, whisk the corn syrup, sugar, eggs, margarine and vanilla in a bowl until blended. Stir in the pecans. Pour the pecan mixture over the crust and spread evenly. Bake for 30 to 35 minutes or until set. Immediately run a sharp knife around the edge of the pan. Cool in the pan on a wire rack and cut into squares. Store in an airtight container.

The Pat Walker Tower, a five-floor expansion of the Jones Eye Institute, was dedicated. For the fourth year in a row, the UAMS College of Medicine's geriatrics program named one the of country's ten best in the U.S. News & World Report *list of "America's Best Graduate Schools."*

2006

Pumpkin Bars

Yield: 36 bars

Nutrients per bar
Calories 159
Protein 1 g
Carbo 22 g
Total Fat 8 g
Saturated Fat 2 g
Cholesterol 20 mg
Fiber 1 g
Sodium 118 mg

1	(16-ounce) can pumpkin
1/3	cup vegetable oil
1/3	cup sugar
3	eggs
1	tablespoon pumpkin pie spice
1	(2-layer) package butter recipe cake mix
1	(16-ounce) can vanilla frosting
3	ounces cream cheese, softened

Combine the pumpkin, oil, sugar and eggs in a mixing bowl and beat at high speed for 1 minute. Add the pumpkin pie spice and cake mix and beat until moistened. Beat at high speed for 2 minutes, scraping the bowl occasionally.

Spread the batter in a greased and floured 10×15-inch baking pan. Bake in a preheated 350-degree oven for 25 to 35 minutes or until a wooden pick inserted in the center comes out clean. Cool in the pan on a wire rack.

Beat the frosting and cream cheese in a mixing bowl at low speed until smooth. Spread the frosting over the baked layer and let stand until set. Cut into bars. Store, covered, in the refrigerator. You may substitute homemade butter frosting, cream cheese frosting or confectioners' sugar frosting for the prepared vanilla frosting.

Cowboy Cookies

Yield: 48 cookies

Nutrients per cookie
Calories 161
Protein 2 g
Carbo 21 g
Total Fat 8 g
Saturated Fat 3 g
Cholesterol 13 mg
Fiber 1 g
Sodium 66 mg

2 1/2	cups all-purpose flour
1 1/8	teaspoons baking soda
1/2	teaspoon (heaping) baking powder
1/2	teaspoon (heaping) salt
1	cup plus 2 tablespoons granulated sugar
1	cup shortening
8	ounces dark brown sugar
3	eggs
2	tablespoons vegetable oil
1 1/4	teaspoons vanilla extract
2	cups old-fashioned oats
2	cups (12 ounces) chocolate chips
1/2	cup chopped pecans

Sift the flour, baking soda, baking powder and salt together. Beat the granulated sugar, shortening, brown sugar, eggs, oil and vanilla in a mixing bowl until creamy. Add the flour mixture and beat until blended. Stir in the oats. Mix in the chocolate chips and pecans.

Drop the dough by scant 1/8 cupfuls onto a greased cookie sheet. Bake in a preheated 350-degree oven for 12 minutes or until the edges turn brown and the centers still look chewy. Cool on the cookie sheet for 5 to 6 minutes and remove to a wire rack to cool completely. Store in an airtight container. These cookies contain no preservatives so they are best if eaten within a couple of days. Or, freeze for future use, if desired. The dough may be frozen in cookie-size balls and baked at a later date.

2006

The College of Pharmacy, College of Medicine's primary care program, and the College of Nursing's master's degree programs also named as some of the country's best in the U.S. News & World Report list of "America's Best Graduate Schools."

Magical Peanut Butter Cookies

1   cup Splenda or any equivalent
1   cup creamy or chunky peanut butter
1   egg
1   teaspoon vanilla extract
1/3 cup granulated Splenda

Combine 1 cup Splenda, the peanut butter, egg and vanilla in a bowl and stir until incorporated. Shape the dough into 1-inch balls and arrange 2 inches apart on a greased cookie sheet.

Using a fork dipped in 1/3 cup Splenda make a crisscross pattern on each cookie. Bake in a preheated 350-degree oven for 12 minutes. Immediately sprinkle the cookies with additional Splenda. Cool on the cookie sheet for 2 minutes. Remove to a wire rack to cool completely. Store in an airtight container.

Yield: 24 cookies

Nutrients per cookie
Calories 72
Protein 3 g
Carbo 3 g
Total Fat 6 g
Saturated Fat 1 g
Cholesterol 9 mg
Fiber 1 g
Sodium 53 mg

Coconut Pie

3/4   cup sugar
1/4   cup cornstarch
2 1/4 cups milk
3   egg yolks, beaten
1/4   to 1/2 cup cream of coconut
1   (7-ounce) can flaked coconut
1/4   cup (1/2 stick) margarine
1   teaspoon vanilla extract
1   baked (9-inch) pie shell
8   ounces whipped topping
1/2   cup flaked coconut, toasted

Mix the sugar and cornstarch in a microwave-safe bowl and stir in the milk. Add the egg yolks and cream of coconut and mix well. Microwave for 6 to 8 minutes, stirring occasionally and adding additional milk if needed for a thinner consistency. Mix in 7 ounces coconut, the margarine and vanilla.

Spoon the coconut mixture into the pie shell and cool slightly. Spread with the whipped topping and sprinkle with 1/2 cup toasted coconut. Store, covered, in the refrigerator.

Yield: 8 servings

Nutrients per serving
Calories 556
Protein 6 g
Carbo 55 g
Total Fat 34 g
Saturated Fat 21 g
Cholesterol 84 mg
Fiber 2 g
Sodium 227 mg

The Jeff Banks Student Union and student dormitory were imploded on February 19, 2006, using about sixty-five pounds of explosives to bring down the 15,000-ton building. The Central Arkansas Veterans Health Care System, a UAMS affiliate, named "Best in Quality" throughout the VA System.

2006

Creamy Lemon Raspberry Pie

Yield: 8 servings

Nutrients per serving
Calories 420
Protein 5 g
Carbo 58 g
Total Fat 18 g
Saturated Fat 11 g
Cholesterol 30 mg
Fiber 1 g
Sodium 336 mg

1/4	cup seedless red raspberry jam
1	baked (9-inch) shortbread pie shell
3/4	cup fresh red raspberries
4	ounces cream cheese, softened
1	(12-ounce) can evaporated milk
2	(4-ounce) packages lemon instant pudding mix
~	Grated zest of 1 lemon
8	ounces whipped topping
1/4	cup fresh red raspberries for garnish
~	Grated lemon zest for garnish

Spread the jam over the bottom of the pie shell and sprinkle with 3/4 cup raspberries. Beat the cream cheese in a mixing bowl until creamy. Add the evaporated milk, pudding mixes and grated zest of 1 lemon gradually, beating constantly at medium speed until combined. Fold in half the whipped topping.

Spoon the cream cheese mixture into the prepared pie shell and spread with the remaining whipped topping. Chill for 2 hours or until set. Garnish with 1/4 cup raspberries and lemon zest just before serving.

166

Bavarian Strawberry Pie

Yield: 8 servings

Nutrients per serving
Calories 375
Protein 3 g
Carbo 35 g
Total Fat 26 g
Saturated Fat 18 g
Cholesterol 61 mg
Fiber 3 g
Sodium 72 mg

2 1/2	cups flaked coconut
1/3	cup butter, melted
1	quart strawberries, sliced
3/4	cup sugar
1	envelope unflavored gelatin
1/2	cup cold water
2	teaspoons lemon juice
1	cup heavy whipping cream, whipped

Combine the coconut and butter in a bowl and mix well. Press over the bottom and up the side of a greased 9-inch pie plate. Bake in a preheated 300-degree oven for 30 to 35 minutes or until light brown, covering the edge loosely with foil to prevent overbrowning if needed. Cool on a wire rack.

Toss the strawberries with the sugar in a bowl and let stand for 15 minutes. Sprinkle the gelatin over the cold water in a small saucepan. Let stand for 1 minute. Cook over medium heat until the gelatin dissolves, stirring constantly. Stir in the lemon juice. Add to the strawberry mixture and mix gently. Let stand until room temperature and fold in the whipped cream. Spread in the prepared pie plate. Chill, covered, for 4 hours or longer.

2006

Dr. Bart Barlogie voted National Physician of the Year by his peers. The new UAMS Residence Hall opened at the corner of Markham Street and Hooper Drive.

Nutritional Profile Guidelines

The editors have attempted to present these family recipes in a form that allows approximate nutritional values to be computed. Persons with dietary or health problems or whose diets require close monitoring should not rely solely on the nutritional information provided. They should consult their physicians or a registered dietitian for specific information.

Nutritional information for these recipes is computed from information derived from many sources, including materials supplied by the United States Department of Agriculture, computer databanks, and journals in which the information is assumed to be in the public domain. However, many specialty items, new products, and processed foods may not be available from these sources or may vary from the average values used in these profiles. More information on new and/or specific products may be obtained by reading the nutrient labels. Unless otherwise specified, the nutritional profile of these recipes is based on all measurements being level.

* **Artificial sweeteners** vary in use and strength so should be used "to taste," using the recipe ingredients as a guideline. Sweeteners using aspartame (NutraSweet and Equal) should not be used as a sweetener in recipes involving prolonged heating, which reduces the sweet taste. For further information on the use of these sweeteners, refer to package information.
* **Alcoholic ingredients** have been analyzed for basic ingredients, although cooking causes the evaporation of alcohol, thus decreasing caloric content.

* **Buttermilk, sour cream,** and **yogurt** are the types available commercially.
* **Cake mixes** which are prepared using package directions include 3 eggs and 1/2 cup oil.
* **Chicken,** cooked for boning and chopping, has been roasted; this method yields the lowest caloric values.
* **Cottage cheese** is cream-style with 4.2% creaming mixture. Dry curd cottage cheese has no creaming mixture.
* **Eggs** are all large. To avoid raw eggs that may carry salmonella, as in eggnog or 6-week muffin batter, use an equivalent amount of commercial egg substitute.
* **Flour** is unsifted all-purpose flour.
* **Garnishes,** serving suggestions, and other optional additions and variations are not included in the profile.
* **Margarine** and **butter** are regular, not whipped or presoftened.
* **Milk** is whole milk, 3.5% butterfat. Low-fat milk is 1% butterfat. Evaporated milk is whole milk with 60% of the water removed.
* **Oil** is any type of vegetable cooking oil. Shortening is hydrogenated vegetable shortening.
* **Salt** and other ingredients to taste, as noted in the ingredients, have not been included in the nutritional profile.
* If a choice of ingredients has been given, the nutritional profile reflects the first option. If a choice of amounts has been given, the nutritional profile reflects the greater amount.

Cover Artist

Keith Runkle is an established designer and has been working in the Little Rock area since 1991. Prior to that, he lived and worked in Williamsport, Pennsylvania. Keith holds a Bachelor of Fine Arts degree from Edinboro University in Erie, Pennsylvania, with a concentration in graphic design and painting.

Since graduating from art school in 1986, Keith has worked for agencies in both Pennsylvania and Arkansas and has won numerous awards for his work in graphic design. In 2006, he was recognized by the Arkansas Advertising Federation with a Gold Addy for a magazine he designed for the University of Arkansas for Medical Sciences College of Medicine.

Keith currently serves as the Creative Director for the Creative Services Department at UAMS, where he has been working since 1997.

Keith can be reached by e-mail at runklekeitha@uams.edu.

From a Friend

Cooking with my grandmothers and mother started at a very young age of five and influenced my interest and ability in cooking, especially baking. From about the age of five, I can remember being involved in some culinary aspect with my grandmothers and mother, small initially in my mind, but still a contribution. I can still remember scooping out a cup of chocolate chips and sitting by the oven, looking through the glass with the oven light on, and watching the cookies bake.

My first solo cooking experience was baking cakes in my Easy Bake oven and serving them to my parents. From these small steps grew a passion for being in the kitchen and providing for neighbors, friends, colleagues, and most importantly, family. Generations of tried-and-true recipes have been passed down over the generations and many of them are the most often requested.

Dr. Claudia Barone, Dean, College of Nursing

Sponsors

Major Underwriting Sponsor

A Friend of the College of Nursing Who Loves to Cook

Corporate Logo Sponsor

UAMS Department Sponsors

UAMS Library

Corporate Sponsors

Arkansas Hospital Association • ASCO Hardware Company Incorporated
DHL • LaHarpes Office Furniture • Little Rock Departmental Club

Individual Sponsors

Dr. Robert Kennedy • Dr. Jean McSweeney & John Holtam
Dr. Donna J. Middaugh • Mary G. Robertson • Dr. Tricia Satkowski
Drs. Cheryl and Michael Schmidt

Contributors à la Mode

1620 Restaurant
Dana Abney, Alumni
Mark Abernathy, Friend of UAMS
Acadia
ACRC Auxiliary
Barbara Adams, UAMS Hospital
Joan Adkins, Alumni
Marilyn Ahring, Arkansas Cancer Research Center (ACRC)
Margaret Alexander, Friend of UAMS
Patre Allen, UAMS Hospital
American Cancer Society
American Heart Association
Raymond Anderson, Academic Affairs and Research Administration
Andre's
Gaylynne Anglin, Support Services
Sandy Annis, Academic Affairs and Research Administration
Marzella Backus, UAMS Hospital
Annette Bailey, UAMS Hospital
Melanie Bainter, College of Public Health
Helen Baldwin, Friend of UAMS
Kristin L. Baldwin, College of Medicine
Susan Ball, College of Nursing
Nola Ballinger, College of Nursing
Nina Barnard, UAMS Hospital
Bart and Kathy Barlogie, Myeloma Institute
Claudia Barone, College of Nursing
Jennie Beard, UAMS Hospital
Sondra Bedwell, Regional Programs
Jane Benton, Support Services
Rose Bernath, UAMS Hospital
Virginia Bost Berner, Alumni
Representative Marion Berry
Mary Betts, Friend of UAMS
Claudia Beverly, College of Nursing
Don Bingham, Friend of UAMS
Robert W. Bishop, Academic Affairs and Research Administration
Lee Blackwood, College of Nursing
John Blohm, Development and Alumni Affairs
Nicole Boddington, Little Rock Family Magazine
Representative John Boozman
Boulevard Bread
Bendi Bowers, UAMS Hospital
Charlene Uthoff Bradham, Friend of UAMS
Evette Brady, Friend of UAMS
Paige Bramlett, UAMS Hospital
Brave New Restaurant
Peter Brave, Friend of UAMS
Cathy Brothers, UAMS Hospital
Lana Brown, UAMS Hospital
K. Browing, UAMS Hospital
Dolores F. Bruce, College of Public Health
Barbara Brunner, UAMS Hospital
Becky Butler, College of Health Related Professions
Tom Butler, Administration and Governmental Affairs

Cathy Buzbee, College of Medicine
Marilyn Byrd, UAMS Hospital
Linda Calhoun, College of Nursing
Johnsye Campbell, Friend of UAMS
Roxie Campbell, Regional Programs
Pam Cannefax, Regional Programs
Mary Cantrell, College of Medicine
Deborah Carman, College of Nursing
CJ Carrell, College of Health Related Professions
Danna K. Carver, Academic Affairs and Research Administration
Kari Cassel, Information Technology
Andrea Cassinelli, Friend of UAMS
Cassinelli 1700
Nelia A. Chambers, UAMS Hospital
Martha Chamness, UAMS Hospital
Carrie Chiaro, College of Nursing
E. LaVerne Chitwood, Friend of UAMS
Kim Clement, College of Medicine
Tomika Clark, Friend of UAMS
Lori Cline, College of Nursing
Ramanda Cody, Communications and Marketing
Elizabeth Ann Coleman, College of Nursing
Nancy K. Compton, College of Medicine
Deidre Connell, Administration and Governmental Affairs
Candace Conners, UAMS Hospital
Imogene Conway, College of Nursing
Jennifer Cotton, UAMS Hospital
Charles Cranford, Area Health Education Centers
LaQuita Croswell, Friend of UAMS
Lesa Culp, Friend of UAMS
Ethel Roberts Curry, Friend of UAMS
Linda Curtis, College of Medicine
Pearlie Daulton, UAMS Hospital
Debby Dean, Arkansas Cancer Research Center (ACRC)
Phil Deloney, Friend of UAMS
Linda Deloney, College of Medicine
Brian Dinsmore, Arkansas Cancer Research Center (ACRC)
Debbie Dinsmore, UAMS Hospital
Leslie Doan, Academic Affairs and Research Administration
Patty Dufrene, College of Nursing
Brenda Duhamel, Jones Eye Institute
April Dumond, Friend of UAMS
Angela Duncan, College of Nursing
Mica Dunn, UAMS Hospital
Sarah Dunn, UAMS Hospital
Robin Easley, College of Nursing
Toni Emerson, Academic Affairs and Research Administration
Susan Erickson, UAMS Hospital
Jane Evans, College of Nursing
Sally Everson-Bates, UAMS Hospital
Kathryn Felton, Arkansas Cancer Research Center (ACRC)

R T Fendley, UAMS Hospital
Eunice Ferguson, UAMS Hospital
Donnie Ferneau, Friend of UAMS
Ferneau
Mary Fine, Friend of UAMS
Kim Finne, UAMS Finance and Administration
Debra Fiser, College of Medicine
Gaye Fleming, UAMS Hospital
Mary Helen Forrest, UAMS Hospital
Betty Foster, Support Services
Sheila Fox, Friend of UAMS
Tom Fox, Friend of UAMS
Paul Francis, College of Nursing
Donna Frank, Friend of UAMS
Jennifer L. Franklin, Stephens Spine Center
Kim Freeman, UAMS Hospital
Sheryl French-Young, UAMS Hospital
Anne Fruge, Little Rock Family Magazine
Rowena M. Garcia, UAMS Hospital
Stephanie Gardner, College of Pharmacy
Barbara E. Garot, Information Technology
Felece Gassman, Communications and Marketing
Jan Gattis, Friend of UAMS
Leo Gehring, Campus Operations
Darlene Giffin, Friend of UAMS
Imogene Gillmore, Friend of UAMS
Carol Godfrey, Arkansas Children's Hospital
Amy Godfrey, Arkansas Cancer Research Center (ACRC)
Marvin Golden, College of Medicine
Melony Goodhand, UAMS Finance & Administration
Bob Goza, UAMS Hospital
Angela Green, College of Nursing
Eula Green, UAMS Hospital
Anita Griffin, UAMS Hospital
Paul Gubbins, College of Pharmacy
Riesa Gusewelle, College of Nursing
Matthew Hadley, College of Nursing
Jacque Hale, Regional Programs
James Hale, Friend of UAMS
Buster Hall, Communications
Carla Halpine, Friend of UAMS
Polly Haney, Friend of UAMS
Jennifer Hankins, College of Medicine
Eleanor Hannah, Friend of UAMS
Joyce Harms, Friend of UAMS
Kim Harris, UAMS Hospital
Paula Harris, Friend of UAMS
Jan Hart, UAMS Library
Cheri Hatfield, UAMS Hospital
Jeanie Hayden, Friend of UAMS
Virginia Henker, Friend of UAMS
Russell Hill, UAMS Get Healthy
Nicki Hilliard, College of Pharmacy
Leslie Hitt, College of Public Health
Dana Hobby, UAMS Hospital
Linda C. Hodges, College of Nursing
Susan Holmes, Friend of UAMS

Diana Hopper, Friend of UAMS
Sarah Hopper, UAMS Hospital
Pamela Horton, Alumni
Arlyn Howard, Stephens Spine Center
Debbie Cooley Huff, College of Medicine
Crystal Hunnicutt, Academic Affairs and Research Administration
Laura Hunt, UAMS Hospital
Brenda Iannacone, College of Medicine
Tim Irby, Communications and Marketing
Eric Isaac, Friend of UAMS
Paige and Pat James, Friends of UAMS
Laura Jennings, UAMS Hospital
Alissa "Lisa" Jensen, UAMS Hospital
Frances Jernigan, Friend of UAMS
Delores Jester, Myeloma Institute for Research and Therapy
Tanya Jewell, UAMS Hospital
Deborah Johnson, UAMS Hospital
Jill Johnson, College of Pharmacy
Valerie Johnson, UAMS Hospital
Melissa Johnston, Support Services
Holly Jones, UAMS Hospital
Lesa Jones, UAMS Hospital
Bobby Justus, UAMS Hospital
James Keaton, UAMS Hospital
Natalie Kay Kelley, College of Public Health
Karen Kemp, Arkansas Cancer Research Center (ACRC)
Lauren Kemp, College of Nursing
Margaret Kenner, Friend of UAMS
James and Elizabeth LaBorde, Friends of UAMS
Pam LaBorde, UAMS Hospital
Linda Laney-Rogers, College of Medicine
Tricia Langston, Support Services
Elizabeth Laurenzana, College of Medicine
Erin Lawrence, UAMS Hospital
Louanne Lawson, College of Nursing
Suzanne Leslie, Support Services
Shannon Lewis, UAMS Hospital
Phyllis Ann Lewis, Regional Programs
Henry Lile, UAMS Hospital
Senator Blanche L. Lincoln
David Lipschitz, Don W. Reynolds Institute on Aging
Little Rock Departmental Club
Little Rock Family Magazine
Sandie Lubin, College of Nursing
Loca Luna Restaurant
Sandy Young Long, Alumni
Kristy Loper, Friend of UAMS
Jane Lowe, ACRC
Robbie N. Lynn, UAMS Hospital
Bea Magers, Friend of UAMS
Joan Manderson, Friend of UAMS
Sara Marecki, UAMS Hospital
Connie Marendt, College of Medicine
Brenda Martin, UAMS Hospital
Greg Matthews, Friend of UAMS
Becky May, Alumni
Jeff Medbury, Friend of UAMS
Stephanie Melchert, Friend of UAMS
Mike's Place Restaurant
Celia McCaslin, Support Services
Robert McGehee, Graduate School
Scott McGehee, Friend of UAMS
Bill McIntyre, UAMS AHEC-SW
Betty W. McLeod, Friend of UAMS
Ruby Lynn McNamara, UAMS Hospital
Jean McSweeney, College of Nursing
Christie McWilliams, Friend of UAMS
Kim Miller, UAMS Hospital
Larry Milne, Academic Affairs and Research Administration
Margaret Mitchell, Friend of UAMS

Phylis Mitchell, Friend of UAMS
Roberta Monson, College of Medicine
Sarah (Kay) Morris, College of Medicine
Debbie Bellisle Morrison, Alumni
Gloria Mugno, Regional Programs
Paula Mullins-Welch, College of Medicine
Val McEntire Neal, Regional Programs
Virginia Neill, Friend of UAMS
Mildred Newton, Friend of UAMS
Sharon Newton, UAMS Hospital
Paul Novicky, Friend of UAMS
Olan and Nancy Nugent, College of Medicine
Lalit Oberoi, College of Pharmacy
Diana Oden, UAMS Hospital
Linda Owens, Friend of UAMS
T. Glenn Pait, Jackson T. Stephens Spine Institute
Brittani K. Paris, Finance and Administration
Donna Parnell-Beasley, Arkansas Children's Hospital
Becky Patterson, College of Nursing
Marie Patterson, UAMS Hospital
Delma Perrot, Friend of UAMS
Gary Perrot, Friend of UAMS
Joseph G. Perrot, Friend of UAMS
Linda Perrot, College of Medicine
George Peters, U.S. Ambassador's Residence, Monrovia, Liberia
Dick Pierson, UAMS Hospital
Rebecca Pillert, College of Medicine
Susan Porter, UAMS Hospital
Mary Prewitt, Support Services
Garland E. Primm, Friend of UAMS
Senator Mark Pryor
Purple Cow Restaurant
Jennifer Pyron, Little Rock Family Magazine
Melissa Qualls, Graduate School
Tina Rachley, UAMS Hospital
James Raczynski, College of Public Health
Anna Radominska-Pandya, College of Medicine
John G. Ragsdale, Friend of UAMS
Tenille Rauls, College of Medicine
Linda Ray, College of Medicine
Aldo Reyes, UAMS Hospital
Debbie Riddling, UAMS Hospital
Dan Riley, UAMS Hospital
Susan Ritchie, College of Nursing
Judge Rick and Cheryl Nicholas Rodery, Friends of UAMS
Mary Robertson, College of Nursing
Megan Robertson, Friend of UAMS
Lynda Rogers, UAMS Hospital
Jan Rooker, College of Nursing
Representative Mike Ross
Ristorante Capeo
Pam Rossi, College of Pharmacy
Shayne Rothwell, Regional Programs
Janie Runkle, UAMS Hospital
Keith Runkle, Creative Services
Naomi Miller Rush, Friend of UAMS
Mary L. Ryan, Academic Affairs and Research Administration
Daniel Sahn, U.S. Ambassador's Residence, Monrovia, Liberia
Deanna Sanders, Regional Programs
Tricia Satkowski, College of Nursing
Clara Saxton, UAMS Hospital
Nikki Schee, Friend of UAMS
Cheryl Schmidt, College of Nursing
Sharon Schneider, UAMS Hospital
Eric Scroggin, UAMS Hospital
Lea Seago, Friend of UAMS
Michael Selig, Friend of UAMS
Erinn Shaver, Friend of UAMS
Nancy Shaver, College of Nursing
Sara Sherman, Regional Programs

John and Nancy Shock, Jones Eye Institute
Linda Shock, College of Nursing
Dana M. Smith, UAMS Hospital
David Smith, Red Apple Inn
Elizabeth Thomas Smith, General Counsel
JoAnn H. Smith, College of Nursing
Judy Smith, UAMS Hospital
Richard Smith, College of Nursing
Rick Smith, College of Medicine
Tameka M. Smith, College of Nursing
Representative Vic Snyder
Linda South, UAMS Hospital
Spaule Restaurant
Carol Beth Stewart, College of Nursing
Allison Streepey, Academic Affairs and Research Administration
Judy Stolz, Friend of UAMS
James and Karen Suen, Arkansas Cancer Research Center (ACRC)
Cathy Sundermann, Friend of UAMS
Connie Sundermann, Friend of UAMS
Martha Sundman, UAMS Hospital
Larry J. Suva, College of Medicine
Sunghee Tak, College of Nursing
Sara Tariq, College of Medicine
Lesley Taylor, College of Nursing
Leslie Taylor, Communications and Marketing
Tim Taylor, Communications and Marketing
Alma Tedder, College of Medicine
Jane Teed, Friend of UAMS
Jerri Jackson Terry, Communications and Marketing
Martha Thannisch, Arkansas Cancer Research Center (ACRC)
Evelyn Thomas, Friend of UAMS
Katy Thomas, College of Nursing
Reba Thomas, Support Services
Cindy Thomasson, Regional Programs
Pat E. Thompson, College of Nursing
Pat Torvestad, Communications and Marketing
Marsha Trammel, UAMS Hospital
Mandy Trantham, UAMS Hospital
Maria J. Trias, Alumni
Mary Twedt, College of Medicine
UAMS Chancellor's Cabinet
Dick and Patti Upton, Friends of UAMS
Ralph Vogel, College of Nursing
Vermillion Water Grill
Karen Stoner Von Kanel, Friend of UAMS
Carol L. Wallis, College of Medicine
Shelia Watts, UAMS Hospital
Kelley Weatherly, UAMS Hospital
Anita Westbrook, UAMS Hospital
Donna West, College of Pharmacy
Wild Oats
Mary Jane Willard, UAMS Hospital
Katey Williams, College of Nursing
Claibanne J. Williamson, Academic Affairs and Research Administration
I. Dodd and Ginger Wilson, Chancellor
Ronald Winters, College of Health Related Professions
Frankie Wolfe, Support Services
David Woodbury, Friend of UAMS
Hester Woodbury, Friend of UAMS
Ross Woodbury, Friend of UAMS
Gail Woodward, UAMS Hospital
Fann Woodward, UAMS Hospital
Mary Jo Worley, College of Nursing
Randall G. Wright, Friend of UAMS
Greg York, Friend of UAMS
Cathy Young, UAMS Hospital
Gary Young, Friend of UAMS
Heather Zimmerman, College of Nursing

Index

175

For additional copies of *Culinary Prescriptions*

Please contact:
University of Arkansas for Medical Sciences
C/o UAMS College of Nursing/Cookbook
4301 West Markham #529
Little Rock, Arkansas 72205
www.nursing.uams.edu

$25.00 plus $5.00 postage and handling per
book. Arkansas residents add $2.00 sales tax.
Make checks payable to UAMS Cookbook.

Please include your e-mail address if
interested in future communications about
the cookbook.